Self-Esteem Research, Theory, and Practice

About the Author

Christopher J. Mruk, PhD, was trained in general learning and cognitive psychology at Michigan State University, where he received his undergraduate degree in 1971, and in humanistic clinical psychology at Duquesne University, where he received his graduate degree in 1981. His first clinical position was working in a closed inpatient psychiatric unit at Cottage Hospital in Grosse Pointe, Michigan, which led to supervising an outpatient heroin addiction treatment program in Detroit. From there, he became a therapist in a 24-hour comprehensive psychiatric emergency service in Lansing, Michigan, which was one of the nation's first models recognized by the National Institute of Mental Health (NIMH). He then provided a wide range of psychological testing and therapeutic services in various community mental health centers, which led to directing the Counseling Center at St. Francis College in Pennsylvania. After doing some private practice, he now works as a consulting psychologist to Firelands Regional Medical Center in Sandusky, Ohio. He is licensed as a clinical psychologist in Ohio and Pennsylvania.

Dr. Mruk's academic experience includes more than 20 years of teaching psychology and training mental health professionals. Currently, he is a full-time Professor of Psychology at Bowling Green State University Firelands College in Ohio, where he has received the college's Distinguished Teaching and its Distinguished Creative Scholarship awards. His publications include a number of academically oriented refereed articles, several invited chapters, and *Zen and Psychotherapy: Integrating Traditional and Nontraditional Approaches* (Springer Publishing Company, 2003), a book that he authored with Joan Hartzell, RN, MA. Dr. Mruk may be reached at cmruk@bgsu.edu.

Self-Esteem Research, Theory, and Practice

Toward a Positive Psychology of Self-Esteem

3rd Edition

Christopher J. Mruk, PhD

SPRINGER PUBLISHING COMPANY

NEW YORK

Springer Publishing Company, Inc.
11 West 42nd Street
New York, NY 10036

Acquisitions Editor: Sheri W. Sussman
Production Editor: Alison Trulock
Cover design: Joanne Honigman
Composition: Graphic World Inc.

06 07 08 09 10 / 5 4 3 2 1

Library of Congress Cataloging-in-Publication Data

Mruk, Christopher J.
  Self-esteem research, theory, and practice: toward a positive psychology of self-esteem
  /Christopher J. Mruk.—3rd ed.
    p. cm.
  Includes bibliographical references and index.
  ISBN 0-8261-0231-X
  1. Self-esteem. 2. Positive psychology. I. Title.

BF697.5.S46M78 2006
155.2—dc22

                                                2005057597

Printed in the United States by Maple-Vail Book Manufacturing Group

Contents

Preface

The third edition of this book is different from the other two. In fact, I talked with Sheri Sussman, my perspicacious editor at Springer Publishing Company, about whether it should be given a new title to reflect that fact. She said that in some ways the book is a defense of self-esteem and could well be titled differently to reflect that, but that we needed to think about it. In the end, the structure of the book seemed to be consistent enough among all three editions to warrant using the original title, but with the addition of a subtitle to reflect the new focus on positive psychology. Chapter 1, which still concerns defining self-esteem, is almost completely rewritten. It no longer needs to focus on justifying self-esteem as a balance of competence and worthiness because now I can show how this two-factor approach constitutes a legitimate tradition in the field. Instead, it is important to present new work of this type, its major authors, their crucial findings, and how such an approach is superior to defining self-esteem in terms of either competence or worthiness alone. Chapter 2 remains largely focused on methodological issues facing self-esteem work. However, it now includes new material about a more sophisticated way of understanding the self. Chapter 3, which concerns updating research findings, received extensive revision because so much has happened in the field during the past few years. For example, I have added nearly 150 new references to the book.

The first and largest portion of Chapter 4 has received considerable revision, mainly because it concerns major theories of self-esteem and several new ones that have appeared in the recent past. Some of them, such as Terror Management Theory and Sociometer Theory, are exciting and represent huge theoretical advances even in a field as old as this one. Chapter 5, which presents my own theory of self-esteem, is largely the same.

However, due to the stunning work of Susan Harter, I have been less concerned with the early development of self-esteem in childhood and more concerned with its management in adulthood. This progress is reflected in a new chart on how self-esteem is lived over time. The only things that are new about Chapter 6, which concerns the self-esteem enhancement program, are a few new research references on its efficacy and some additional material (which I find exciting) on how to apply the program in the individual setting. The new Chapter 7 aims at taking the field of self-esteem in an important direction: right into the new positive psychology. Thus, it begins by comparing the original humanistic positive psychology with the emerging positivistic positive psychology and ends with attempting to show how self-esteem should occupy a prominent place in the new one, just as it does in the older version.

Over the years, I have come to find that good therapists of all ilk have some important things in common and that no discipline is big enough to do it all alone. Thus, as before, this edition is oriented toward both academic and clinical audiences, especially those from counseling, education, nursing, psychology, and social work. Academics and researchers will probably find Chapters 2 through 5 most interesting because they cover research and theory. Clinicians are likely to find themselves drawn more toward Chapters 4 through 6 because they address how self-esteem works in relation to problems of living and how to help people deal with them more effectively. Chapters 1 and 7 should be of equal interest to both groups because defining self-esteem may be the most crucial issue in the field right now, and the relationship between self-esteem and the new positive psychology could become the most important one for the future. Finally, it might be helpful to say a word about writing style. Moving all the way from research, through theory, and then to practice is an unusual approach in this field, as most of its books emphasize only one, or sometimes two, of these themes. However, as a clinician, I know that the best practical tools come from a good theory, and as an academician I have learned that the best theory comes from good research, so for me, there is no alternative. Consequently, I try to find a "middle path" in style and tone that is compatible with key expectations of both audiences. Because the approach covers a lot of ground, I try to proceed in a logical, systematic fashion: from research issues and findings, through theory, to practice, and beyond to new issues with which the field must deal.

Acknowledgments

Naturally, it takes more than one person to write a book, even though most of the credit (or blame, as the case may be) falls on the author. First and foremost, of course, is Marsha, my wife, who has had the patience to put up with my odd hours while writing. I owe her a vacation of her choice for tolerating an author-in-residence yet again. As always, thanks to my original family, consisting of Steven, Veronica, and Joseph Mruk, my brother, mother, and father, respectively; my second family, which includes Dee Mruk, Tina Bradshaw, and Pam and Curt Pawloski; and my married family, especially Virginia, Carl, and Sylvia Oliver.

Friends who helped during the process this time include Bob Noe, as well as Frank and Mary Ann Salotti, Joan Hartzell, JoEtta Crupi, Mia Bartoletti, Tony Barton, Connie Fischer, and Scott Churchill. Karen Page Osterling, my colleague at work, friend outside of it, and personal copy editor for both of my books in all their editions, has done much writing with me over the years. I am sure her presence can be detected in the book if one looks closely enough, and always for the better. Finally, I would like to mention Will Currie and the staff at the library of Bowling Green State University Firelands College who were all more than helpful in finding sometimes obscure references. They also offered warm hospitality as I often read, wrote, and sipped tea in the back area of the stacks.

I am grateful to the staff of Springer Publishing Company for their interest and help over the past decade of work together. This time, Sheri Sussman gets special thanks for carefully listening to the idea of a third edition and helping to realize the project. Dr. Ursula Springer, who stands as something of a David facing the Goliath of gigantic for-profit publishing houses in her dedication to bringing scholarly work to psychology, nursing, and related fields, deserves special recognition. Dee Delassandro, who encouraged me to set up my first self-esteem workshops while director of the counseling center at St. Francis College, and Jack Howard, who helped me see the importance of self-esteem long ago, are also worthy of mention. Special thanks goes to Alison Trulock of Graphic World Publishing Services for her dedication to high-quality work. Last, but closer to first than least, it is important to thank clients and students who are now too many to name, for without them there would be nothing to say nor any reason to say it.

Introduction

Perhaps the most important question to ask about a third edition is why should anyone invest the time and energy to read or to write one? Of course, the most common answer is to update and expand a particular body of work or line of thought. That rationale was certainly true of the second edition, which was aimed at adding more recent research findings and defending the concept of self-esteem against the onslaught of criticism that arose in response to what is commonly referred to as the self-esteem movement. However, this third edition has different origins.

Over the past few years, the approach to the research, theory, and practice of self-esteem presented here seems to have generated some interest. Sometimes, for instance, I would see reference being made to it in a number of professional articles. Various Web sites started to refer to the model of self-esteem being developed here. Then, the self-esteem matrix appeared in college texts. More important, major researchers in the field also seemed to take notice. One of them, Michael Kernis (2006), went so far as to invite me to write a couple of chapters for a book he is authoring that I believe is sure to be a classic in the psychology of self-esteem.

Just then, I was also in a position to take a sabbatical from Bowling Green State University Firelands College, where I work as a professor of psychology, and was in need of a project to work on during that period. At the same time, I started to explore Romin Tafarodi's work. Between Kernis' new material on optimal self-esteem and Tafarodi's two-factor approach, I realized that there is an entire line of research and theory on the psychology of self-esteem into which my more phenomenological work could fit and make a contribution, particularly in terms of enhancing self-esteem. That moment brought with it a breath of fresh air and renewed inspiration.

For the next several months, I read more than 2,400 pages of new self-esteem work and also explored related material on what is being called "positive psychology." When Jim Smith, the dean of my college at Bowling Green State University, asked my wife, Marsha, how I was doing on sabbatical, she said with a smile and laughter, "I don't know. He never comes out of his study!" I've certainly not heard the last of that comment, but during that time I saw a number of things that would influence the design of the third edition. First, although I had feared that the field of self-esteem would only be damaged by the devastating popular and professional criticisms continually being leveled against it during the 1990s, self-esteem survived as a viable topic. Moreover, that onslaught, which was well deserved in more than one way, seems to have forced the field to look at itself anew and with a more demanding eye. The result seems to be that the psychology of self-esteem has matured since the last edition, to the point where it is once again thriving with new ideas, theories, and research. Thus, in part, the third edition was necessary because the older ones were simply out of date in ways that could not be ignored.

The other thing that I found during this time is that the field is now facing a new kind of challenge or danger. I was in the audience when the new vision of positive psychology was presented to the general membership of the American Psychological Association. Having been trained in humanistic, as well as traditional, empirical psychology, I was thrilled to hear so many familiar themes being revitalized and believed that psychology was finally getting on the right track again. After reading the new studies and literature on this version of positive psychology, however, I soon realized that self-esteem was not a major part of it. I think that is a terrible mistake and decided it was necessary for someone to demonstrate how self-esteem is and should be an important part of any positive psychology, whether conceived in the twentieth century by the humanistic perspective or in the new millennium by a more traditional approach to psychology. Thus, the new edition includes a seventh chapter, instead of the previous six, dedicated to this issue.

CHAPTER 1

The Crucial Issue of Defining Self-Esteem

One of the most striking things about the field of self-esteem is its vitality and resilience as a topic for social scientists and clinicians alike. For example, if history is an indication of the significance of a phenomenon, then self-esteem easily stands out as an important subject. After all, William James (1890/1983) first introduced the topic more than a century ago in what is often regarded as the first American textbook on psychology, which makes self-esteem one of the oldest themes in social science, at least in this country. In addition to historical depth, the breadth of a topic, or how much attention it receives, is another good indicator of vitality. Even a cursory database search of PsychINFO will reveal that in the time between James' work and this investigation, scholars, researchers, and practitioners have written more than 23,215 articles, chapters, and books that directly focus on self-esteem as a crucial factor in human behavior. The fact that the number seems to grow substantially each time the database is updated further supports the claim that self-esteem is a basic, if not fundamental, topic in the social sciences. In fact, Rodewalt and Tragakis (2003, p. 66) stated that self-esteem is one of the "top three covariates in personality and social psychology research," along with gender and negative affectivity. The ability to endure controversy is another good indicator of importance, and self-esteem appears to be resilient in this regard as well. Indeed, we shall see that work on self-esteem is characterized by a diversity of opinion strong enough to generate a lively and continuing exchange among researchers, theorists, and laypeople alike. Self-esteem is one of those rare topics for which controversy, even heated controversy, only seems to stimulate more interest in the subject over time. When all things are considered, then,

1

self-esteem certainly seems to warrant additional attention as we move into the twenty-first century.

What accounts for such vitality in a psychological topic? Perhaps it is that self-esteem is one of those few dimensions of behavior that stretches across the full spectrum of human existence that creates so much interest for such a long time, much like the topics of personality or identity. At one end of the human behavioral continuum, for instance, low self-esteem is often mentioned in regard to various mental disorders, such as depression, anxiety, and learning problems. We can also find self-esteem more toward the middle of the spectrum in terms of many of the more ordinary problems of living, including difficulties dealing with failure, losses, and other setbacks that are sure to challenge most of us during the course of our lives. Finally, self-esteem is also found at the other end of the continuum because it is often talked about in relation to such things as being mentally healthy, successful, living effectively, and even the "good life." In light of such a rich historical and contemporary context, the first question to ask of new work in the area, let alone a third edition, could be a rather poignant one: Why is there a need for more work on self-esteem given all the attention it has received to date, and what can be gained by the individual reader, researcher, or practitioner by taking the time to become familiar with it (Aanstoos, 1995)?

The answer to this question is the central aim of this book, which involves presenting, supporting, and advancing an integrated, systematic, two-factor approach to self-esteem research, theory, and practice. However, the nature of such a query is such that it must be addressed before proceeding any further, so let us consider a brief response to it, one that may be further developed as we proceed. Succinctly stated, there are at least three good reasons to continue the pursuit of self-esteem and each one of them is discussed throughout this chapter. First, today, self-esteem may be more important for individuals and the society in which they live than ever before, especially in terms of what is typically described as "self-regulation" and "quality of life." Second, the research and ideas that historically characterized this field have undergone a striking period of rapid growth and severe critique. This re-examination of self-esteem is beginning to result in the development of more sophisticated research, more comprehensive theories, and more effective tools for enhancing self-esteem. Finally, new influences, such as the advent of positive psychology, are beginning to affect the field in ways that must be examined and understood to make sense of the changing face of self-esteem in modern psychology. It is helpful to elaborate each of these three points to clarify what they mean before we venture into this rich and vibrant field any farther.

In whatever way one defines self-esteem, and we will take on this important task in the course of this chapter, it is usually understood as something that is especially meaningful to the individual. Whether self-esteem has to do with an abiding sense of worthiness as a person or the experience of being able to solve problems competently, or both, self-esteem is intensely personal, in part because it says something about who we are and how we live our lives. One reason to continue to study it, then, is the hope that understanding self-esteem will help us to learn things about ourselves: important things, such as who we are as unique individuals and how we are faring in life in terms of the meanings of our actions, our short- and long-term goals, our relationships with others, and the direction in which our lives are heading. Another thing that makes self-esteem especially significant may also be that it is one of those rare human qualities that is active in both negative and positive situations, experiences, and states of being, making it relevant to a wide range of behavior. Reading any list of characteristics commonly associated with low self-esteem clearly makes this point. For example, Leary and MacDonald noted that,

> People with lower trait self-esteem tend to experience virtually every aversive emotion more frequently than people with higher self-esteem. Trait self-esteem correlates negatively with scores on measures of anxiety (Battle, Jarrat, Smit & Precht, 1988; Rawson, 1992), sadness and depression (Hammen, 1988; Ouellet & Joshi, 1986; Smart & Walsh, 1993), hostility and anger (Dreman, Spielberger & Darzi, 1997), social anxiety (Leary & Kowalski, 1995; Santee & Maslach, 1982; Sharp & Getz, 1996), shame and guilt (Tangney & Dearing, 2002), embarrassability (Leary & Meadows, 1991; Maltby & Day, 2000; Miller 1995), and loneliness (Haines, Scalise & Ginter, 1993; Vaux, 1988), as well as general negative affectivity and neuroticism. (Watson & Clark, 1984) (2003, pp. 404–405)

In all fairness, it is necessary to point out that we will see some authors who report that low self-esteem does not necessarily lead to such forms of human misery. Instead, low self-esteem is seen as the result of adopting certain self-protective strategies that limit reductions in self-esteem (Snyder, 1989; Tice, 1993). But it is still acknowledged that low self-esteem has its costs, such as missed opportunities or lack of spontaneity. Even more to the point, it is difficult to dismiss the fact that low self-esteem has been identified as either a diagnostic criterion for, or associated feature of, some 24 mental disorders in the fourth edition of the *Diagnostic and Statistical Manual of Mental Disorders* (American Psychiatric Association, 2000), according to O'Brien, Bartoletti & Leitzel (2006).

Moreover, if it is true that at least 15 percent of Americans meet criteria for a diagnosable mental health condition in a given year (Regier et al., 1993) and if it is true that self-esteem is involved in many other less severe conditions, then it stands to reason that self-esteem is of considerable social significance, too. This aspect of low self-esteem is put into even greater relief when we remember that most people who suffer mental disorders are also connected to many others through families, friendships, and other relationships. The result is that low self-esteem probably touches most of us either directly through personal experience or indirectly through such things as rising insurance premiums or tax dollars spent on mental health services. Finally, if self-esteem does span a continuum as was mentioned earlier, then it may also tell us something about how life is lived at the other, healthier end and the positive psychology that addresses it.

In addition to the meaning of self-esteem at the lived level of everyday life, a second reason for taking another look at self-esteem concerns several events that seem to be creating important changes in the field. One of them, for instance, involves challenging basic assumptions of self-esteem work in a way that is giving rise to substantial growth in research and theoretical activity. Although the historical roots of self-esteem run deep and long, until the 1960s they were relatively quiet and, at times, almost hidden. After James, self-esteem appeared to recede from the academic stage, only to be taken up by psychodynamic theorists and clinicians, most notably Alfred Adler (1927) and Karen Horney (1937). No doubt, much of the low profile that self-esteem occupied in social science during these middle years had to do with the dominance of behaviorism, which eschewed such phenomena as consciousness and instead focused on the observable (Harter, 1999; Mruk, 1999).

However, a sudden eruption of interest in self-esteem and related phenomena occurred in the mid-1960s, somewhat analogous to what biologists call the "Cambrian Explosion," which is a segment of geological time when life suddenly diversified into many forms all over the planet. For self-esteem, this period was led by such figures as Stanley Coopersmith (1959, 1967), who began to look at self-esteem from a learning theory perspective and in the laboratory. Carl Rogers (1951, 1961) explored self-esteem from a humanistic perspective and created considerable interest in its therapeutic possibilities, as well as how genuine self-esteem facilitates living a healthy, authentic, or optimal existence. Around that time, Morris Rosenberg (1965) developed a 10-item, easy-to-administer self-esteem survey that became the "gold standard" for self-esteem research. Indeed, it may have been used in as much as a fourth of all the considerable research that exists on self-esteem today (Tafarodi & Swann Jr., 1995). Finally during this rather amazing period in the development of the field, Nathaniel Branden (1969) introduced self-esteem to popular culture through his best selling book, *The Psychology of Self-Esteem*. All of these things and more occurred in just a 10-year period, and their impact was so great that it is still reverberating throughout the field today.

During the late-1980s to mid-1990s, two converging forces worked together to push the social significance of self-esteem into a much larger social arena. One of them originated with a group of academicians and politicians in California who emphasized to the general public the possibility of a link between individual self-esteem and major social problems, such as substance abuse, welfare, and teen pregnancy. As Mecca, Smelser, and Vasconcellos said,

> The well-being of society depends on the well-being of its citizenry. . . .
> The more particular proposition that forms our enterprise here is that
> many, if not most, of the problems plaguing society have roots in the low
> self-esteem of many of the people who make up society. (1989, p. 1)

Perhaps in response to the zeitgeist of the time, maybe as a result of the high profile from which this group benefited, or simply because it seemed to make so much "common sense," this position generated a broad base of political and social support. For the first time, self-esteem work received considerable financial backing. Like never before, interest in self-esteem made its way to other parts of society, particularly into the educational setting (Beane, 1991; Damon, 1995). At the same time, self-help and popular psychology markets got aboard the self-esteem bandwagon and spread interest in the topic to even wider social arenas, including the media. The result of such a concatenation of events was a dramatic rise in programs aimed at enhancing self-esteem in primary school systems and a significant increase in the number of books and discussions on self-esteem throughout the nation. In short, the large but once quiet field of self-esteem achieved social significance through what is now commonly known as the "self-esteem movement."

However, popular interest is a double-edged sword. In addition to obvious benefits, such as more research funding and more people working in the field, bringing a scientific concept to the public forum can also result in negative forms of attention. The most important of these appears to have been a second, countervailing, social force operating on self-esteem during this period that took the form of a backlash against the topic. Early signs of what might be called "self-esteem bashing" or even an "anti–self-esteem movement" began to appear in social commentaries with eye-catching titles such as, "The Trouble with Self-Esteem" (Leo, 1990) or "Education: Doing Bad and Feeling Good" (Krauthammer, 1990) that appeared in popular weekly news magazines. Such criticism of self-esteem spread to various segments of the popular media during the remainder of the 1990s (Johnson, 1998; Leo, 1998). However, a more substantial line of scientific work criticizing the merit of self-esteem research and practices also appeared in professional literature at the same time. For example, the psychologist Martin Seligman (1995b, p. 27) said in a book on child rearing that by focusing on self-esteem "parents and teachers are making this generation of children more vulnerable to depression." William Damon (1995, p. 72) criticized self-esteem work in the educational setting even more strenuously when he called it a "mirage" for those who work with children, and "Like all mirages, it is both appealing and perilously deceptive, luring us away from more rewarding developmental objectives."

Perhaps the most significant and influential scientific work of this type was led by Roy Baumeister, one of the major authorities in self-esteem work today. Although earlier a strong advocate supporting the importance of self-esteem for understanding human behavior (Baumeister, 1993), a turning point seemed to occur in 1996. It was at this time that in major scientific journals Baumeister and colleagues (1996) suggested that high self-esteem appears to be associated with certain undesirable forms of behavior, most notably egotism, narcissism, and even violence. They termed these negative findings as the "dark side" of self-esteem. Other scientifically oriented work also criticized the importance of self-esteem in these and other ways (Emler, 2001). Although we will find that this phenomenon can be understood in a different way than the one proposed by such critics, the phrase caught the eye of the popular media and press mentioned earlier, thereby helping to create an atmosphere that was far less receptive to self-esteem work than ever before. In short, the combination of poignant empirically based criticism from within coupled with a reversal of fortune in the popular media from without, seemed to result in challenging the foundations of self-esteem and work in this area. In fact, there are those who even question the merit of pursuing any form of self-esteem (Crocker & Nuer, 2004).

Fortunately, science can be unrelenting in its pursuit for more information. At the turn of the twenty-first century the same self-correcting power of the scientific method that exposed the dangers of over generalizing the virtues of self-esteem also placed the claims of those who criticize it into question as well. The result of this progressive process is that over the past few years there have been a number of research and theoretical advances in the psychology of self-esteem that make it absolutely necessary to examine the topic anew. For example, some new research focuses on the possibility that various types of self-esteem can be associated with negative outcomes, such as anxiety, depression, narcissism, or aggression. But other work indicates that another type of self-esteem is associated with desirable characteristics, something that is generally referred to as "healthy," "genuine," or "authentic" self-esteem

(Deci & Ryan, 1995; Kernis, 2003b). Also, recent developmental work seems to be making considerable progress in terms of understanding the antecedents of self-esteem (Harter, 1999), something that Stanley Coopersmith (1967) called for decades ago. Perhaps even more important, the ongoing critical look at self-esteem that has come to characterize much of the field today has not only led to re-examining old theories, but has also stimulated the formation of some powerful and exciting new ones, such as Self-Determination Theory, Terror Management Theory, or Sociometer Theory. In other words, recent events in the field are so important that they must be considered when thinking about self-esteem today.

The third and final reason for taking another look at self-esteem is that several new, positive forces are now at work in the field that may create exciting possibilities that were out of reach in the past. These developments arise from within the field, but also they come to the psychology of self-esteem from outside the discipline. For example, it is already well established that there is a relationship between self-esteem and happiness that even critics recognize (Baumeister et al., 2003). Other work suggests that self-esteem can affect, or at least interact with, immunocompetence (Bartoletti & O'Brien, 2003), which implies that self-esteem may be related to physical, as well as mental, well-being. Still other material points to a relationship between self-esteem and authenticity (Kernis, 2003a, 2003b), which brings up interesting possibilities concerning self-actualization and the "good life." The point is that although it is necessary to continue to appreciate the limits of self-esteem as its critics point out, it is just as important to make room for more developments. Why should the critical attitude that challenges old work on self-esteem stop there? It may well turn out to be that the phase of re-examining work on self-esteem prepares the way for a new period of refinement and growth. After all, separating the next crop of wheat from the chaff is the hallmark of the scientific method because that is how it creates progress in a given field.

In addition, new developments can also mean new synergies. The relationship between self-esteem work and the new positive psychology is an area to explore in this regard. Like many others, I was first introduced to the contemporary version of this term while in the audience of Martin Seligman's presidential address to the American Psychological Association. In that speech, he called for the kind of psychology that would

> Articulate a version of the good life that is empirically sound and, at the same time, understandable and attractive. We can show the world what actions lead to well-being, to positive individuals, to flourishing communities, and to a just society. (Seligman, 1999, p. 2)

Since that time, positive psychology has grown to the point where it has identified many key issues and concerns. For instance, we find that in the classic *The Handbook of Positive Psychology* (Snyder & Lopez, 2002) such topics as subjective well-being, positive affectivity, and authenticity are included in the field, all of which have been a part of self-esteem work for a good while. Perhaps now it is the time to see whether these two overlapping fields may be integrated in meaningful ways. In sum, these three factors (the importance of self-esteem for negative and positive qualities of life; the development of more sophisticated research methods, findings, and theories; and the advent of a new positive psychology) work together to create the need to look at self-esteem anew.

THE CENTRAL ISSUE OF DEFINING SELF-ESTEEM

In one sense, we all know what self-esteem "really is" because it is a human phenomenon, and we are all human beings. But like much common sense knowledge, there are serious limits to such understanding that become apparent as soon as we begin to examine them more closely. As Smelser observed,

> We have a fairly firm grasp of what is meant by self-esteem, as revealed by our own introspection and observation of the behavior of others. But it is hard to put that understanding into precise words. (1989, p. 9)

A simple but revealing way to explore this problem is to ask almost any reasonably mature undergraduate psychology class to do the following exercise.

At the beginning of the class or lecture ask each person to write down his or her own definition of self-esteem. Then, invite the students to either read their definitions aloud or to hand them in to be read aloud. As the information comes in, write the key components of each definition on the board so that they can be examined publicly. After that is done, ask the group to develop a single definition of self-esteem. The typical class sees the point almost immediately: What seems so familiar and easy at the beginning of the activity quickly shows itself to be quite complex and difficult. They also tend to be struck by the diversity of definitions, and for some it may even seem as though there are as many ways to define self-esteem as there are people trying to do so! Similarly, the class tends to notice that, although different, several definitions appear to have some merit because they all suggest, capture, or describe an important aspect of the phenomenon.

If the class spends enough time with this exercise, the students also begin to notice that definitions can be grouped on the basis of key characteristics that various approaches tend to emphasize over others. One individual might see that some depictions focus on values such as self-respect. Another person might notice that some definitions center on the feeling or affective dimension of self-esteem. Somebody else is likely to point out that some of the definitions emphasize cognitive factors such as the attitudinal components of self-esteem. Often, a participant sees that particular definitions focus attention on the behavioral aspects of self-esteem such as being more independent or assertive. The lesson, however, really begins to solidify when they are asked to defend the definitions they developed while the others offer critique. By the end of this activity, of course, two things usually become apparent. The first thing is that developing a good definition of self-esteem is difficult because people tend to focus on and emphasize different aspects of it when they put their thoughts into words. The other is that how one defines self-esteem is a crucial issue because definitions have power: They help shape what we see and fail to see, which methods we choose and decline, and the standards of proof that we use to accept or reject evidence or conclusions (Mruk, 2006).

The reason that the exercise is mentioned here, of course, is because *it is a microcosm of what actually seems to happen among writers, researchers, and clinicians in the field* (Wells & Marwell, 1976; Smelser, 1989). Unfortunately, what typically seems to be so clear to beginners often appears to be forgotten by experts. For it turns out that some researchers define self-esteem in one way, others define it in different ways, and many either take the term for granted or define it as broadly as possible. The result is that the concept loses specificity: Although a lot of people may talk about self-esteem, little communication occurs. Thus, there are several good reasons to pause for a moment and to consider why defining self-esteem is a necessary, even crucial, first step when investigating this phenomenon. First, definitions open up pathways of understanding, in part because they *name* things and "naming" shapes perception. In this sense, every major definition is important because each one can show us some things about self-esteem that can only be seen from that particular point of view. At the same time, of course, definitions also create limits. Although each particular definition opens up one way of looking at a phenomenon, it closes off other perspectives that can lead to different insights or understandings. Phenomenologists call this aspect of human perception "perspectivity," (Gurwitsch, 1964), which means that it is necessary to fully appreciate the ways in which each approach or definition both reveals and conceals.

Second, even though we are limited in this fashion, we must take some direction in beginning any kind of a journey, even one of understanding, so it behooves us to select the best definition possible. The problem in this field is that there is much variation in this process. Indeed, there is so much of it that defining self-esteem involves entering what Smelser (1989) terms a "definitional maze" that causes considerable confusion. Given the need to define terms as accurately as possible in scientific research and the need to do that as a first step, it is surprising to find that, "Of the thousands of entries listed in ERIC on some aspect of self-esteem, only a few are listed that target its definition" (Guindon, 2002, p. 205). One way to deal with such definitional problems is to examine the major definitions of self-esteem that are in use to see whether any of them proves to be better than others.

TYPES OF DEFINITIONS

Wells and Marwell attempted to organize definitions of self-esteem on the basis of two psychological processes: evaluation (which emphasizes the role of cognition) and affect (which prioritizes the role of feelings) as they pertain to self-esteem.

> In our description, we distinguish between two main underlying processes—evaluation and affection. . . . Like most conceptual distinctions, the one between evaluation and affection is not always easy to make consistently and clearly. However, emphasis upon one or the other process leads to different forms of description, explanation, and sometimes, measurement. Self-evaluation generally involves more mechanistic, causal descriptions, while self-affection tends to elicit more "humanistic" conceptualizations of behavior. (1976, p. 62)

The result is a typology of definitions that consists of four ways of defining self-esteem. The first and the most basic definition is to simply characterize self-esteem as a certain attitude. As with any other attitude that is held toward a given object, this one can involve positive or negative cognitive, emotional, and behavioral reactions. A second type of definition is based on the idea of a discrepancy. In particular, it is the discrepancy between the self that one wishes to be (the "ideal" self) and the self that one currently sees oneself as being (the "real" or "perceived" self) that matters. The closer these two percepts are, the higher the individual's self-esteem is thought to be, and the wider the gap between the two, the more self-esteem suffers. A third way to go about defining self-esteem focuses on the psychological responses a person holds toward himself or herself, rather than attitudes alone. These responses are usually described as feeling-based or affective in nature, such as positive versus negative or accepting versus rejecting. Finally, Wells and Marwell maintained that self-esteem is understood as a function or component of personality. In this case, self-esteem is seen as a part of the self-system, usually one that is concerned with motivation or self-regulation, or both.

There are other well-accepted ways to approach making sense out of the definitional maze. Instead of looking at types, for instance, Smelser (1989) seeks to identify the "almost universally accepted components of the concept." He began by presenting three of them.

> There is first, a cognitive element; self-esteem means characterizing some parts of the self in descriptive terms: power, confidence, and agency. It means asking what kind of person one is. Second, there is an affective element, a valence or degree of positiveness or negativeness attached to those facets identified; we call this high or low self-esteem. Third, and related to the second, there is an evaluative element, an attribution of some level of worthiness according to some ideally held standard. (p. 10)

He went on to note that definitions vary as to whether they focus on self-esteem as a global or situational phenomenon. That is, some definitions see self-esteem as being reasonably stable over time, whereas others regard self-esteem as being responsive to situational and contextual influences, which means that it fluctuates. Today, this aspect of self-esteem is seen in such phrases as "trait versus state" self-esteem (Leary & Downs, 1995), "stable versus unstable" self-esteem (Greenier, Kernis & Waschull, 1995), or "global versus situational" self-esteem (Harter, 1999).

In fact, neither developing typologies nor identifying basic elements can offer us the one thing that is needed most: a clear statement concerning what self-esteem is as it is actually lived by real human beings in real life. Although typologies of self-esteem reduce the number of definitions with which we must contend, they offer us no criteria for identifying one as being more valid than another. Similarly, although identifying common elements is a necessary step toward developing such a definition, it is also necessary to work them into an integrated, comprehensive form; otherwise, the elements simply constitute a list. Clearly, then, we are in need of another method. The approach that we use to reach this goal consists of moving in two steps. First, we examine three definitions of self-esteem that seem to run throughout the depth and breadth of the field. This activity involves analyzing the theoretical strengths and weaknesses of each one to assess their potential usefulness. The second step takes us into the lived character of self-esteem, or how it is actually experienced by real people in real life, particularly in terms of what phenomenological psychologists call the "general structure" (Giorgi, 1971) of the experience. At this point, we will be able to evaluate the definitions and find out whether one of them turns out to be superior to others empirically, as well as theoretically.

At first glance, it might seem as though identifying major definitions, significant findings, or leading theories of self-esteem is an arbitrary process. However, using time as a criterion to "measure" such things is one of the most useful and accepted ways of identifying important themes. Time is helpful in this task because the field is old enough to have undergone several scientific "shake outs." In other words, once a definition, finding, theory, or technique is formed, other researchers tend to come along and re-examine such work. In doing so, the particular item in question is confirmed, modified, or discarded, on the basis of current evidence or understanding. Those that withstand scrutiny over a long period of time and yet remain relatively intact may at least be considered to be *persistent* or reliable enough to be useful, although certainly not necessarily valid. Another test offered by time concerns breadth rather than duration. Definitions, findings, theories, or techniques that are able to stimulate meaningful research and give rise to entire schools of thought over time demonstrate another valuable characteristic, namely *significance*. Of course, items of scientific discourse that are both persistent (i.e., enduring) and significant (i.e., generative) are likely to warrant the status of existing as a "standard" in the field. Three such definitions appear to occur in the psychology of self-esteem (Mruk, 1999, 2006). In this section, then, I present each of these major, classical, or standard definitions in some detail, offer what I hope to be sufficient evidence that each approach generates a significant line of work in self-esteem so as to constitute its major schools, and conclude each presentation with a critique of its strengths and limitations. This procedure helps us reach the first part of determining whether one definition is superior to others and why.

Self-Esteem as Competence

Time and history are good places to begin when looking at previous work, so it seems most appropriate to start with the oldest definition, which was developed by William James more than a century ago.

> So our self-feeling in this world depends entirely on what we *back* ourselves to be and do. It is determined by the ratio of our actualities to our supposed potentialities; a fraction of which our pretensions are the denominator and the numerator our success: thus,
>
> $$\text{Self-esteem} = \frac{\text{Successes}}{\text{Pretensions}}.$$
>
> Such a fraction may be increased as well by diminishing the denominator as by increasing the numerator. (James, 1890/1983, p. 296)

This definition presents a number of things worth our consideration. First and foremost is that James defined self-esteem in terms of action, in particular, action that is successful or competent. In this case, we see that self-esteem depends on two things: an individual's hopes, desires, or aspirations, which are termed "pretensions," and his or her ability to realize them, which in turn requires competence. Thus, work that stems from James' definition tends to focus on behavioral outcomes and the degree of discrepancy between one's "ideal" self and "real" self.

However, James went on to considerable length to make sure we understand that general success or overall competence is not what constitutes self-esteem. Rather, it is competence in areas that matter to the individual as a unique and particular human being that determines whether success (or failure) in them has meaning for one's self-esteem. In his words

> I, who for the time have staked my all on being a psychologist, am mortified if others know much more psychology than I. But I am contented to wallow in the grossest ignorance of Greek. My deficiencies there give me no sense of personal humiliation at all. Had I 'pretensions' to be a linguist, it would have been just the reverse. (James, 1890/1983, p. 296)

Thus, when we say that a definition of self-esteem is a competence-based definition, we also automatically maintain that it is a certain type of competence, namely, competence in areas that matter to an individual given his or her developmental history, personality characteristics, values, and so forth. By contrast, general competence or even high degrees of success in areas that are not important to a particular individual are not necessarily related to self-esteem when it is defined this way. Finally, in presenting self-esteem as a ratio, James (1890/1983, p. 292) defines self-esteem in a way that means it tends to be fairly stable as a trait may be, which is referred to as "a certain average tone of self-feeling." However, like all ratios, the number of successes or failures one has can change as well, which means that self-esteem is also a dynamic phenomenon and must be maintained, especially during times of challenge or threat.

After the beginning of the twentieth century, self-esteem became an important psychological theme again, but this time it was carried by the psychodynamic tradition. For example, Alfred Adler (1927) emphasized the importance of success for building a positive sense of self, particularly in terms of overcoming feelings of "basic inferiority" that are seen as playing a large role in determining human behavior. Karen Horney (1937) focused on the difference between real and idealized selves as the central variable in developing and maintaining self-esteem. However, Robert White's (1959, 1963) work is probably the most articulate psychodynamic expression of self-esteem, and it is clearly tied to competence.

His approach went far beyond Freud's (1914/1957) original discussion of self-regard as a function of narcissism and the meeting of ego ideals. White began by noting that both traditional behavioral and classical psychodynamic psychologists suffer a central contradiction when it comes to their theories of motivation. In one way or another, both models of human behavior are based on drive reduction theory. In this case, when a need is not met, it disturbs homeostasis, which generates a negative tension or affective state. That stress, in turn, motivates behavior in a way that seeks to discharge the tension, which is done through acting in ways that aim at restoring homeostasis. White pointed out that the problem with homeostatic theories of motivation is that they have great difficulty accounting for a set of behaviors that seems to do just the opposite. Even in animals, play, curiosity, and exploration all involve disturbing homeostasis. Yet, instead of creating negative affect states, this type of tension results in positive ones. Such behaviors, he argues, are also need-based, but cannot be explained in terms of tension reduction because the organism actually seeks them out or creates them, even though they stimulate the sympathetic nervous system and can often involve risk. Therefore, he argued that "It is necessary to make competence a motivational concept; there is a *competence motivation* as well as competence in its more familiar sense of achieved capacity" (White, 1959, p. 318). Satisfying this need through the mastery of developmental tasks and experiencing other successes in childhood results in feelings of "effectance" and a sense of self-respect. In other words, "self-esteem . . . has its taproot in the experience of efficacy" (White, 1963, p. 134).

The most recent manifestation of seeing self-esteem largely in terms of competence does not come from a psychodynamic perspective, but it does take us to what might be the ultimate expression of this definition. Crocker and Park, for example, began their work on self-esteem by basing it squarely on James' definition when they said that

> Our central proposition is that people seek to maintain, protect, and enhance self-esteem by attempting to obtain success and avoid failure in domains on which their self-worth has been staked. Contingencies of self-worth, then, serve a self-regulatory function, influencing the situations people select for themselves, their efforts in those situations, and their reaction to successes and failures. (2003, p. 291)

If it is true that self-esteem is strictly based on success and failure in domains that are of particular significance to an individual alone, and if it is true that people must have self-esteem, then in some sense we are bound to these particular areas of life. Some people may even become so invested in success in these areas that they become "enslaved" to them.

In other words, instead of being a positive developmental and motivational force, Crocker and Park (2003, 2004) took the competence model to its final conclusion and pointed out that self-esteem could actually drive people to seek success and avoid failure in ways that are harmful to themselves or to others. They referred to this aspect of self-esteem as the "problem of pursuing self-esteem" and went on to list its many costs. Potential problems involved in pursing self-esteem when it is defined this way include risking a loss of autonomy caused by being driven toward success instead of just desiring it; having a lowered capacity to learn or take risks that results in chronic failure or an incapacitating fear of it; developing conflicts in relationships that are created by the need to defend against losing self-esteem when honesty and openness would serve one much better; experiencing difficulty with self-regulation that might lead to negative outcomes, such as becoming overly aggressive, and so forth. These authors even discussed how various clinical problems could result from an unhealthy pursuit of self-esteem that is connected with a drive toward perfection, such as is found in eating disorders, or how failure to achieve one's goals may be associated with substance abuse problems or other ways of masking a sense of failure.

We can see three things that result from defining self-esteem primarily in terms of competence. First, the approach certainly merits the status of a major school of thought and work on the topic. After all, seeing self-esteem in terms of competence not only was the first way to conceive of it, but it is still very much alive today. Second, there are considerable advantages to this approach. By understanding self-esteem in relation to success and failure, for example, we are able to appreciate it in terms of human motivation and motivational psychology. People do seek various forms of success, we may come to avoid taking advantage of opportunities to reduce the possibility of failure, and we often react powerfully when self-esteem is threatened. In addition, this vision of self-esteem allows us to appreciate how unique individual self-esteem is for each of us: We all care deeply about success and failure in areas that are personally significant to us on the basis of our particular constellation of history, circumstances, interests, and pursuits.

Unfortunately, there is a glaring problem with this approach to self-esteem that cannot be ignored. Crocker and Park (2003, 2004) capture it most convincingly: If self-esteem is defined in terms of competence alone, then it is truly contingent on our successes and failures. Because success never lasts forever and because failure is always possible, this view of self-esteem means that success is a fragile foundation on which to build an identity or a life. Although plausible, defining self-esteem in terms of competence, then, takes one in a rather narrow, predictable, and "dark" direction. If that is the only way of defining self-esteem, then it would indeed be rational to give up its pursuit, just as Crocker and Park (2003, 2004) strongly recommend.

Self-Esteem as Worthiness

Morris Rosenberg (1965) introduced another way of defining self-esteem that led to the development of the next major school of thought and work in the field. He defined it in terms of a particular type of attitude, one that is thought to be based on the perception of a feeling, a feeling about one's "worth" or value as a person. Hence,

> Self-esteem, as noted, is a positive or negative attitude toward a particular object, namely, the self. . . . High self-esteem, as reflected in our scale items, expresses the feeling that one is "good enough." The individual simply feels that he is a person of worth; he respects himself for what he is, but he does not stand in awe of himself nor does he expect others to stand in awe of him. He does *not* necessarily consider himself superior to others. (1979, pp. 30–31)

One thing to notice about understanding self-esteem as an attitude is that this view casts it in a light where cognition plays a greater role than affect. This shift to a more cognitive focus on self-esteem means that it is possible to see it in terms of the psychology of attitude formation. Of course, forming attitudes about the self is more complex than doing so for anything else, largely because the perceiver is also the object of perception (Wylie, 1974). However, even then social scientists were reasonably familiar with the formation of attitudes, how they work, and especially how to measure them, which marked a significant change of direction in the field.

The second distinguishing feature of defining self-esteem and working from this position is that self-esteem is seen primarily in terms of a certain attitude. It is one that concerns a person's evaluation or judgment of their own "worth," which brings the notion of values into play in self-esteem work. Whereas the chief value question for a competence-based approach is whether some particular domain of behavior matters to an individual, one's worth as a person is a more basic and rather universal issue. That is, it matters to most of us whether we are worthy or unworthy because one is generally recognized as being inherently more desirable or "good" and the other is generally viewed as being distinctly undesirable, inferior, or perhaps even "bad." Of course, at some point, seeing self-esteem in terms of worthiness involves dealing with all the issues associated with cultural relativity and the question of whether there are any universal values. However, this approach also yields at least one tangible power: Viewing self-esteem in terms of an attitude means that it can be measured. In fact, most of the early measures of self-esteem come from this position and, as noted earlier, Rosenberg's scale alone has been used in about a fourth of self-esteem studies between 1967 and 1995.

A more contemporary example of understanding self-esteem in terms of worth or worthiness, as I prefer to say it, may be found in cognitively oriented theorists and researchers, such as Seymour Epstein's Cognitive-Experiential Self-Theory (CEST) (Epstein, 1980; Epstein & Morling, 1995). In this case, worthiness takes on a much more powerful motivational connotation that is central to one's personality. In addition to saying that self-esteem is something that occurs at the explicit level of awareness, Epstein stated that this assessment of oneself also takes place implicitly, which is to say non-consciously. Moreover, this position holds that self-esteem is a fundamental schema of human perception, experience, and motivation at both levels, which makes self-esteem an important dimension of human behavior, especially in relation to identity and self-regulation. Finally, others who work on the basis of this definition go so far as to suggest that "implicit" self-esteem can be even more powerful than "explicit" self-esteem. In this case, the former is understood to be more spontaneous, reactive, or "hotter" and, therefore, more directly connected to the self. As such, these implicit processes can override the "cooler," more explicit cognitive processes of thinking, reason, and so forth (Campbell, 1999; Devos & Banaji, 2003; Dijksterhuis, 2004).

Perhaps the most striking and important work resulting from defining self-esteem largely in terms of worth or simply feeling good about oneself is seen when this approach is taken to the extreme. For example, Baumeister, Smart, and Boden (1996) investigated self-esteem when it is defined this way.

> Although some researchers favor narrow and precise concepts of self-esteem, we shall use the term in a broad and inclusive sense. By *self-esteem,* we mean simply a favorable global evaluation of oneself. The term *self-esteem* has acquired highly positive connotations, but it has ample synonyms the connotations of which are more mixed, including pride, egotism, arrogance, honor, conceitedness, narcissism, and sense of superiority, which share the fundamental meaning of favorable self-evaluation. (1996, p. 5)

In later work, Baumeister and colleagues (2003, p. 2) modified their definition somewhat, but it is still "literally defined by how much value people place on themselves. . . . Self-esteem does not carry any definitional requirement of accuracy whatsoever." When seen this way, it is no wonder that self-esteem can be said to have the "dark side" that this line of work has been so instrumental in pointing out. I would fully agree that such a definition would mean that self-esteem can be associated with either positive characteristics, such as dignity, honor, conscientiousness, and so forth, as well as negative ones, such as egotism, narcissism, or aggression that this tradition focuses on so pointedly. Although Baumeister and colleagues (2003) took some pain to point out that they are *not* saying self-esteem causes narcissistic, defensive, or violent behavior, they made it clear this "heterogeneous" way of defining self-esteem results in the mixed picture that we often see today. In fact, I argue that much of the work on self-esteem that has been criticized is based on defining self-esteem in terms of worth or worthiness alone.

Recognizing that the most common way of defining self-esteem is to understand it as a form of worth or worthiness can help us to understand another important problem in the field. Although "common sense" suggests that self-esteem is important because it plays a major role in human behavior, social scientists have been puzzled by the general lack of empirical support for such a position. Even those who are sympathetic to self-esteem work note this condition. For example, when reviewing the literature concerning the social importance of self-esteem for a study commissioned by the State of California, Neil Smelser said, "The news most consistently reported . . . is that the associations between self-esteem and its expected consequences are mixed, insignificant, or absent" (1989, p. 15). Nicholas Emler (2001) did an independent report examining the correlations between self-esteem and behavior in England and reached the same conclusion. Finally, Baumeister and colleagues (2003, p. 37) conducted a highly structured review of self-esteem literature done in a given period and found that, "With the exception of the link to happiness, most of the effects are weak to modest. Self-esteem is thus not a major predictor or cause of almost anything."

This line of work leaves us with several possibilities to consider. One of them is that self-esteem is not a particularly significant phenomenon. If so, then we should move beyond discussions about self-esteem. Another possibility is that even if self-esteem is significant, it is too difficult to untangle it enough to tease out clear relationships between self-esteem and behavior. If this position is correct, then we must await new methodological breakthroughs as Smelser (1989) or Wells and Marlow (1976) recommend. Of course, it could be that, as some conclude, self-esteem is more of an outcome than a cause (Seligman, 1995a). In this case, we should look for the variables that affect self-esteem instead of focusing on self-esteem per se. Finally, if any of these possibilities are true, we must conclude along with Scheff and Fearon Jr. (2004, p. 74) that work on self-esteem, which "probably represents the largest body of research on a single topic in the history of all of the social sciences," has not paid off to say the least.

However, it is also possible that just as defining self-esteem in terms of competence leads to one kind of scientific or behavioral dead end, so does seeing it largely in terms of worth or worthiness. If this position is correct, then many of the difficulties that we have been encountering may actually be the result of partial or lopsided ways of defining and understanding self-esteem more than anything else. To be sure, such a realization would not mean that all the problems involved in researching self-esteem or measuring its significance will be solved. However, it is necessary to consider this alternative for two reasons. First, there may be a more effective way of defining self-esteem that leads to progress in the field. Second, if such an approach does show us that self-esteem is an important aspect of human behavior, then failing to consider it is scientific "bad faith."

Self-Esteem as Competence and Worthiness

Fortunately, one more definition of self-esteem seems to have withstood the test of time as indicated by the fact that a distinct body of work has developed around it: Defining self-esteem in terms of competence *and* worth or worthiness. Nathaniel Branden first offered such a definition in 1969 when he said that

> Self-esteem has two interrelated aspects: it entails a sense of personal efficacy and a sense of personal worth. It is the integrated sum of self-confidence and self-respect. It is the conviction that one is *competent* to live and *worthy* of living. (p. 110)

Branden's way of defining self-esteem is based on philosophical foundations, particularly that of what is known as Objectivism, rather than on empirical study. Working from this position, he held that human beings have a fundamental need to feel worthy but may only achieve that goal by acting competently, which is to say rationally, when making decisions. Competence, in this case, means facing reality directly and then making rational decisions, which are those that allow an individual to solve problems realistically. Rational goals are those that are personally significant, life affirming, and do not compromise one's integrity as a person either in design or execution. Self-esteem, then, is a precious psychological resource that must be won, can be lost, and needs to be maintained at all times. Tying competence to worth in this fashion distinguishes this view of self-esteem from mere competence. In this new sense, competence must be behavior that in some way reflects or involves worth or worthiness to matter for self-esteem. Tying a sense of worth to competence in this way means that just feeling good about oneself does not necessarily reflect self-esteem: Such a feeling must also be rational, which is to say based on appropriately corresponding behavior. In other words, worth results from engaging in healthy actions and avoiding destructive ones, a condition that makes it difficult to connect self-esteem to such things as narcissism or other "dark" phenomena.

Perhaps because Branden offered more philosophical than empirical support for his definition, it did not receive the kind of attention in the field as did the others. However, other work that is based on a similar understanding of self-esteem has been going on since the 1970s. More empirical studies of self-esteem that define it in terms of competence and worth or worthiness have achieved a level of credibility that is at least equal to the other traditions. This third force in self-esteem is described as a "dual model" of self-esteem (Franks & Marolla, 1976), a "two-factor" theory (Tafarodi & Swann Jr., 1995), or as a "multidimensional approach" (Harter, 1999; O'Brien & Epstein, 1983, 1988). Empirical work in this tradition seems to have begun in 1971 with Victor Gecas when he was researching factors that affect self-esteem in adolescence. After exhausting other possibilities, he found that only a two-factor approach accounted for the variables that were showing up in the study. Later, he noted that his work was not alone.

> Increasingly, however, various aspects of self-esteem have been differentiated—e.g. sense of power and sense of worth (Gecas, 1971); "inner" and "outer" self-esteem (Franks & Marolla, 1976); evaluation and affection (Wells & Marwell, 1976); sense of competence and self-worth (Smith, 1978); self-evaluation and self-worth (Brissett, 1972); and competence and morality (Rokeach, 1973; Vallacher, 1980; Hales, 1980). Common to these subdivisions is the distinction between (a) self-esteem based on a sense of competence, power, or efficacy, and (b) self-esteem based on a sense of virtue or moral worth. (Gecas, 1982, p. 5)

Gecas went on to talk about how it is that each factor involves different psychological and social processes. For example, the competence dimension of self-esteem is connected to performance, whereas virtue or the worthiness factor is grounded in values, particularly those that govern interpersonal conduct. Like Branden, he also pointed out that competence and worthiness are greatly intertwined in self-esteem: It is their reciprocity that creates self-esteem and makes it a unique phenomenon.

Today, modern researchers whose work is as empirically rigorous as any in the field are using this dual, two-factor, or multidimensional approach. However, it is disappointing to see that such work is often conspicuously absent in the reference sections of work that is done from the other two perspectives or in work that criticizes self-esteem research for its "weak" findings. Yet, it is clear that Romin Tafarodi and several

researchers have shown just how inadequate and ineffective unidimen-
sional approaches to defining self-esteem are in theory and in research.
For example, Tafarodi and Swann Jr. (1995) examined Rosenberg's Self-
Esteem Scale and found that its questions actually load in two directions.
To be sure, some items seem to assess factors that are associated with
worthiness, which was the original intent. However, others clearly tap
into competence even though the instrument was not designed to do that.
Noting that researchers have been aware of the need to consider two axes
of self-esteem since Diggory's critique of the self-concept in 1966, they
maintain that, "Rather than experiencing ourselves as simply positive or
negative, we experience ourselves as globally *acceptable–unacceptable*
(referred to here as *self-liking*) and globally *strong–weak* (referred to here
as *self-competence*). Together these dimensions are held to constitute
global self-esteem" (Tafarodi & Swann Jr., 1995, p. 324).

The term self-esteem, then, actually turns out to be an efficient way
of talking about an interaction between these two variables. As Tafarodi
and Swann Jr. most elegantly said, self-esteem "may simply be an expe-
dient of discourse, in the same way that one speaks of the *size* of a
person's build rather than the person's (constitutive) height and girth"
(Tafarodi & Swann Jr., 1995, p. 337). Thus, those who work within this
school often note that the two-factor approach has the ability to bring
two major streams of the field together much more than do the other
ways of understanding self-esteem. For example, they work together well
conceptually.

> Self-competence, as the valuative experiences of one's own agency, is
> closely linked to motivational concepts such as effectance (White,
> 1959, 1963), personal causation (de Charms, 1968), and striving for
> superiority (Adler, 1931/1992). It is the self-valuative result of acting
> out one's will on the world—of being effective. Self-liking, in contrast,
> is the valuation of one's personhood—one's worth as a social object as
> judged against internalized social standards of good and bad. This
> social worth dimension of self-esteem figures prominently in accounts
> of the genesis of the ethical self, as offered by Baldwin (1899/1973) and
> Cooley (1902/1992), among others. (Tafarodi & Vu, 1997, p. 627)

In addition, it is important to appreciate the fact that this dual model
of self-esteem also takes the field in new directions. One of them concerns
the relationship between culture and self-esteem. This work is typically
discussed in terms of individualist versus collectivist societies and their
respective approaches to providing the foundations for healthy identities.
For instance, Tafarodi and Swann Jr. (1996) found that whereas both
types of cultures appreciate the need for an individual to demonstrate competence and to feel worthy, each one tends to emphasize one component of

self-esteem over the other, namely the one that is most characteristic of the general social orientation of the culture. Americans, of course, tend to stress the role of competence in self-esteem because it emphasizes the individual and success. Asians, however, are more apt to emphasize worth and worthiness because these cultures are more group oriented and make greater use of interpersonal relationships to hold the social fabric together.

Other areas of research that characterize this school include investigating such things as how self-competence and self-liking affect success and failure over time (Tafarodi & Vu, 1997); how such a dual model accounts for types of self-esteem (Mruk, 1999; Tafarodi & Milne, 2001); and how to use a two-factor definition of self-esteem to effect change in the clinical setting (Hakim-Larson & Mruk, 1997). Finally, it is helpful to realize that much of the work that is based on understanding self-esteem in terms of competence and worthiness does not use the phrase "two-factor" or "dual." Although still reflecting these two factors as crucial, the term "multidimensional" is sometimes used to distinguish the work from that which is based on only one of the other two unidimensional definitions. For example, although Susan Harter (1999) uses the terms "self-esteem" and "self-worth" interchangeably, her multidimensional approach to self-esteem clearly includes competence and worth as two primary components. Similarly, modern methods of measuring self-esteem eschew the unidimensional approach in favor of a multidimensional one. For instance, the Multidimensional Self-Esteem Inventory developed by O'Brien and Epstein (1983, 1988) assesses several dimensions of affect and behavior that are related to self-esteem. Later we see that most, if not all, of the various dimensions or domains used in "multidimensional" work can be grouped into those that emphasize competence and those that focus primarily on worthiness (Mruk, 1999).

In sum, the two-factor approach to defining self-esteem is more complex than unidimensional approaches because it involves always keeping in mind that there are variables to consider when researching or measuring self-esteem. Competence, for instance, is based in part on the degree to which an individual is capable of initiating action and carrying it through to a successful conclusion, especially in regard to dealing with problems effectively and in terms of reaching significant personal goals. Competence thereby includes such things as motivation, self-efficacy, and other aspects of cognitive style, as well as actual abilities, all of which are largely intrapersonal psychological processes. In contrast, worthiness, or simply "worth" as it is more commonly termed in the literature, is more of a feeling than a behavior, more of an evaluation than an outcome, and it always involves subjective appraisals of value. Such concepts as "right" or "wrong," "good" or "bad," or "healthy" or "unhealthy," and so forth imply more interpersonal and social foundations.

In addition, there is another richer but more complicated way in which there are two factors in the two-factor approach. At one level, the dual model seems to only involve identifying competence and worthiness as the two factors that are involved in self-esteem. But virtually everyone in this school also recognizes that the connection between them is also central to the model. In this sense, we could also say that the two factors may actually be (1) the individual components (competence and worth); and (2) the relationship between them. Perhaps the term "three-factor model" is more accurate in this regard (competence, worthiness, and their dynamic reciprocity), but I do not wish to add to the variations on the theme in the name of consistency. Suffice it to say that although this dimension of the two-factor approach is often overlooked, it may arguably be the most important part of the definition because it is the relationship between competence and worthiness that actually creates or generates self-esteem.

A TWO-FACTOR DEFINITION OF SELF-ESTEEM AND THE WORLD OF EVERYDAY LIFE

The final task of this chapter is to examine the three standard ways of defining self-esteem in the hope that one stands out as more accurate (valid) or at least more comprehensive (useful) than the others. It should be fairly clear that defining self-esteem primarily in terms of either competence or worthiness (worth) alone offers no advantage because they both seem to have reached a serious impasse, even a dead end. After all, success is never guaranteed and is always fleeting even when it is achieved. Therefore, basing self-esteem largely on competence means that the individual must live in a constant state of vigilance and always be on the lookout for threats and then be willing to act against them in one way or another. If this view of self-esteem is followed to its logical conclusion, then Crocker and Park (2003, 2004) are quite correct: The pursuit of self-esteem is far too "costly" and we should be studying ways to get rid of it rather than means of enhancing it.

Similarly, understanding self-esteem in terms of feeling good about oneself without connecting such belief or experience to reality through the expression of appropriate, corresponding behavior is also a lopsided way of understanding self-esteem. As we have seen, Baumeister and colleagues (1996, 2003), Damon (1995), Seligman (1995b), and others point out that such a "feel good" approach can only result in confusing self-esteem with things like narcissism, egotism, conceit, and other undesirable or "dark" states. Unfortunately, the largest portion of work on self-esteem seems to be based on the heterogeneity of such worthiness-based definitions, so it is no wonder that the entire field has come to such negative attention. As suggested earlier, then, one reason to pursue self-esteem that is based on competence and worthiness is that otherwise there is simply no reason to go any further with work based on the other definitions.

The second reason to define self-esteem in terms of competence and worthiness is more substantial: This way of understanding self-esteem is inherently more comprehensive than the others, which means that it offers different or perhaps even new possibilities in terms of integrating the disparate literature of the field. However, it is not the case that two factors are simply more powerful than one, because that could mean inheriting both sets of limits that we discussed earlier. Rather, it is the idea that competence and worthiness work together to create self-esteem that makes the definition different, dynamic, and powerful. Tafarodi and Vu (1997, p. 627) use an analogy of the difference between rectangles and the lines that create them to help understand this relationship and why it is so important for self-esteem. Studying only the lengths or widths of such a figure will never give us a sense of its true shape and characteristics. Putting them together, however, not only creates something that is much greater than the sum of its parts but also allows us to understand much more accurately the area that is opened up by them. In other words, competence and worthiness together define the "semantic space" (Tafarodi & Vu, 1997, p. 627) of the thing we call self-esteem: Defining it in terms of competence *and* worthiness rather than either term alone allows us to view the phenomenon more completely and, therefore, puts us in a much better position to understand it more fully.

Even so, the crucial test of any definition of self-esteem is how well it makes sense of the phenomenon at the lived level of real life. Although we discuss the methods used to research self-esteem as it is lived in everyday life in the next chapter, it is necessary to bring some of the results forward here so that we can take a position on which definition of self-esteem has the most empirical validity. Fortunately, a surprising number of studies have investigated self-esteem in this way. Epstein (1979) is one of the pioneers of empirically rigorous experiential work in this area. For example, in *A Study of Emotions in Everyday Life* he asked female and male participants to track daily experiences for a month and asked them to record the ones that enhanced or lessened the participant's self-esteem in detail. In brief, he found that there are at least two types of experiences that people report as being particularly thematic in terms of their self-esteem. I like to call these and other such poignant self-esteem experiences "self-esteem moments," which can be defined as situations in which one's experience of his or her own self-esteem becomes particularly active, thematic, and alive, or simply "lived." Epstein found that situations capable of generating success or failure in areas that are important to a given person constitute one set of self-esteem experiences. As might be expected, when outcomes are positive or successful, participants reported an increase in self-esteem, and when they are not, a corresponding decrease occurred. The other type of situation identified by Epstein that has such an effect on self-esteem are those that involve acceptance or rejection by significant others. Like before, the link to self-esteem in these moments is that situations leading to acceptance result in reports of increases in self-esteem and those that involve rejection were associated with reports of decreases in it. Others have done work that comes to similar conclusions. For instance, Tafarodi and Milne (2002) asked 244 students to respond to a retrospective measure of life events on two separate occasions, some 4 weeks apart. Their results correspond to Epstein's, with failure affecting participants' sense of "self-competence" and negative social events affecting their reports of "self-liking." Clearly, this work offers support for the position that both competence and worthiness are linked to self-esteem at the lived level of human experience.

In addition to affirming that competence and worthiness are linked to self-esteem, other related work reveals that it is actually the relationship between competence and worthiness that creates self-esteem. For example, in another study entitled, "Experiences That Produce Enduring Changes in Self-Concept," Epstein (1979, p. 73) asked a total of 270 college participants to describe in writing "the one experience in their lifetime that produced the greatest positive change in their self-concept and the one experience that produced the greatest negative change in their self-concept." The analysis of this data, which were gathered from almost equal numbers of men and women, identified that there are three types of such experiences that occur most often in adulthood. They are having to deal with a new environment, responding to a challenging problem that requires the person to acquire new responses, and gaining or losing significant relationships. Using smaller numbers of subjects but studying them in a much more in-depth fashion, Mruk (1983) examined another class of self-esteem experiences, one that seems to be powerful enough to change it at the deepest levels, a possibility that is extremely important in this field if it is to help people live better.

This work was conducted with a small number of participants who were reasonably well diversified in terms of age, gender, and socioeconomic status. They were asked to describe in detail a time when they were pleased with themselves in a biographically crucial way and a time when they were displeased with themselves in the same fashion (Mruk, 1981, 1983). Then, they were interviewed extensively about these powerful self-esteem moments. The experiences spontaneously chosen by all the subjects can be described as encountering a situation that challenged them to deal with what could be called a strong approach–avoidance situation, but one with unusually powerful biographical implications that tie the entire situation to important dimensions of their histories and identities as persons. This dimension of the situation called into question who the people knew themselves as being at deeper levels in a way that can be described in terms of "authenticity." That is, each subject was faced with a situation where, on one hand, they desperately wanted to do what they believed to be the "right thing" and where, on the other hand, doing so meant facing a personal limitation they had worked hard to avoid facing for most of their lives. In other words, situations where their self-esteem was genuinely "at stake," tied to both competence and to worthiness, and completely in their own hands.

One example involves an older woman with a traditional sense of gender who had to choose between complying with a male supervisor's legitimate work request to give up her current duties for others, or to take a stand and argue vigorously against changing positions based on the fact that she liked her job and did not want the new duties. On the surface, the immediate problem is a relatively simple one of compliance versus risk taking. Analysis revealed, however, that she had a long history of complying with authority figures, particularly males, beginning with her father, sometimes even to the point of abuse. In her life, then, such decisions inevitably led to her giving up what she really wanted and feeling terrible about doing so. Another example concerns a much younger man who had a clinically significant fear of public speaking. In the past he always avoided situations in which speaking publicly was necessary, sometimes at a cost of considerable psychological pain and missed financial opportunities. However, this individual also had a strong commitment to his career and work. Then, one day life suddenly challenged him on both levels when his career and personal development came together in a situation that required him to either defend his work in public forums or lose any hope of staying in the field that he loved the most. In these two examples the individuals faced their particular challenge of living and handled them in a way that was appropriate for a mature adult. They both experienced a concomitant increase in their self-esteem that lasted well into the future because each of them demonstrated competence at living in ways that are worthy of a decent, healthy, and functional human being.

Of course, facing such existential dilemmas does not always end on a positive note. One negative example involved a woman who had a life theme of loneliness around the holidays connected with the fact that her entire family died when she was young. One holiday season, she was facing the possibility of terrible isolation yet again. At that moment, a certain colleague made advances toward her. She did not care for the individual in any special way and was also aware that the circumstances were such that fellow workers would know of any intimate contact. Even so, the thought of being alone again seemed too overwhelming and the immediate possibility of comfort seemed too appealing to resist. Giving into these biographic forces, she slept with the colleague, much to her own chagrin. Similarly, a young man had a negative biographic theme that involved neglecting his physical well-being in certain situations. He subjected an already injured back to additional stress rather than allowing himself the time to rest because doing so would have meant thinking about the loss of an important relationship he could not bear to face. Unfortunately, this decision led to the development of a chronic illness and continual pain. In both instances, the person took what at first appeared to be the easy way out, failed to deal with the deeper challenge life presented in a way that demonstrated competence and worthiness, and subsequently suffered negative consequences, especially inauthenticity and a loss of self-esteem.

The analysis of this type of self-esteem experience or moment involves a six-stage process that the individual goes through when facing such a major challenge of living, which we examine later in Chapter 5. The point here is that we do seem to be able to find evidence supporting the position that self-esteem involves competence *and* worthiness at the lived level, in ways powerful enough to have a transforming effect on people. As before, this kind of work has also been done by others and supports its conclusions, meaning that this third force in the psychology of self-esteem is not just a collection of isolated findings. For example, Michael Jackson (1984) also looked at situations that involved intense biographic conflicts and came to similar conclusions concerning the unique character of self-esteem. In short, we may say that there is empirical evidence to support this definition of self-esteem.

A PHENOMENOLOGICAL, MEANING-BASED APPROACH TO A TWO-FACTOR DEFINITION

The two-factor approach to defining self-esteem seems to be more comprehensive theoretically because it is capable of handling material from either of its single-factor counterparts. The approach also appears to be in a position to be more empirically accurate than the others when they are examined at the lived level. Therefore, there is only one more task that needs to be completed before taking this way of defining self-esteem to the field. It is here that we will find whether this two-factor approach has the power to make real advances in terms of generating insights or establishing new levels of integration. This step involves fleshing the definition out so that we can see what is meant by competence and worthiness, as well as how their relationship works to create self-esteem in positive or negative ways. Phenomenological psychologists often use what is called the "general structure" of the phenomenon (Giorgi, 1971, 1975) to complete this process. A general or fundamental structure is a succinct description of all the elements that are necessary to give rise to a given human phenomenon or experience. It also describes how the individual components work together to create the phenomenon in the lived world. When properly done, such a complete description also makes an excellent definition of a phenomenon because it is more substantial than a mere concept.

Because fundamental structures are only found in the life world, their descriptions can only emerge from data generated at this level. The investigation that I conducted into more poignant self-esteem moments presented earlier also led to the development of a fundamental structure, and it has been refined over time (Mruk, 1981, 1995, 1999). As it is used here, then, *self-esteem is the lived status of one's competence at dealing with the challenges of living in a worthy way over time.* One of the valuable things about succinct descriptions of fundamental structures is that they show what is both necessary and sufficient for a particular phenomenon to occur, which means that they can also be unfolded in a way that reveals the inner workings of the phenomenon, as well as its basic components. The lived structure of self-esteem consists of five key elements which can be unpacked in the following fashion.

The first one, "status," concerns a particular state of being. The word was chosen to represent this aspect of self-esteem because status implies something that is reasonably stable while still being open to change under certain conditions. One's economic or marital status are examples of this condition. In this sense, each of us tends to live a relatively stable degree, level, or type of self-esteem that we characteristically bring to the world. The word "lived" is added to status to express that self-esteem cannot be avoided: It is grounded in the past, becomes alive in the present, and follows us into the future in one form or another. Yet, like other dynamic conditions, sometimes self-esteem is lived in a way that is more important for particular situations than others, such as the ones that have been identified as self-esteem moments.

Competence, of course, is a familiar term. It is often used in this field to refer to an individual's particular set of physical, cognitive, and social skills or abilities, as well as weaknesses in these areas. However, it is also important to realize, as developmental psychology does, that competence is also a process: It takes time and practice to learn how to master the tasks of life. Competence is connected to self-esteem because individuals deal with the various challenges of living on the basis of what specific skills are available to them but also through one's particular level of maturity as an individual. Sometimes the challenges of living are small, or at least normal, such as learning to walk, growing up, and acquiring the survival skills that are necessary in a particular culture. We also encounter much larger challenges such as finding and maintaining meaningful relationships, earning a living, raising a family, and so forth. In addition, at yet other times, life presents us with challenges that are especially powerful because they mobilize who we are at the deepest or most authentic levels. In all three cases, the word "challenge" is appropriate. After all, by definition, a challenge involves facing a task that has an uncertain outcome, taxes us in terms of our current abilities, and gives us the opportunity to reach higher levels or fall back to lower ones, but not without considerable cost.

The concept of worthiness is important in describing the structure of self-esteem because it expresses the fact that self-esteem does not occur in a vacuum. Rather, it is tied to the value or quality of our actions. Competent behavior tends to result in positive feelings, and poor performance often creates negative ones. But worthiness is far more than a mere outcome because worthiness concerns the meaning of our actions. Instead, worthiness is the value dimension of self-esteem and ranges from low to high. More mature or "authentic" actions are superior to others because they are less common, deserve more respect, and demonstrate virtue. The particularly intense self-esteem moments examined earlier demonstrate that the feelings of worth that are associated with self-esteem reflect the quality or meaning of certain behaviors. For example, some types of actions, such as "doing the right thing," generate positive self-esteem because they have positive value or meaning. Other behaviors result in a loss of self-esteem because of the lack of such value or because they are of genuinely negative or dishonorable value.

In relationship to self-esteem, then, competence is needed for worthiness because only certain types of actions have such a positive meaning. However, worthiness also balances competence because not all things that one does effectively are necessarily meritorious. Talking about competence or worthiness without stressing their relationship could mean that we are not talking about genuine self-esteem at all. After all, competence without worthiness can result in negative acts of human behavior, such as injuring others for personal gain, and feelings of worthiness without doing something to earn them is, at best, narcissistic. It is the relationship between competence and worthiness that is at the heart of self-esteem, as we saw in Tafarodi and Vu's rectangle. I would add that because they are equal, the only way to show the particular nature of the relationship between competence and worthiness using the metaphor of lines and figures is to point out that only one such form captures such balance: that of a square, which may express the lived character of self-esteem a bit more completely.

Time is the last term in the fundamental structure of self-esteem and it pertains to this phenomenon in several ways. First, it takes time to develop a stable form of self-esteem because, in the largest sense, it is the result of a developmental process. Rather than being born with self-esteem, when it is defined this way self-esteem emerges in the space created by competence and worthiness as they stand in relationship to each other over time. Second, time is also that which carries us into the future, which is to say toward self-esteem moments that have yet to come to us as adolescents, adults, and as older people. This aspect of the relationship between time and self-esteem means that time is both an adversary and friend when it comes to self-esteem. The bad news is that when we fail to act in ways that are competent *and* worthy, we suffer a loss of self-esteem and experience corresponding pain. The good news is that at other times we have the opportunity to demonstrate higher levels of competence and to thereby affirm, regain, or even to increase our sense of worth as human beings by our own hands. In either case, time is important to the fundamental structure of self-esteem because it shows us that it is something that deserves our attention throughout the entire cycle of life.

By now it should be clear that there are ways in which defining self-esteem in terms of a relationship between competence and worth or worthiness is more comprehensive than basing it on either competence or worthiness alone. Similarly, it should seem plausible that defining self-esteem in terms of at least two factors (three, if one counts the relationship as a factor) is also more accurate at the lived level, which is the basic source of data for understanding human behavior. In the following chapters, we see that understanding self-esteem in terms of competence and worthiness together help us to deal more effectively with other problems in the field as well.

CHAPTER 2

Self-Esteem Research Problems and Issues

Like most investigations into human behavior, understanding self-esteem involves dealing with several major research problems and issues particular to a field. They can be grouped into two types in the case of self-esteem work. The first set arises out of the characteristics of the phenomenon itself, such as the problem of defining self-esteem, how self-esteem is a dynamic phenomenon with existential relevance, and so forth. The other group of difficulties stem from using the scientific method to study something such as self-esteem in the first place. These issues involve such things as the many methods that have been used to research self-esteem, each of which has its own strengths and weaknesses; certain methodological challenges that arise when researching or measuring self-esteem; and some special problems that concern validity in self-esteem work. It is important to understand both sets of issues so that we have a framework in which to evaluate the many findings that characterize this field.

MAJOR SELF-ESTEEM PARADOXES

The first set of issues concerns self-esteem as a phenomenon. Is there really such a thing as self-esteem, or is it an artifact of culture as some suggest (Hewitt, 2002)? If there is, and the research on self-esteem moments makes us adopt this position, then how does one go about looking at self-esteem? For that matter, what is the difference between self-esteem and self-regard, self-respect, self-acceptance, self-love, self-confidence, self-efficacy, or self-image? How is self-esteem connected to these things? Although no one has all the answers to these questions, it is important to appreciate their presence in the field because they help in creating the definitional maze that Smelser (1989) noted earlier in Chapter 1.

Another layer of complexity is that all self-related phenomena are connected to a much larger philosophical and scientific set of questions that concern such things as consciousness itself, identity, and meaning making (Diggory, 1966; Harter, 1999; Jackson, 1984; Mecca, Smelser & Vasconcellos, 1989; Wells & Marwell, 1976; Wylie, 1974). Of course, it is not realistically possible to address these matters in a definitive way in this or any other book: Western philosophy has tried to deal with some of them for 2500 years (Miller, 1992). However, we do need to find a way of standing in the face of such complexity so that we do not become lost in it. Defining self-esteem in terms of competence and worthiness gives us a firm place to stand because it emerges from the fundamental structure of self-esteem, which is grounded in the human "life-world." Because description seemed to help when accessing that dimension, perhaps it will assist us in understanding the complexity of researching self-esteem, especially in terms of what can be called "self-esteem paradoxes," a term that Bednar, Wells, and Peterson (1989) offered in a related context.

Is the "Self" in Self-Esteem Primarily Psychological or Sociological?

As Bhatti, Derezotes, Kim, and Specht (1989) pointed out, there are two basic ways of looking at self-esteem and of doing work in this field.

> We have also noted that there are many different conceptions of self-esteem—some primarily psychological and others primarily sociological—all dealing with different dimensions of the phenomenon . . . various perspectives on self-esteem lead us to emphasize one or another policy direction. The sociological perspective tends to support policies and programs that will increase self-esteem by reducing environmental pressures on vulnerable persons (e.g., provision of child care for single teenage parents); the psychological perspective tends to support policies and programs that will increase self-esteem by changing individuals (e.g., counseling and psychotherapy). (p. 60)

Each perspective involves a different vision of what the "self" in self-esteem means and how to understand it. The psychological approach to the self and self-esteem focuses largely on the individual, intrapsychic developmental processes, the role of the individual in the creation of the self through decision making, and specific behaviors, particularly those that involve success, mastery, and achievement. We saw that this influence is alive today in psychological approaches to self-esteem, especially among those who define it primarily in terms of competence. However, it is interesting to note that starting at nearly the same time, a more socio-logical approach to the self also began to develop through what is often regarded as the Cooley–Mead tradition in sociology (Cooley, 1909; Meade, 1934). Here the self is held to be a largely interpsychic phenom-enon that develops in a social context. As such, the focus is on how others react to us, how we react to their reactions, and how those processes lead to the development of self and one's worth or value in a social context. This sociological view of self-esteem can easily be seen running through the work developed by Rosenberg (1965, 1986), Smelser (1989), and others who tend to emphasize the worthiness component of self-esteem.

Whether the self is primarily a psychological or social phenomenon makes dealing with the self complicated because no matter which per-spective one starts from, it always leads to the other. The additional fact that this phenomenon may be studied from two overlapping but dis-tinctly different disciplines adds even more complexity to the picture. When psychologists study self-esteem, the methods of introspection, case study, and interviews, as well as experimental design, are likely to be used. In contrast, when self-esteem is studied from a sociological per-spective, conducting surveys, looking for group norms, and establishing correlations among various demographic variables such as race, gender, socioeconomic status, and so on, are more likely to come into play. The paradox is, of course, that both approaches are valid because the self is the product of both types of forces from its beginning. However, starting from different positions, using different assumptions, having separate priorities, and working with different methods, serves to create a bewil-dering range of hypotheses, data, and findings to deal with when trying to understand either self-esteem or the work that has been done on it.

Self-Esteem as a Trait versus a State

For a good while, self-esteem was understood to be a relatively stable characteristic, something like personality or intelligence, which gave it the form of a trait. As such, it was possible to think of self-esteem in terms of degrees: high, medium, and low. Historically, much self-esteem research, especially that which was based on assessing self-esteem with a unidimensional scale of worthiness, views self-esteem in this way. However, now we know that self-esteem is much more complicated than that. For example, it became apparent that self-esteem could also be thought of as involving several factors, or as being multidimensional, with each component making a specific contribution to self-esteem.

Another complication is that although people have talked about levels and types of self-esteem for a long time now, these two terms were often used interchangeably. Recently, however, researchers began to notice that some people's self-esteem appeared to fluctuate considerably with certain situations, or even in general (Greenier, Kernis & Waschull, 1995). Thus, it becomes meaningful to see self-esteem in terms of states, as well as traits. Instead of understanding self-esteem as ranging on a continuum of high to low levels, it may also be necessary to see it in terms of ranging from being relatively stable to unstable. This approach means that there are distinctly different types of self-esteem and that they cannot be ordered along a simple continuum. Instead, types and levels can be thought of as two intersecting or overlapping continua. The paradox in this regard is how can self-esteem manifest itself in such different ways? It would be helpful if we could simply determine that one view is superior to the other because that would reduce the complexity of the field. However, it is more likely that we need a way of making sense of self-esteem that integrates all of the possibilities.

Is the Function of Self-Esteem a Motivational Need or a Calling?

Although there are exceptions, the majority of those who research and otherwise investigate self-esteem approach it in terms of a need, which is the most basic type of motivation (Bednar, Wells & Peterson, 1989; Branden, 1969; Leary & Downs, 1995; Mecca, Smelser & Vasconcellos, 1989; Wells & Marwell, 1976). However, there are two ways of seeing self-esteem as a need that must be reconciled if we wish to understand it in a comprehensive fashion. On one hand, people are thought to need self-esteem because it maintains the self and a sense of self-sameness over time, or an identity. In this sense, self-esteem acts as a shield: it defends the self against insults from the environment and protects the integrity of the self during more stressful times (Coopersmith, 1967; Newman & Newman, 1987). Another way in which self-esteem can work to protect the individual is to function as a gauge, one that helps us regulate behavior to keep it in a certain safe or comfortable zone, especially in terms of social functioning (Leary, 2004a, b). In this case, low self-esteem, for instance, would be a signal to stop engaging in a certain kind of behavior and to start engaging in other more prosocial actions.

In contrast, many others (Deci & Ryan, 1995; Kernis, 1995; Rogers, 1961; Ryan & Deci, 2003, 2004) suggest that instead of just maintaining the self, self-esteem also motivates us to expand the self and selfhood. Here, the need for self-esteem takes on the character of a "calling" or an intrinsic motivation to reach a higher level of mastery and growth. Such motivation pushes the individual to face challenges rather than avoid them, keeps the person plugging away at an obstacle instead of giving up, and encourages them to take risks to "be all one can be" rather than to shy from such possibilities in life. In this case, self-esteem is seen as helping the person to be "authentic" and to live "authentically." Once again, a simple dichotomous approach to the question of whether self-esteem is related primarily to self-maintenance or self-enhancement is somewhat misleading because it oversimplifies matters. The paradox is that there is good evidence for each possibility and it is likely self-esteem works in both ways, which means that a comprehensive model will have to find some way of incorporating both motivational structures into its approach.

Is Self-Esteem a Developmental Product or Process?

The next puzzling characteristic of self-esteem to consider concerns its nature as a developmental phenomenon. On one hand, it can be said that self-esteem develops in a certain direction and then stays relatively consistent thereafter for most people (Trzesniewski, Robins, Roberts & Caspi, 2004). Hence, we can talk about the developmental processes and events that lead to various types or levels of self-esteem as possibilities or destinations. If so, then where a person ends up developmentally depends on the usual set of factors working together such as temperament, environment, reinforcement, choices, good fortune, and so forth.

However, we have also seen that it is possible to focus on self-esteem as an ongoing developmental process, one that is open to change in certain situations, even in adulthood. Otherwise, there is no need to talk about changing self-esteem once we move past adolescence, which would make most of the empirically supported work on changing self-esteem in adulthood (Bednar & Peterson, 1995; Bednar, Wells & Peterson, 1989; Frey et al., 1992; Hakim-Larson & Mruk, 1997) meaningless. From this point of view, self-esteem is not just a fixed quality that, once set, shapes perception and behavior in one direction. Instead of being simply global, self-esteem also responds to various situations that arise in life and in response to certain types of developmental challenges. This "global versus situational" characteristic of self-esteem, as it is known in testing literature, is also relevant to assessing or measuring self-esteem (Harter, 1999). For example, if we are to design an instrument that genuinely assesses self-esteem, we must be sure that it is not constructed in a way that is too sensitive to situational fluctuations in self-esteem or the instrument will be unreliable.

Is Self-Esteem an Independent or a Dependent Variable?

Finally, we encounter what might be the most challenging paradox of all. This issue involves understanding how self-esteem works in everyday life.

Kitano (1989) presented the problem clearly when he pointed out that self-esteem is a complex variable.

> From a sociocultural perspective, it is a dependent variable, that is, self-esteem is the result of a person's ethnic, social class, or gender group. . . . Another aspect of self-esteem is self-esteem that is in progress or in process. Individuals are perceived and judge themselves in relation to yet-to-be fulfilled goals and activities. . . . Self-esteem is also used as an independent variable—that is, as the "cause" of behavior. An individual is said to behave in a particular manner because of a high or low level of self-esteem. Through knowledge of the variable, then, we can try to predict and understand behavior. (p. 318)

In other words, one reason that it is difficult to research self-esteem is because there are several ways of hypothesizing how it works.

The relationship between self-esteem and academic achievement is a good example of this paradox in action. First, there are those who see self-esteem as playing a causal role, meaning that changes in one factor ought to produce changes in the other. If so, then increasing self-esteem should lead to corresponding increases in grades. Second, there are those who take the position that self-esteem is a dependent variable, which means that the relationship works in the other direction (Baumeister, Campbell, Krueger & Vohs, 2003). In this case, academic achievement is the independent variable that affects self-esteem. If so, then enhancing academic skills should be a way to increase self-esteem. The paradox is that self-esteem may work in both ways, or "directionally" (Harter, 1999). Thus, in understanding self-esteem we must either determine which of the first two views is correct or understand how self-esteem can appear to change from one type of variable to the other.

Summation of the Paradoxes

Determining whether self-esteem is primarily a psychological or social phenomenon; a trait or a state; a need or a call; a product or a process; or an independent, dependent, or mediating variable is an overwhelming task if we think in traditionally dichotomous ways. However, we can also examine the work that has been done on each theme and see if it is possible to clarify them any further at this point in the development of the field. At least the process of combing the current field of research to identify these themes is a valuable endeavor because each one of them brings our attention to a different aspect of self-esteem that has research, theoretical, and perhaps even practical significance. In addition, these themes also have to be accounted for in any kind of comprehensive or integrated theory of self-esteem, which is our basic goal. Thus, even clarifying one of them is worth the while. Fortunately, we will find that in the past few years especially, the field has made some advances in this regard.

PROBLEMS WITH ASSESSING SELF-ESTEEM

Much of the empirical work on self-esteem involves testing someone's self-esteem, measuring self-esteem across samples, or assessing self-esteem in relation to other variables, especially clinical or academic ones. Therefore, it is important to focus on the fact that it is difficult to develop a good (i.e., reliable, valid, and useful) instrument to measure this basic human characteristic. Unfortunately, although there are dozens, if not hundreds of self-esteem tests available, few are worth considering because the majority of them succumb to problems in one or more of the areas described in the following sections. These design features can also be used as criteria for determining whether an instrument is a good one.

Measuring the Right Things

The first factor to consider in developing, using, or evaluating a test or measure is to make sure that the instrument actually assesses what it claims to assess, in this case, self-esteem. Our work on defining self-esteem lets us know, for example, that self-esteem is often thought about in terms of competence or worth, or both. Therefore, one thing we need to do when examining an instrument is to determine which definition of self-esteem it is based on. The problem is much more complex than one of mere definitional preference: although most of the instruments that have been constructed to measure self-esteem are unidimensional in their design, self-esteem seems to be multidimensional, thereby rendering most of the tests as inadequate from the beginning.

Rosenberg's Self-Esteem Scale (1965, 1979) is a major case in point because it has been the most widely used measure. Both Gecas (1971) and Tafarodi and Swann Jr. (1995) have investigated that instrument independently and found that even this scale of global self-esteem actually consists of two dimensions.

> Contradicting the scale's assumed unidimensionality, factor analyses have revealed that the items reduce to two correlated but distinct factors. Generally, it has been found that items with high loadings on one factor are all positively worded, whereas items with high loadings on the other factor are all negatively worded. . . . Evidence for two underlying factors raises the possibility that there may be two distinct global dimensions of self-valuative feeling. That is, global self-esteem may be experienced in two distinct senses. (Tafarodi & Swann Jr., 1995, pp. 323–324)

In all fairness to Rosenberg, it must be said that he was aware of this issue, which he talked about in terms of "baseline" (overall or global) self-esteem and "barometric" (domain-specific or situational) self-esteem (Rosenberg, 1986) later in his work. Fortunately, Harter (1985), Tafarodi and Swann Jr. (2001), and O'Brien and Epstein (1983, 1988) developed approaches to measuring self-esteem that were based on multiple dimensions or "domains" from the ground up. Such "multidimensional" tools may turn out to be more accurate instruments, which is of great importance if one chooses to do work that involves measuring self-esteem. The point is that the instruments used to assess self-esteem may be unidimensional, unidimensional in intent but actually multidimensional in practice, or explicitly multidimensional. Which form is used in a given work makes an important difference in terms of how and whether self-esteem is actually being assessed.

Dealing with Dynamic Factors

The dynamic nature of self-esteem is another issue with which test designers must contend. It should be recalled that self-esteem is a phenomenon that may be seen as being global or situational in nature because we live out a certain basic level of self-esteem most of the time, but in a way that also involves the potential to fluctuate or change. The simplest example of how this factor affects a testing situation is when the subject has experienced a recent loss, gain, failure, or success, any of which can affect self-esteem test scores. Unfortunately, many self-esteem tests are too general and fail to tell us about the particular situations or specific areas of life that are important for an individual's self-esteem. This testing challenge is a difficult one to overcome because it requires identifying areas of life that can contribute to, or have an effect on, self-esteem before constructing the instrument, and all but a few instruments do not seem to have done that.

The Development of Norms

There appears to be some consensus that a good instrument has at least three normative characteristics. First, the selection processes for finding subjects from which to obtain norms must be random so that the test does not reflect a bias for any group. Second, the subject pool must be stratified so that the normative sample is genuinely representative of the general population of those who will be examined by the test once it is developed. Third, the size of the normative sample must be large enough so that the test can be used with a wide range of individuals and backgrounds: If we are interested in assessing self-esteem for the general population, then the normative samples must also be sensitive to age, gender, culture, and so on.

Unfortunately, individual researchers develop most self-esteem tests for specific purposes rather than for general use by major research facilities or clinicians (Wells & Marwell, 1976). This situation usually results in tests that are normed on relatively small numbers of subjects. Consequently, even well-known self-esteem tests are normalized against no more than a thousand participants and the majority use many less. Yet, a small number of subjects cannot hope to provide good norms for the major social, ethnic, economic, or other socially based variables that affect self-esteem. Similarly, developmental factors affecting self-esteem pose a normative challenge. For example, Pope, McHale, and Craighead (1988) and Harter (1999) pointed out that developmental age is a factor that needs to be included in normalizing a self-esteem test, especially in regard to younger people. For instance, it is likely that a 6-year-old has different self-esteem issues than a 12-year-old and using the same set of norms to evaluate both individuals is simply inappropriate. The problem of normalization is compounded by the fact that many self-esteem tests do not even report how, and sometimes even whether, they were standardized in relation to any particular criteria (Sappington, 1989). The result is that most of the instruments are nearly useless.

Self-Report Problems

The problem with most psychological tests is that they are subjective in that we must use an individual's report of his or her own experience, behavior, or characteristics to draw conclusions about that person. The responses of even the most well-meaning subjects are going to be filtered by all kinds of factors usually involved in self-perception, not to mention the additional problems that can occur when an individual is anxious, angry, suspicious, or mentally ill. Even under the best circumstances, for instance, self-esteem tests are vulnerable to the "ceiling effect," or the tendency to see oneself in a positive light when reporting about oneself. The most common problem that arises from this factor is that most people tend to rate themselves more favorably on positive qualities and less unfavorably on negative ones than they are likely to actually merit when compared with external standards (Wells & Marwell, 1976).

In addition, self-esteem tests are also vulnerable to what social psychologists call the "social desirability" effect (Baumeister, Campbell, Krueger & Vohs, 2003). In regard to self-esteem, however, such an effect is extremely important because it can generate "false positives" in addition to simply elevating scores in general (Greenier, Kernis & Waschull, 1995). That is, some people, particularly those who suffer some from unstable, fragile, or pseudo self-esteem, are defensive. They resist admitting to ordinary human failings let alone low self-esteem, consciously or otherwise. Instead of reporting such insecurity about their competence or worth or both, they deny it and can even overcompensate instead. The result is that not only are their scores elevated, but also more importantly, they are simply wrong. In addition to creating difficulties in terms of developing good norms, such a problem can present crucial issues in clinical work. In other words, without tests that have some means of identifying such "defensiveness," as it is often called, these complications are sure to cause the researcher or clinician to miss an entire range of serious self-esteem problems. Probably the best way to deal with the issue is to develop validity scales, such as those of the Minnesota Multiphasic Personality Inventory (Hathaway et al., 1989). Although such an exhaustive approach is not practical, it is reasonable to expect a good self-esteem test to at least alert us to the possibility of excessive deception and defensiveness. Sadly, few tests even come close to being helpful in this regard.

Test Validity: A Question of Limits

Even if a self-esteem test addresses all of the issues mentioned earlier, we still have to know whether, and to what extent, a given instrument is valid. Although written more than 3 decades ago, the review by Wells and Marwell (1976) still does an unparalleled job of examining the technical difficulties involved in developing self-esteem tests. Their work described how self-esteem measures can be evaluated against three traditional indicators of test validity. The highest type of validity such an instrument can have occurs when test items or tasks predict a particular outcome accurately. Unfortunately, such "criterion validity" is unlikely to occur with self-esteem tests, in part because it is such a complex phenomenon.

Content validity is another approach and is based on whether the test questions are connected to self-esteem in some logical way. For instance, it is possible to define what kinds of behaviors or attitudes are most likely to be associated with high and low self-esteem, and then design questions that ask about them. This type of validity increases with the thoroughness of the questions: The more the test covers the whole range of factors thought to reflect self-esteem, the greater the validity of the instrument. We know that there are a good number of such self-esteem tests, but with the exception of a few, most of them are so brief that they cannot hope to be considered valid because they are based on an incomplete definition of self-esteem. Furthermore, even when both competence and worthiness are covered by a test, brevity often takes precedence over comprehensiveness because short tests are easier to administer and score than longer ones.

Construct validity, or "the degree to which certain explanatory concepts or constructs account for performance on the test" (Wells & Marwell, 1976, p. 153), is another way to achieve a meaningful degree of validity in self-esteem testing. This type of validity is based on the connections between a particular self-esteem test and the theory or definition of self-esteem that a researcher or clinician is using in his or her work. If the theory is well constructed and if the test questions embody the major components of self-esteem as they are expressed by the theory, then the measure at least has a certain logical integrity or theoretical validity. Unfortunately, such tests are usually transparent and easily manipulated by the subject. Even so, they can be useful, providing a clinician is only interested in using the instrument to open up a discussion of self-esteem or to develop a general sense of it. This "practical" approach to validity is often favored by clinicians, because the here-and-now concerns of identifying basic self-esteem issues and problems for clients are more important than measuring self-esteem with academic precision or waiting for researchers to achieve a meaningful degree of consensus on a particular issue. Not surprisingly, such face validity is by far the most common one in this field.

PROBLEMS GENERATED BY USING THE SCIENTIFIC METHOD

The next group of problems faced by self-esteem researchers occurs when we try to investigate this phenomenon scientifically. Proponents of so-called "pop psych" (self-help) approaches to self-esteem do not have to deal with these knotty issues. For the rest of us, there are certain methodological problems that invariably arise in self-esteem research and assessment due to the presence of two scientific paradigms (one quantitative, the other qualitative) and the question of their validity.

Methodological Diversity in Researching Self-Esteem

A few major self-esteem researchers and theoreticians grapple with the fact that there is considerable methodological diversity in the psychology of self-esteem. The most thorough and comprehensive work in this regard is that of Wells and Marwell (1976), whose entire book is devoted to the subject. Rather than attempt to duplicate this classic, I will refer to it as the leading authority. *The Social Importance of Self-Esteem* (1989) by Mecca and colleagues updated this information but did not change it. The list of methods used to study self-esteem is fairly typical of the social sciences in general. It has been studied introspectively (Epstein, 1979), with case studies and interviews (Bednar, Wells & Peterson, 1989;

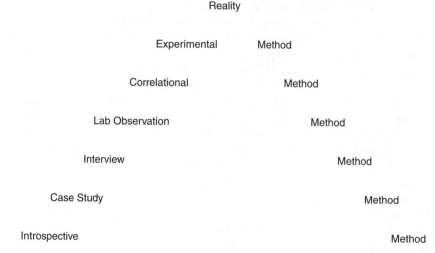

Figure 2.1   The Traditional Methodological Pyramid.

Branden, 1969; Pope, McHale & Craighead, 1988), through surveys and tests (Rosenberg, 1965), experimentally (Coopersmith, 1967), and phenomenologically (Jackson, 1984; Mruk, 1983). One way of understanding such methodological diversity in the social sciences is to organize it in terms of increasing degrees of objectivity (measurability), which results in a kind of pyramid, as shown in Figure 2.1.

According to this arrangement, the most subjective (qualitative) methods are placed lowest on the hierarchy and the most measurable or objective (quantitative) ones are placed at the top, with the experiment standing as the epitome of the scientific method. Let me move quickly through this pyramid in terms of the strengths and weaknesses of the various methods as they are used for researching self-esteem. In the next section, I examine the range of methods from a different, more revealing angle.

Introspection

This approach was first used by James (1890/1983) to study self-esteem more than a century ago. However, examining one's own experience by simply describing it is rarely used in self-esteem research today because the method is considered to be extremely subjective. For example, classically introspective research depends on one individual's perception of his or her own experience and is therefore vulnerable to problems with reliability and validity associated with having a sample of only one. Nevertheless, it is instructive to note that some of James' early findings based on this technique turn out to be central today in terms of defining self-esteem and its major dynamics. Thus, we must conclude that although introspection is at the bottom of the traditional research hierarchy, it is not without value, at least as a source of insight.

Case Study

This method, especially clinical case study, is another "soft" technique used in the psychology of self-esteem and is also quite low on the standard methodological hierarchy. However, case study is important even today because it allows us to investigate problems with self-esteem when looking at individual lives. Case study, for example, helps us to explore the relationship between self-esteem and psychological functioning by comparing individuals and noting regularities or variations from regular patterns. Indeed, Branden (1969) pointed out that this approach is useful in the clinical or applied settings. In fact, many, if not most, self-esteem enhancement programs rely on case study evidence as the main source of support for their therapeutic efficacy. Finally, case study is an integral part of good clinical training. However, it is important to appreciate the limitations of this method of researching and enhancing self-esteem. Although studying several cases can expand the subject base, such work is time consuming and results in a number that is far too small to allow one to generalize very far. Also, the data generated and the procedures for analysis are not often amenable to duplication.

The Interview Method

Interviewing subjects is better for studying self-esteem than introspection or case study because this method can correct some of the weaknesses of the other approaches. For instance, structuring the interview in advance helps to make it more reliable, and an interview can be recorded and transcribed so that others have access to the data, which reduces some subjectivity. The major limitations of doing research this way include the fact that sample sizes are still relatively small and that establishing cause-and-effect relationships is another matter: Although a hypothesis can be formed, confirmation is difficult. Also, the time that is involved in conducting interviews can place additional burdens on valuable resources.

Laboratory Observational Method

Because it is not possible to see self-esteem directly, laboratory-based observational methods are not used often in researching self-esteem. However, there is some work that focuses on direct observation of children and other work that involves asking parents, teachers, and even peers to evaluate the behavior of others in terms of self-esteem (Coopersmith, 1967; Harter, 1999). Perhaps one of the more important uses of the method is in the clinical setting, where a clinician actually asks the parents and teachers of children about domains where the child is experiencing success or difficulty (Pope, McHale & Craighead, 1988). This method is limited in terms of its ability to tell us about cause and effect or why something happens, but it does offer the important advantage of offering more concrete information than previous approaches provide.

Correlational Method

Much of the work on self-esteem involves the use of surveys and testing as ways of gaining access to the phenomenon. Surveys and tests are an especially attractive way to study self-esteem because once an assessment instrument has been developed it can be used to establish correlations in many types of situations. We use such measures to assess an individual's self-esteem, for instance, in relation to their behavior, performance, grades, or even personality. We can also set up pre- and post-testing situations for measuring self-esteem under experimental conditions or in relation to therapeutic manipulations. High versus low self-esteem is the most frequent type of comparison made in this regard, but researchers have focused on behavioral correlates of medium and defensive self-esteem as well (Kernis, 2003a).

Studying self-esteem by measuring it is important for research and for theoretical reasons. For example, establishing correlations reduces some of the subjectivity of the research process. Measurements also have practical value for a clinician or educator in that they can be used to target areas or behaviors in need of assistance. Furthermore, showing statistically significant links between self-esteem and well-being, performance, mental health, or any number of clinical conditions is also valuable. Unfortunately, this approach is difficult to implement because, as we saw earlier, developing good self-esteem measures means facing some serious research problems. Moreover, even when correlations are found, the old adage "a correlation does not a cause make" is still at play.

Experimental Research

Finally, we come to the experimental method and the top of the methodological pyramid. According to Wells and Marwell (1976), there are two basic types of experiments used to research self-esteem and both of them usually involve some pre- and post-test measures of self-esteem. The most straightforward format is to set up an experiment so that subjects are engaged in an activity; the outcome of which they believe depends on their efforts. However, it is actually the experimenter who controls the results, meaning that success and failure can be manipulated so that their effects on self-esteem can be observed. The other format differs in that subjects are given information about themselves or their personalities either just before or while attempting a task or activity. In this situation, the information is manipulated so that, for instance, a low self-esteem subject hears positive comments or a high self-esteem subject receives negative personal feedback as a manipulation. Either way, the experimental situation helps the researcher to observe or measure changes in behavior that may be linked to self-esteem and exciting work is being done using this method. For example, research on Terror Management Theory (Pyszczynski, Greenberg & Goldberg, 2003) and work that investigates what is called "implicit versus explicit" self-esteem (Devos & Banaji, 2003; Dijksterhuis, 2004) may be making headway using this approach.

The strength of this method is that it allows us to test for causal links between self-esteem and other phenomena or behavior. In addition to research and theoretical value, such information is important at the practical level. A self-esteem enhancement program that has this kind of evidence to back it is going to be seen as more valid than those that do not. However, we also know there are some real difficulties in applying this method in self-esteem research: It is time-consuming, labor intensive, expensive, and limited in terms of its level of generality beyond the laboratory situation. According to Scheff, Retzinger, and Ryan,

> The rich diversity of experimental research in this area is impressive, and certainly much is owed to the investigators for their ingenuity and persistence. It is therefore especially disheartening that the experimental studies have tended to be inconclusive, often demonstrating effects that are weak, nonexistent, or sometimes contradictory. Although much has been learned, the parts still fail to add up to a recognizable whole. Furthermore, because these studies are conducted in laboratory settings, the extrapolation of results to real situations is uncertain. Such studies may lack what is called "ecological" validity. (1989, p. 167)

Finally, researching self-esteem places especially severe demands on the method. Epstein, for example, points out some of those that occur when the researcher wants to examine emotionally significant human phenomena in the lab setting.

> How does one investigate love in the laboratory, or threats to an individual's ego that produce such high levels of anxiety as to produce enduring changes in personality? Obviously, for both practical and ethical reasons, such states cannot be studied in the laboratory. (1979, p. 50)

The significance of this limitation is important in regard to self-esteem research, especially when it comes to trying to demonstrate the link between self-esteem and behavior, which seems to stand as the major criticism against the field.

THE PROBLEM OF SCIENTIFIC PARADIGMS AND SELF-ESTEEM RESEARCH

Examining the methodological diversity in this field suggests that each approach offers a way of finding out valuable information about self-esteem. In fact, every method has generated an entire stream of self-esteem research and findings. Yet, we also saw that each approach also has serious limitations, including difficulty in achieving any type of consensus about the findings that are generated from such diverse work. Indeed, some self-concept experts suggest that investigating this class of phenomena using the scientific method is essentially a hopeless task (Diggory, 1966). Others regard the methodological difficulties in researching self-esteem as reflecting the limits of our quantitative sophistication and, therefore, call for "improved" statistical methodologies as the only hope (Smelser, 1989).

Today, there is a general recognition from both sociologists and psychologists studying self-esteem that the field is in a state of methodological flux. Scheff, Retzinger, and Ryan (1989), for instance, examined six major reviews of the methodological issues facing such research. Four reached a negative conclusion about the possibility of resolving the problems effectively, whereas two were hopeful about it. Scheff and colleagues conclude that

> Even reviewers who are completely sympathetic to the intentions of the quantitative studies acknowledge that these studies have produced no results. In our opinion, the implication of all six of the general reviews is not that the field is healthy but that it is in a state of crisis, and has been for some time. . . . We do not claim that the quantitative studies have been useless. On the contrary, we believe that they were necessary. Their very lack of success suggests the need for new directions in theory and method that might be more suited to the problem at hand. . . . Perhaps what is needed is a new paradigm more closely connected with the particular problem of self-esteem. (1989, p. 177)

Indeed, the situation may have become even more acute over the past few years given the continuation of the "anti-self-esteem movement." Yet, a crisis for one methodological paradigm can be an opportunity for another (Kuhn, 1962), and one way to see this possibility in terms

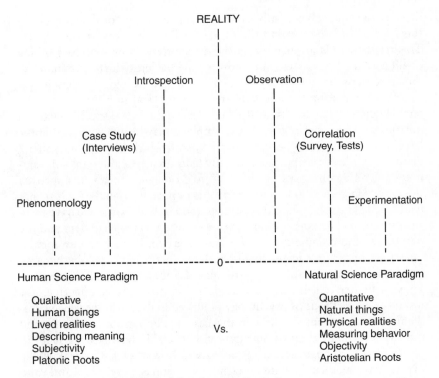

Figure 2.2   A Methodological Continuum.

of self-esteem work is to turn the traditional methodological pyramid on its side. Instead of a simple hierarchy, this literal shift in perspective results in a continuum of methods, as shown in Figure 2.2.

Figure 2.2 shows us that scientific methods actually have a range of characteristics when applied to understanding human phenomena. To the right of the midpoint, for instance, we encounter a focus on external realities and their measurement that is characteristic of the natural sciences. This approach begins with observation and progresses toward an increasing degree of "objectivity" that culminates with the experimental method. Such a progression in quantitative sophistication helps us to understand the natural world by observing properties, measuring characteristics, and discovering cause-and-effect relationships, often in that order.

People exist as objects in this world, so the methods of natural science may be applied to us too. However, it is also true that human beings are unique in that we are conscious, which means we live in a world of experience and meanings, as well as one consisting of physics and biology. The methods to the left of the midpoint reflect more of a human science paradigm and are better able to access internal realities because the focus is on the experiencing subject (subjectivity, which is to say "of the subject" in this case), lived reality, and the fundamental structures of experience. This time, there is an increase in the descriptive richness offered by the qualitative methods as we move toward the far left, which culminates in the more rigorous techniques of classical phenomenological psychology.

It is interesting to reflect on the metaphorical implications of the terms "left" and "right" because in a real sense they are perfectly balanced mirror images of one another. For example, it may be no accident that the left side of the diagram becomes more liberal, which is to say a "softer," Platonic, or idealistic approach to knowledge; whereas the right side connotes a certain conservative, "harder," Aristotelian, or realistic approach (Mruk & Hartzell, 2003). Therefore, it is important to make it clear that neither side of the line should be seen as good or bad: For as we have seen, such simple dichotomies do not work well when trying to understand the paradoxes and complexities of human behavior. Rather, the important question concerning scientific methods and paradigms is whether one technique is more suitable to a particular task than another. If we want to know whether a self-esteem enhancement program is effective, for instance, the methods of psychology practiced in the natural science paradigm make good sense because in this case it is important to identify and measure outcomes in terms of causes and effects. If, however, we want to know what self-esteem actually is in terms of how it is lived by real people in everyday life, then the human science paradigm is more useful and valid because it is able to access the lived world of experience more directly.

Phenomenological Methods

We have already investigated traditional methods for researching self-esteem from the paradigm of psychology practiced as a natural science, so let us now examine the qualitative paradigm by looking at the methods used by modern phenomenological psychology. There are several reasons to look at this material when investigating the psychology of self-esteem. For one thing, it is difficult to dismiss the value of paying attention to the qualities of experience in this field. For example, Harter (1999) uses the term "phenomenology" to remind us that even if we wish to dismiss such "fuzzy" or subjective aspects of self-esteem as "non-scientific," we cannot do so because self-esteem and its components "do represent a phenomenological reality for individuals" (p. 192). In later work she said,

> However, it is very important to emphasize that, in our zeal for parsimonious explanatory models, we must not ignore the fact that the *phenomenological* self-theory as experienced by children, adolescents, and

adults is not necessarily parsimonious. Self-evaluations, including global self-worth, are very salient constructs in one's working model of self and, as such, can wield powerful influences on affect and behavior. Thus, the challenge is to develop models that identify the specific antecedents of different outcomes while preserving the critical role of self-representations as phenomenological mediators. (Harter, 2003, p. 635)

Devos and Banaji (2003) made a similar point when discussing an individual's immediate, non-reflective reaction to various events. Such phenomenological experience, they noted, is an important factor in experimentally contrived situations but is usually not taken into account by researchers who do such work.

However, the term "phenomenology" is not only used in a descriptive sense as we have just seen. It is also used as a technical term that refers to an entire approach to psychology, one that goes beyond mere symptomology or only subjective experience. Giorgi's work (1971, 1984) is especially helpful in this regard because he was also trained in traditional empirical psychology. This approach begins by pointing out what phenomenological psychology is not to be mistaken as. Modern phenomenological psychology is not introspectionism because we want to investigate the structure of a given experience, not just a particular incidence of it. Individual experience, I like to say to my students, is a good starting place, but unless we are working in a clinical setting, a sample of one cannot take us far in terms of knowledge. What if, for example, the person whose experience was used turned out to be emotionally upset at the time the experience was described or under the influence of a drug such as alcohol or a psychotic state? Although it is true that investigating a person's experience of something by having him or her describe it is the beginning of phenomenological research, that is only the first step. Phenomenological inquiry is interested in understanding both how an experience or phenomenon is lived concretely in a person's life *and* how it is that a certain experience is possible in the first place. Instead of merely analyzing components of an experience as we might with content analysis, phenomenology attempts to describe what gives rise to these elements in a way that allows them to form a particular type of human experience.

Giorgi also pointed out that, contrary to some characterizations, phenomenological methods are not "anti-scientific." Quite the contrary: as we just indicated, phenomenological description and analysis are just as rooted in the scientific method as naturalistic or traditional psychology, a point that I try to make throughout this book. Indeed, qualitative methods can actually be very formal as we move toward the extreme left of the continuum.

> If anything, a phenomenological approach is even more rigorous than
> a traditional approach because it tries to account for more of the phe-
> nomenon. . . . Traditional psychology has avoided the major psycho-
> logical issues by either ignoring the peculiarly human phenomena or by
> reducing them to such an extent to fit the strict scientific method that
> they were no longer recognizable. A phenomenological approach to
> human phenomena insists that the phenomenon cannot be essentially
> distorted. . . . From a phenomenological viewpoint measuring a phe-
> nomenon is not the same as determining its meaning. These are two
> separate perspectives that must be balanced in every research. (Giorgi,
> 1971, p. 14)

Like its natural science counterpart, the phenomenological method
involves a step-by-step approach to collecting observations of experience,
analyzing them, and presenting findings in a way that can be confirmed
or challenged by others who replicate the steps.

A related misconception, Giorgi noted, is that phenomenological psychology is sometimes thought to be largely speculative. Although developing theories from one's analysis and findings is always speculative in
some sense, phenomenological analysis itself is a disciplined activity
bound by identifiable rules. The most important of these is that research
must remain faithful to the phenomenon, which is captured by the phenomenological adage of making sure that a phenomenon is described in a
way that allows the experience to "show itself from itself in the very way
in which it shows itself from itself" (Heidegger, 1927/1962). We cannot
simply impose description on a phenomenon as an operational definition
might do, because a phenomenological description must arise from the
thing itself. This means that phenomenological psychology is not anti-
data, which is another misconception. In fact, the descriptive power of
this approach may be capable of handling more diverse forms of data than
its natural scientific counterpart, a feature that is particularly important
for dealing with the diverse methods and findings concerning self-esteem.
Similarly, Giorgi (1984) stated that phenomenological psychology is not
anti-traditional, "Rather it is willing and able to dialog with traditional
psychology" (p. 14), which is an important part of integrated description.
(To give credit where it is due, I should mention that Giorgi was one of my
professors in graduate school and that I first learned how to do phenomenological research using his method.)

Of course, the nature and merits of psychology envisioned as a
human science versus natural science is a topic that is discussed in great
depth. Those who are interested in understanding more of this approach
are invited to do so by investigating Giorgi's work already cited, as well as
that of Heidegger (1927/1962), Husserl (1954/1970a), Gurwitsch (1964),
and Merleau-Ponty (1945/1962). The basic point is really quite simple:

There is a limit to researching self-esteem or any other human phenomenon for that matter by insisting on the methods of the naturalistic paradigm. There are, of course, serious limits to the human science paradigm as well. For example, the human science approach does not establish cause and effect relationships easily, and its work can be more difficult to replicate. The question becomes, then, how do we go about studying self-esteem qualitatively in ways that make a contribution to the field?

Qualitative Advances in Researching Self-Esteem

The recent past has seen some genuine advances in applying qualitative methods to studying self-esteem. For example, several researchers have used them to investigate important aspects of self-esteem that are not otherwise amenable to traditional methods. Epstein, for instance, took issue with the appropriateness of doing experimental research on self-esteem. His alternative is an ecological one that may be done in two ways. One is to manipulate self-esteem in what he called "natural laboratories," where it is possible to obtain

> Measures of behavior in specially selected situations where manipulations could be introduced in a natural manner. Such research can be regarded as using certain events as natural laboratories for the study of behavior. We had previously studied sport parachuting as a natural laboratory for the study of anxiety. . . . Unfortunately, natural laboratories can be found for only limited phenomena. For other events, we turned to self-observation of experiences in everyday life. (1979, p. 51)

Of course it is desirable to take advantage of such natural laboratories. However, it is difficult to do so with something like self-esteem. For instance, it is hard to predict when a naturally occurring self-esteem situation is about to present itself, let alone to identify control versus experimental subjects or to repeat events enough times to obtain reliable findings. Nevertheless, Epstein's point is a good one: Having subjects report on their own self-esteem experience in a way that is relatively structured and that occurs right after an appropriate event does increase the value of such results.

In Chapter 1 we saw that another version of Epstein's (1979) ecological approach is to have students track self-esteem over a period of time. The technique may be used for short periods or longer ones, which means that such a chronicling of self-esteem may be helpful in designing longitudinal studies, and they are greatly lacking in this field. If self-esteem is a vital force that is generally present in behavior over time, then what better way to study self-esteem in real life than to have people report on it? One advantage of researching self-esteem in this fashion is that the paradoxes mentioned earlier are more likely to show themselves as they are actually lived, which gives us the opportunity to study them better. Another reason to use such qualitative methods is that these data can be more "objective" than expected. For example,

> Self-report estimates are usually based on impressions gained over repeated observations, whereas laboratory studies usually investigate responses in a single setting on a single occasion. On this basis alone there is reason to suspect that laboratory findings, as customarily obtained, are often low in replicability and generality, and cannot therefore establish strong relationships with findings obtained on other occasions by other means. (1979, p. 52)

It is also worth noting that Epstein fully recognized the limits of using self-reports as data. In spite of them, he concluded that research based on self-reports should not be so readily dismissed.

In general, the qualitative approach is capable of putting us in close proximity with the link between self-esteem and behavior as it actually occurs, which is something that more traditional work seems to find so elusive. For instance, Tafarodi and Milne (2002) asked 244 participants to record negative experience over a 4-week period. They were asked to fill out the Life Events Record (LER) at the beginning and end, and those records were analyzed by judges who were trained to look for the effect of negative experiences on self-esteem. Similarly, Scheff and Fearon, Jr. (2004) take the fascinating approach of combining both qualitative and quantitative techniques. This work involves asking participants to take a standard self-esteem test and then interviewing each person about how they answered the questions. This technique can result in a measurable evaluation of self-esteem *and the reasons for it* because discussing the meaning of each response through the interview method takes us to the one place more traditional or objective methods cannot go, which is the lived world. Clearly, just because the qualitative approach is experiential rather than experimental in nature does not mean that it is methodologically undisciplined: Qualitative work simply has different strengths and weaknesses.

Phenomenological psychologists also investigate real-life human experiences, such as various emotional states, certain types of decisions, and even learning and thinking (Aanstoos, 1984; Colaizzi, 1973; Costall & Still, 1987; Dreyfus & Dreyfus, 1986; Giorgi, 1970, 1975, 1984; Wertz, 1984). The basic form of this method involves what can be thought of as a stepwise process. Typically in this format, the researcher begins by identifying the phenomenon to be studied, then finds suitable subjects for its investigation. The study might simply be a retrospective look at experience or it could involve a host of contrived situations or manipulations designed to elicit or test responses. Data are usually generated by asking subjects for an initial description of the experience or event, then expanding on this material via interview. Each initial description and its related interview are transcribed as a single body of data. This narrative or "extended protocol" of behavior is then examined for individual units of meaning, which are often identified by turning points in the narration.

These results, in turn, are used to develop a description of a given subject's experience as a situated instance of the phenomenon, or how it is lived by a particular subject at a particular time. Next, these individual records of the phenomenon are examined for regularities that occur between subjects. The recurring themes that arise from this step are then identified as being basic to the phenomenon and are known as its essential or constitutive elements. Finally, these components, and the relationships between them, are worked into a final phenomenological description, usually identified as its fundamental structure, or that which is necessary and sufficient to give rise to the phenomenon for any given individual. Of course, all the while the researcher attempts to suspend his or her own judgments and preconceptions as much as possible, which requires considerable attention to the researcher's own thinking processes each step of the way. This method was the one that was used in analyzing the self-esteem moments discussed in Chapter 1 and that led to the fundamental structure presented there.

Like their natural science counterparts (Howard, 1985), human science researchers recognize that in all cases the best research method is the one that is most suited to working with the particular phenomenon in question. When studying experience, this axiom means that the method must be flexible as well as rigorous, because experiences are more fluid than experiments. These two characteristics of the phenomenological method allow it to be faithful to the phenomenon, wherever it may lead. Michael Jackson's *Self-Esteem and Meaning: A Life Historical Investigation* probably represents the most in-depth and articulate discussion of the value of using qualitative methods to research self-esteem in this way. In dealing with the problems and limits encountered when researching it from the natural science paradigm Jackson noted that,

> The problem seems rather to lie in experimentation itself—or more correctly, in the application of the experimental method to the investigation of self-esteem. . . . Self-esteem is not a determinate process like the ones studied in the physical sciences; its nature lies rather in its subjective character and in its ever-changing manifestations and implications. Confronted by a phenomenon so elusive and so dynamic, the experimental method is, as it were, overpowered. (1984, pp. 4–5)

He made it clear that, above all, self-esteem is a meaningful phenomenon: It is literally filled with living implications concerning our worthiness as individuals when facing vital challenges of living and whether we do that competently over time. Jackson also discussed in detail the types of problems studying such phenomena present for traditional methods, particularly those involving the experiment. For example, he pointed out that one of the greatest limitations in approaching human phenomena quantitatively is that this approach tends to break living wholes down into observable but broken parts. Although their sum may turn out to be correct in number, it is always less than the lived realities people actually experience.

Scheff and Fearon Jr. presented a similar case more recently in a critique of using the methods of psychology envisioned as a natural science while researching self-esteem and the perennial search for statistical significance, even when effect size is not forthcoming.

> This report on reviews of the field of self-esteem makes two main recommendations. 1. The conventional approach, based on scales and significance tests, should be discontinued, or at least be made to compete with alternative directions. 2. As an alternative to existing studies that are static and correlational, studies of the dynamics of discourse on topics relevant to self-appraisal and self-feeling might help new conceptions of self-esteem, and generate important and testable hypotheses. (2004, p. 87)

In short, Jackson did not say there is no value in knowing about the parts. Rather, he concluded that it is important not to mistake them for the whole. Scheff and Fearon, Jr. made the point that even if one continues to use traditional methods, there is value in exploring alternatives, too. In light of this situation, I will take the position that self-esteem work can benefit most from using a method capable of integrating both quantitative and qualitative findings, such as the one that is proposed below.

Integrated Description

In all fairness, I must say that phenomenologists sometimes focus so much on meaning that they become just as biased as their natural scientist counterparts in insisting that one approach is better than another. Indeed, much of what passes for phenomenological research today seems to suffer from an overemphasis on one of two things. On one hand, many contemporary phenomenologists emphasize individual or personal experience so much that their work leads back to phenomenalism, which focuses on merely describing someone's experience. On the other hand, they sometimes seem so excessively postmodern that their work lacks methodological rigor: It demonstrates so much relativism that it is difficult to distinguish between psychological research and what might more properly be called literary criticism or even mere opinion, neither of which is grounded in the scientific method. Rather, if we want to be genuinely phenomenological, then we must stay with the thing itself, and self-esteem seems to be telling us that both scientific paradigms are necessary if we wish to do that faithfully.

One way of reaching this goal is to use a form of the phenomenological method I have referred to as "integrated description" (Mruk, 1984, 1994). This approach is based on Giorgi's more scientifically rigorous vision of phenomenological psychology in that it is a step-by-step procedure. However, integrated description is also designed to work with the findings of psychology practiced as a natural science, so the result is a more balanced and comprehensive analysis, which may be just what we need to research self-esteem most effectively. Integrated description is a two-stage research process. First, it is necessary to identify the general structure of a phenomenon by using something like the step-by-step version of the phenomenological method presented earlier. Then, it is possible to proceed to the integration phase. This part of the process involves identifying what Jackson (1984) might call the "parts" of a phenomenon, which are often best determined quantitatively, and then fitting them into their respective places in the "whole" or general structure. I actually began this work in Chapter 1, when the fundamental structure was revealed by analyzing the definitions and checking them against self-esteem as it is lived. In Chapter 5, I will use the general structure to form a theory of self-esteem and show where the self-esteem paradoxes, as well as many significant findings of the field, fit into it in a way that leads to practical applications that are amenable to examination and verification both qualitatively and quantitatively.

It is important to realize that this method of integrated description may be applied to any number of human phenomena. For instance, if we were doing an integrated description of anxiety or an anxiety disorder, I would first attempt to find out what it means to be anxious by asking subjects to describe their experiences and then develop a general structure of it in a step-by-step fashion. Next, I would examine more traditional research on anxiety and show where those results fit into the structure. For example, because anxiety involves bodily sensations and states, I would have to show where and how the biology of anxiety comes into play in "being anxious." Yet, anxiety also affects perception, so I would elaborate the description further by including findings on thinking patterns typically associated with anxiety. Furthermore, because anxiety often affects a person's relationships with others, I would expand the phenomenology to show how the fundamental structure involves the various interpersonal and social dimensions of anxiety. The result would be a more comprehensive picture of anxiety than seeing it only as a "chemical imbalance" or a "lack of meaning;" although both views would be accounted for in the description. The same approach could be used for depression, schizophrenia, love, hope, and many other human phenomena.

However, it is also true that using information generated from both paradigms presents a difficult challenge in two ways. First, it is demanding work because it requires being able to deal with a broad range of material from many points of view. Second, the results are likely to please neither the hard-core empirically oriented, number-crunching social scientist nor the "touchy-feely," literarily inclined, experientially oriented, postmodern counterpart. Even so, as Giorgi (1971, 1984) pointed out there are ways these paradigms can balance each other. For instance, where psychology as a natural science focuses on measuring behavior, a human science approach deals with the meaning of behavior. Similarly, whereas the natural science paradigm looks for determined or causal reactions, the human science approach attempts to account for "free" or intentional ones. Where one method seeks identical repetition of a measure or outcome to reduce uncertainty, the other does so by searching for essential themes that are consistently present in a given phenomenon. In short, human subjects live simultaneously in external and internal worlds, both of which must be described if they are to be understood, let alone integrated. Unfortunately, it is easy to fall prey to methodological tunnel vision if we practice psychology from one perspective and ignore or dismiss the other. Although integrated description has its limits, at least it avoids this common paradigmatic trap and may even be able to help achieve some degree of "consensus" that Wells and Marwell (1976) claim is so important in this field.

THE QUESTION OF VALIDITY
AND RESEARCHING SELF-ESTEEM

We now have an idea of what the phenomenological method looks like and how I am using it here, but the issue of whether such research is valid must also be addressed. If one accepts the scientific method as being empirical, methodical, theory building, and self-correcting, then there can be no doubt that the human science paradigm qualifies, providing one stays with the procedures outlined by Giorgi (1971, 1984). For example, the word "empirical" concerns experience, as well as observation, and we can "observe" experience to a certain degree through techniques such as introspection or interviews. Both external and internal observations are sources of data, at least in the psychological realm, and they are tied to the underlying structures of being human. If we wish to know about something that is human, then we must be faithful to this basic fact to be truly "objective." Of course, it is the case that experiential and observable data are not identical, but that is why we need two paradigms in the first place.

Next, science is a methodological or step-by-step way of knowing, which means that it can be duplicated by others. The research question or hypothesis, how relevant data are generated, what is observed from such activity, and how the material is analyzed to yield regularities are all steps that are identified, recorded, and presented. Although we are most familiar with explicating these steps in laboratory notebooks (which can also be seen as quantitative journals), it is important to realize that phenomenological research follows the same rules. Such descriptive or qualitative activities begin with an idea (or hypothesis, if we wish to use traditional scientific language) concerning what gives rise to a given experience. Then, we implement a program of research that includes specifying how relevant data were gathered, showing how such material was analyzed for regularities, and presenting specific findings, such as fundamental structures. Each step is identified so that the method can be examined by others and replicated, if desired. In fact, most social scientists would welcome people showing more interest in doing just that, including this one.

One advantage of science is that it allows us not only to discover information but to organize it into powerful bodies of ideas called models and theories. These scientific creations, in turn, help generate additional questions and more research. Phenomenological researchers are just as capable of being active at the theoretical level as are their natural science counterparts. In fact, theory building is something qualitative researchers do rather well. Where quantitative theories lead to predictions and the possibility of controlling various domains of the natural world, phenomenological theories also offer an understanding of human behavior that is of practical value. For instance, human science research helps us to see how something is lived both in general and in individual terms. Such knowledge can be used to help in developing clinical interventions that are specifically designed for the unique characteristics of a particular person, group, or culture.

Finally, the scientific method is self-correcting. For example, if a researcher makes a claim, and if someone else duplicates the steps that lead to it and reaches the same outcome, then the original finding is strengthened or validated to some degree and scientific knowledge is advanced. If the steps are repeated and the same outcome is not obtained, then the step-by-step method forces us to reconsider the claim and to look for alternative explanations. The beauty of the scientific method is that it "wins" no matter what the case may turn out to be because either outcome creates better understanding over time. In this sense, science can be seen as a great conversation to which anyone may contribute at any time, regardless of gender, race, culture, or historical period. Although perhaps in a different voice, phenomenologically oriented social scientists are legitimate participants in this great discussion because they follow the same rules of discourse. The presence of this perspective also is beneficial because it helps to keep the other more dominant perspective "honest" by reminding it that it is not capable of doing everything, even in principle.

Validity in Self-Esteem Research

The last set of difficulties generated by using the scientific method to study self-esteem, regardless of the paradigm being used, concerns the question of validity. Of course, this issue is a complex one and has been dealt with extensively in regard to self-esteem, especially by Wells and Marwell (1976) and Jackson (1984), who represent the quantitative and qualitative approaches, respectively. They concluded that validity is not so much a matter of absolute truth but of available proof. In other words, the value of the scientific method is not that it allows us to find hidden answers. Rather, it helps to eliminate possibilities and reduce uncertainty to increasingly manageable levels (Tryon, 1991).

Perhaps a better way of dealing with the concept of validity is to ask, as Jackson (1984) did, *validity for what?* If the goal of research, for instance, is to measure self-esteem in a person, then the quantitative method is more valid because it is capable of dealing with such a task. If, however, we are interested in investigating aspects of phenomena as they are lived by real people, then qualitative methods are more valid both in principle and in practice. Jackson talked about this situation in the following way:

> Experimental investigation is based on the criteria of prediction and replication. . . . But this is only one *kind* of criterion, and it establishes only one kind of knowledge. There are other kinds of knowledge that elude the criteria of prediction and replication; and a specific example is knowledge about self-esteem as a meaningful experience in a person's life. This kind of knowledge resides in a system of relations that is unique and irreducible in each separate instance. Such knowledge cannot be captured by a method that breaks it down into standard components. The experiment, however, is designed to perform exactly this kind of reduction. *It is aimed at washing out the very information which we seek—namely, information about unique and specific constellations of personal meaning.* (1984, pp. 216–217)

If what Jackson said is correct, and I think it is, then we must also add that self-esteem research needs to be concerned with information from both qualitative and quantitative research for two reasons. First, human beings exist in both ways: We are quantitative objects in the world just like any other physical body and all the laws that apply to such entities also apply to us. But we are also what phenomenologists call "body-subjects" (conscious identities that are always also embodied in physical form), and only qualitative research methods help us out with this crucial dimension of self-esteem, just as only quantitative methods help with other tasks. Second, if it is true that the field is in need of consensus, and again I think it is, then we cannot avoid the reality that the psychology of self-esteem is filled with both types of research and findings. In other words, we cannot dismiss one kind simply because it might be convenient to do so. The final question becomes, then, what are the criteria by which qualitative indicators may be said to have validity?

Validity applies to qualitative work as much as to quantitative findings, perhaps even more so. This type of validity is based on evaluating whether a finding is consistent with an explicit conceptual framework or theory. Such correspondence is based more on the rules of logic than on numbers, so we should expect to be held accountable in this way. Thus, fidelity (being "true," i.e., descriptively accurate about the phenomenon) is an important criterion used in phenomenological research (Heidegger, 1927/1962; Marcel, 1964). This type of validity concerns the degree to which a given description of the fundamental structure of a particular phenomenon actually reflects that phenomenon at the empirical (i.e., observed or experienced) level. Although it is assumed that no one description can ever be complete, descriptions vary, and they can be evaluated in terms of how accurate or faithful they are. This means that it is possible to compare qualitative work and determine which description is more accurate, more complete, or more valid.

The difficulty with this form of validation is, of course, how do we check (validate) a finding or description? To paraphrase Husserl (1970b), for this we must return to the facts themselves. If a particular description leaves out something important about a phenomenon, or if it does not account for a major finding, then the validity of that description is weakened. The reader will note that I used this procedure in defining self-esteem. Most of the definitions were invalid or, more properly, less valid because they left out competence, worthiness, or how they relate to one another. By the same measure, the third definition of self-esteem we examined had greater validity because all the components were accounted for in that description, the linkage between them was articulated, and all of the findings corresponded to the general structure of self-esteem as it is lived in real life. We continue to evaluate the validity of this approach as we examine major research findings and major theories of self-esteem in the next two chapters. In other words, the validity of our description of the fundamental structure of self-esteem depends on its ability to show how it is that what is known about the phenomenon is actually located within the structure.

Finally, it is important to keep in mind that in all science, validity is more of a process than an event. In other words, validity is a dialogue between researchers, where convergence (establishing something as being "true" or agreed on) emerges through what Paul Ricoeur describes as "logic of uncertainty and of qualitative probability" (Jackson, 1984, p. 219).

> Ricoeur calls this process of validation—this argumentative discipline—'the method of converging indices'. . . . This dialog is indispensable because it provides the 'logic of argumentation' which leads to increasing validity and secure knowledge about a phenomenon. We assume that our dialogue will be fruitful, that we will move toward progressive agreement, because we live in a common world and we study phenomena that spring from common sources—social, economic, biological, and physical. As we observe the ways different subjects organize a psychological phenomenon in this common objective matrix, and as we discuss this phenomenon from a number of theoretical perspectives, we cannot help but converge on its essential structure. (1984, p. 219)

Just as with the natural science paradigm, the results of such efforts (which may be called findings) become material for further investigation by others. Points of convergence arise through dialogue in either paradigm, which is a social process that is, at bottom, a qualitative endeavor. Thus, uncertainty is reduced via the same process in both paradigms and it is at the core of reaching a scientific consensus.

It would be a mistake, however, to think that we are talking about validity as mere consensus: After all, people used to agree that the world was flat, but consensus did not make it so. Yet, there is a certain way in which all the validity the scientific method can really offer is a process of consensus building, albeit a more demanding one than common sense or mere belief requires. For as Heisenberg (1950) suggested, science does not discover truth: That is the business of religion or philosophy. Instead, empirical work of both the quantitative and the qualitative types continually seeks to refine and expand knowledge through the reduction of uncertainty. As Wells and Marwell pointed out in their discussion of test validity,

> Validity is not something that an instrument 'has,' but a qualitative attribution made to it through investigation, negotiation, and persuasion. Nor is validity attributed to the measure in isolation, but within

the context of a particular interpretive usage. . . . Very briefly put, validity is a joint property of a measurement or observational technique, an interpretive framework, and a scientific audience. (1976, pp. 155–156)

In short, validity involves a process, includes reaching a consensus, and is always a matter of degree. Why should it be different with something as complex as self-esteem?

Conclusion

Much more could be said about validity and self-esteem research. For example, I could talk about the "plausibility" of a theory, which is the type of credibility that comes when ideas are useful in an applied or practical setting, regardless of whether they can be "proven" in the ordinary sense (Wells & Marwell, 1976). However, we are not so much concerned with explicating the scientific method as with understanding how it can be used to research, understand, and enhance self-esteem. By way of sum, then, four things appear to stand out at this second stop of our journey through the field. At this point, we can see that qualitative and quantitative methods have been applied to the topic for a long time. Next, it is clear that there is a substantial amount of research currently available on the subject, even though it is diverse in terms of method. Third, the field suffers from a need for some kind of integration or "consensus" (Wells & Marwell, 1976). Finally, it appears as though reaching this goal depends on using a method that is capable of integrating both qualitative and quantitative data, as doing otherwise is likely to produce an incomplete social science of self-esteem. Accordingly, the next step is to examine the major research findings about self-esteem as they occur today. In Chapter 5 we will attempt to integrate them into our description of its fundamental structure.

CHAPTER 3

Major Self-Esteem Research Findings

The purpose of this chapter is to develop a sense of the major findings in the field of self-esteem, particularly those with clinical relevance because that type of work addresses our practical concern with this topic. One reason to proceed in this fashion is that it should result in a reasonably accurate picture of what is actually known about self-esteem from several different perspectives. In addition, the findings can also act as the building blocks for a comprehensive theory of self-esteem, which is to say one that is capable of integrating them into a meaningful whole. Finally, research findings are useful in evaluating the validity of a theory. For example, the extent to which it is capable of integrating the major "facts" of the field helps us evaluate how robust the theory happens to be.

First, however, it is necessary to develop a method to identify findings that are important or substantial enough to be gathered into such a group. Because we are dealing with both qualitative and quantitative research, the usual definition of findings used in social science needs to be expanded enough to include both types of work. In addition, because we are examining the field as well as its work, specific points of agreement, areas of strong disagreement, and other unique characteristics of self-esteem work may also be considered to be a "finding," although of a different type. In other words, we will continue to use the criteria of persistence and significance in this phase of our look at self-esteem. Even so, it is still important to remember that it is difficult to do a comprehensive review of any field, let alone one as old and as broad as self-esteem.

PARENTAL FACTORS

Genetics

One of the newest trends to appear in the field of self-esteem is the study of possible genetic foundations. Developmental psychology has been interested in how genetics affects the development of temperament and personality for some time now, and its research methods have become quite sophisticated over the past decade or so. Thus, although it was surprising to see work of this type while researching this edition, it makes sense that the genetic tree should be examined in terms of branches that affect self-esteem just as they have for so many other aspects of human behavior. Neiss, Stevenson, and Sedikides (2003) reviewed this small but growing body of literature. In general, they concluded that genetic influences account for 30–40% of the variance among self-esteem levels in siblings. Non-shared environmental factors, such as play, school, peers, work, and so forth, account for the largest portion of the remaining variance, and shared environmental factors explain a relatively small amount of it.

More specifically, biology appears to bring with it certain predispositions such as energy level, basic temperament, and certain physical, social, and cognitive abilities (or the lack of them). If an individual is fortunate enough to be born into a family or culture that appreciates his or her particular constellation of characteristics and abilities, then a good person–environment fit is likely to occur. All things considered, in this case it should be fairly easy to be valued as a worthy person and to acquire the competence necessary for self-esteem. If one is not such a genetic winner, then one's self-esteem story is much more likely to be difficult or at least complex. Although it is important not to make too much of genetic predispositions, they can no longer be ignored in this field.

Parental Support (Involvement)

Parental involvement was one of the first antecedents of self-esteem to receive attention (Coopersmith, 1967) and still does today. Usually, supportive parental involvement is presented as a positive force. For example, Gecas (1971) noted that support from mother correlated more with developing a sense of worth in children, where support from father seemed to be tied more to the development of competence. He also noted that middle class fathers tend to spend more time with their children than working class parents, which increases opportunities for supportive engagement. Burger (1995) pointed out that the efficacious feelings associated with mastery are helpful in the development of self-esteem, and that parents who encourage their children offer more positive support than those who do not. Other work noted the importance of support by the effects of its absence. For instance, parents who are described as being indifferent toward their children, as well as parents who are absent frequently or absent for long periods of time, tend to have children with lower levels of self-esteem (Clark and Barber, 1994; Coopersmith, 1967; Rosenberg, 1965). Moreover, this effect may be particularly important for male children (Miller, 1984).

Parental "Warmth" (Acceptance)

Mere involvement does not seem to be enough. Quality counts, and parental warmth or acceptance appears to be crucial to the development of self-esteem (Bednar, Wells & Peterson, 1989; Coopersmith, 1967; Rogers, 1961). This finding is frequently mentioned throughout several decades of work, but it tends to be a bit vague as a term. Trying to specify the behavioral components of such an attitude is difficult, but the term *acceptance* is used most often to describe a parent's willingness to see a child's strengths *and* weaknesses, potentials *and* limitations. Such acceptance is "warm" in that it is balanced, not blind, which means that simple approval is not associated with self-esteem. By contrast, mere approval or praise is more likely to be associated with problems such as narcissism and so forth. By seeing both the strengths and the limitations of a child in a particular situation, a parent can encourage him or her to explore the world in ways that are based on the child's unique constellation of abilities, preferences, competencies, fears, interests, and so on at any given age, all of which are connected to developing mastery.

This factor can also be illustrated by studying what happens when acceptance is absent. For example, Kernis (2003a) noted that a lack of such warm or loving acceptance is detrimental to self-esteem. He found that when individuals suffer a deficit in this area, they often become more likely to base their sense of worth on extrinsic rather than intrinsic factors, which makes them more vulnerable. Crocker and Park (2003) found that students who place much of their worth on academic performance suffer a greater loss when they do not get accepted into graduate school than those who value other aspects of their person more highly. Finally, it should almost go without saying that parents who are harsh and derogatory or who use name calling and love withdrawal can have a negative effect on self-esteem (Kernis & Goldman, 2003).

Parental Expectations and Consistency

Clearly defined expectations and limits are parental attitudes often associated with developing positive self-esteem in children (Coopersmith, 1967). Setting high but not impossible expectations, for instance, involves providing clear standards of worthiness. Setting goals and holding standards lets the child know that certain forms of behavior are desirable, good, or "worthy" and to be strived toward. Establishing and maintaining limits is important because failing to do so is destructive to self-esteem in the long run. For example, a long line of developmental literature shows that parental over-permissiveness is related to negative behaviors such as impulsivity and aggressiveness. The same literature, which can be found in almost any standard text on child development (Newman & Newman, 1987; Sigelman & Shaffer, 1995), indicates that limits that are too severe or too harshly enforced are also problematic. For instance, they can engender the development of anxious and restrictive behavior, rather than spontaneity and engagement with life.

Parenting Style

Respectful treatment, which involves acknowledging the essential humanity of a child when dealing with him or her, is another positive parental attitude. Research on parental styles of discipline, for instance, suggests that rather than being authoritarian or permissive, a "democratic" (Coopersmith, 1967) or authoritative approach is more conducive to developing self-esteem in children. This means there is a parental willingness to discuss matters and negotiate conflict but not at the expense of violating certain basic standards of behavior such as respecting the rights of others. Of course, few people are naive enough to believe that one must always be democratic or authoritative. Rather, it is a matter of which discipline style one uses most often or of being a "good enough" parent (Winnicott, 1953). This attitude of respectfulness extends to other areas, such as honoring agreements, taking the time to explain things, and accepting (within limits) a child's preferences. Kernis and Goldman (2003) noted that the mother's parenting style may be particularly important. However, Leary and MacDonald may have said it best when they summarized what research has to say about the relationship between parenting style and self-esteem: "Parents who are approving, nurturant, and responsive tend to produce children with higher self-esteem than parents who are disapproving, uninterested, and unresponsive" (2003, p. 413).

Birth Order

There has been a small but consistent stream of research beginning with Coopersmith (1967) suggesting that birth order can have an effect on self-esteem. All things considered, being firstborn slightly enhances the possibility of developing positive self-esteem. Similarly, there is indication that children without siblings tend to have higher self-esteem than those who have them. Although there is no simple causal relationship between birth order and self-esteem, the general understanding seems to be that first and only children receive more attention from and interaction with parents than those who arrive later, which means that more direct or focused parental involvement occurs here than with other ordinal positions. However, it is important to remember that the quality of the interaction is more important for self-esteem than its quantity.

Modeling

Coopersmith (1967) first noticed a positive relationship between self-esteem levels in mothers and their children. But Bednar, Wells, and Peterson (1989) made considerable use of this factor by pointing out that parents actually *show* (i.e., live out, demonstrate, present by example) their children the route to self-esteem (or the lack of it) by how they handle their own challenges, conflicts, and issues. "The impact of parents' behavior upon the child's self-esteem is undeniable; given the immaturity of children, however, parents' expression of their own resolution of the self-esteem question is far more influential than what they teach verbally" (p. 257). Parents who face life's challenges honestly and openly and who attempt to cope with difficulties instead of avoiding them thereby expose their children early to a pro–self-esteem problem-solving strategy. Those who avoid dealing with difficulties reveal a negative route for handling the challenges and problems of life. Either way, it is important to remember that modeling helps set the stage for healthy self-esteem or problems with it.

Summary

Although parents or primary caregivers are the first ones to bring these kinds of social factors into play, it is especially important to remember two things as we move on. First, these social forces never leave us. "Across numerous studies with older children and adolescents, as well as college students and adults in the world of work and family, we have found that the correlations between perceived support from significant others and self-worth range from 0.50 to 0.65" (Harter, 1999, p. 175). Basic human warmth, encouragement, respect, and support are necessary to the development or maintenance of self-esteem over the course of a lifetime. Second, no single family or social factor is overwhelmingly significant. After all, some children with "great" parents turn out to be quite poor in terms of their self-esteem and behavior, whereas many children with poor parenting turn out to be high self-esteeming individuals who demonstrate many desirable characteristics and behaviors.

In general, this problem of weak statistical correlation is common in developmental psychology literature. For example, even basic texts on developmental psychology point out that the work on linking attachment style to adult relationship formation is present but not strong (Sigelman & Shaffer, 1995). Similarly, the emerging research on resilience shows that even when there are strong correlations between negative developmental environments and negative adult behavioral patterns, there are plenty of exceptions (Vaillant, 1995; Werner & Smith, 1992). Such factors are more accurately understood as being predisposing and interactive rather than causal or deterministic. They are *among* those conditions that increase (or, by their absence, decrease) the likelihood of self-esteem. Instead of being dismayed by the weakness of the correlation between self-esteem and family factors as some researchers lament, perhaps we ought to be thankful for it. The indeterminate nature of these variables means that the absence or diminishment of any one of them does not necessarily doom people to a lifetime of low self-esteem.

SELF-ESTEEM AND VALUES

In general, the research seems to indicate that we cannot escape dealing with a relationship between values and self-esteem if we want to understand either self-esteem or its link to motivation and behavior. For example, it is clear that although people exhibiting high or low self-esteem can differ in certain key ways, such as in how likely they are to gain what they value, *what* they actually value is quite the same. As the "expectancy" literature on self-esteem would have it, "Both groups want to feel good about themselves" (Brockner, Wiesenfeld & Raskas, 1993, p. 220). The difference seems to be in what each of these groups tends to expect about their respective chances of really attaining that which is valued. For example, both such individuals value being successful, but the two groups hold different expectations of how likely they are to be successful, so their strategies for filling in this part of the self-esteem picture differ markedly. People with high self-esteem usually feel competent enough to take the risk and worthy enough to sustain a failure, should it occur, so they may set their sights high from the beginning. The others, in contrast, are often just as concerned with avoiding the loss of worthiness as with gaining more, so they may use what is called a "self-handicapping strategy" even as they go about trying to be successful (Snyder, 1989; Tice, 1993). Such a cognitive device allows people to focus on reasons that they are likely to fail so that they may not be as disappointed if it occurs. In either case the value of feeling worthy about oneself is the same.

Social Values

Another set of findings concerns the way more socially derived values affect self-esteem. Historically, there has been debate between two aspects of this dimension of values and self-esteem (Rosenberg, 1979). The "stratification hypothesis" links self-esteem and levels of self-esteem to general social groups such as socioeconomic class. The other, called the "subcultural hypothesis," links self-esteem more closely to primary social groups such as the neighborhood. Like many debates in the social sciences, the answer to the question of which view is right is "both" because each set of factors are active. Researchers recognize a consistent, albeit weak, link between self-esteem and general social class in the expected direction (Coopersmith, 1967; Mack, 1987; Rosenberg, 1965; Schneiderman, Furman & Weber, 1989; Twenge & Campbell, 2002). At the same time, there is agreement among most of the same authors that social factors within a subcultural group are more influential in determining a group member's particular self-experience than the general social values of the larger society: These "local" values are formed earlier, experienced more directly, and reinforced more frequently, so they tend to have a stronger influence. For instance, the family and neighborhood are seen as being a particularly powerful source of self-esteem-related values, particularly if people stay in touch with their roots over time.

Self-Values

Although values are certainly set in a social context, the individual also plays a role in the relationship between self-esteem and values, especially in terms of "self-values" (Pope, McHale & Craighead, 1988; Rosenberg, 1965). Self-values, which are "the conceptions of the desirable that represent the individual's criteria for self-judgment" (Rosenberg, 1965, p. 15), are important for self-esteem because they connect it to one's identity which, in turn, creates a relationship between self-esteem and behavior. However, these values concerning that which is good and desirable are based more on direct, meaningful, and individual experience than are social or even sub-cultural values. Self-values are, therefore, more personal in the sense that they affect us directly, and because they help give us a sense of self-sameness or identity as a unique person, regardless of social class or background.

Research also shows that certain types of experiences can change self-values in ways that affect identity, self-esteem, and behavior. For example, Epstein's research suggests that "there are certain experiences that can be a turning point in an individual's existence" (1979, p. 73). In this case, 270 subjects were asked to fill out forms that required them to describe such an experience and rate it according to various scales. This information was then analyzed to develop a typology of experiences, leading Epstein to conclude that "significant changes in self-concept are produced by three broad kinds of experience, namely, exposure to a new environment, being required to make new responses, and establishment or loss of significant relationships" (p. 79). Similarly, we saw in Chapter 1 that self-esteem seems to be affected by value conflicts within the self (Jackson, 1984; Mruk, 1983). This happens in situations where people hold one basic self-value to be important but also find that it is simultaneously opposed by another deeply held belief. For instance, an individual can hold independence as a self-value worthy of aspiration, but the same person may also value security so much that he or she actually becomes dependent in relationships. Such value conflicts shape identity and create lively self-esteem stories that Jackson calls (1984) "central conflicts" and that I call "self-esteem themes."

The worthiness dimension of self-esteem means that it always involves values. Otherwise, how would we know what is worthy in the first place? But researching values is challenging work. For one thing, values are difficult to measure, observe, or even define. In addition, the problem of relativity is always attached to values. Although learning theory and post-modernism (Gergen, 1991) tempt us to say that all values are culturally relative, it is dangerous to maintain that culture alone determines what is worthy. If we did that, then we would also have to say that people could be worthy (i.e., "good") Nazis, racists, terrorists, and the like, as long as their primary social group promoted such values. Such a relativistic position is deeply disturbing and would contradict the notion of basic human values.

Instead, it might be preferable to maintain that certain pro–self-esteem values are universal. Though proving their existence is a daunting task, one could adopt an evolutionary stance on this issue and say that there are such values. For instance, evolution has shown that sometimes cooperative values have more use than competitive ones, so it might be argued that such values as self-sacrifice and respect for it are more "worthy" of emulation than mere selfishness. It is also possible to think in terms of the humanistic position, which is that human beings are innately disposed toward a hierarchy of intrinsic value. In short, the "value dimension" of self-esteem is always going to be controversial at some level. What I do here is to point out the problem and suggest three things to consider in regard to self-esteem. First, we will see that evidence suggests most people in most cultures seem to be able to distinguish between what is deeply worthy of emulating and what is not. Second, certain values seem to have cross-cultural, if not universal, recognition such as courage, self-discipline, honor, and selflessness. Third, the values involved in acquiring and maintaining self-esteem appear to be more connected to these "deep structures" than to those that are more relative to time, place, and social mores.

GENDER AND SELF-ESTEEM

Rosenberg noticed a possible interaction between gender and self-esteem as early as 1965, and more findings support it. Epstein (1979) found that when female subjects were asked to report on experiences related to self-esteem, they "reported more experiences involving acceptance and rejection, particularly acceptance, than males, and males reported slightly more experiences involving success and failure than females" (p. 62). O'Brien and Epstein (1983, 1988) extended this work into the area of testing and measuring self-esteem and found differences in responses based on gender to be significant enough to require separate norms for males and females. Harter noted that various researchers have also found a gender-based difference in self-esteem and how it seems to persist across the life cycle, although diminishing in strength with time.

> For example, Block and Robins (1993) report that the ability to relate to others in an interpersonally positive manner promotes self-esteem in females, whereas lack of emotion, independence and personal uninvolvement are more highly related to self-esteem in males. In their longitudinal study (age 14 to 23), they find that males and females come to be more similar to one another over time . . . however, the long-recognized basic interpersonal asymmetry is still observed. Block and Robins (1993) observe that females are still socialized to "get along," whereas males are socialized to 'get ahead.' (Harter, 1999, p. 293)

The consensus is that, even in childhood (Pallas, Entwisle, Alexander & Weinstein, 1990), gender is capable of influencing self-esteem to a small but measurable degree, and that this influence occurs in the expected direction.

Like others, Harter (1999) found that there is a drop in self-esteem during adolescence that affects both genders. However, females seem to experience a greater one than males, particularly in the domain of self-esteem that is associated with satisfaction with one's physical appearance. She also discovered that one group of females appears to suffer a particularly large drop: those whose gender identification is strongly based on what might be called "traditional femininity." More androgynous females do not experience such a marked decrease in self-esteem. Harter noted that this finding calls into question some other work on self-esteem and gender. For example, much attention has been given to the idea that women suffer low self-esteem in general, largely because of discrimination, a lack of "voice," and other factors (American Association of University Women, 1991; Sanford & Donovan, 1984). However, Harter's work made the point that it is a particular subset of women who experience these difficulties, not women in general. Those women who live a traditional type of femininity, one that may foster greater dependence on social approval and could put limits on the ability to be assertive, are the ones who seem to be vulnerable to this condition. The result of such a position may be increased difficulty in terms of achieving a healthy degree of success or sense of competence, thereby creating a real self-esteem dilemma if both factors are needed for genuine self-esteem. Similar dynamics may be at work in the findings that suggest that teen pregnancy may be associated with low self-esteem (Emler, 2001).

In terms of the general structure, then, we can say that women in our and most societies seem to gravitate toward the worthiness component of self-esteem (being valued by others in terms of acceptance or rejection), and that men tend to be pulled slightly more by the competence dimension (success or failure). However, it seems just as important to remember that such a distinction applies to some groups much more than to others. It should also be noted that insofar as a society is "sexist" in these ways, it prevents or discourages women from pursuing competence, thereby making them more dependent on worthiness. However, pushing men toward competence is just as negative because it limits one's access to worthiness. Being too "macho" or ignoring one's need to be connected to others also carries great cost. For example, some work indicates that males who are unemployed may suffer some damage to their self-esteem (2001). Fortunately, other work suggests that the gender difference seems to be much less prominent today than was reported in the research of the early 1980s (O'Brien, Leitzel & Mensky, 1996), perhaps reflecting some cultural shifts in this area, at least in America.

RACIAL, ETHNIC, AND ECONOMIC FACTORS AFFECTING SELF-ESTEEM

The questions of whether and how racial, ethnic, and economic forces affect self-esteem have been a part of self-esteem work for some time. The basic issue seemed resolved by Rosenberg and Simmons (1971), who did a large research project involving 1917 students in urban schools, many of whom were African-Americans. They reported that, contrary to popular assumptions at the time, African-American children do not have lower self-esteem than Caucasian children. Indeed, they examined 12 other studies done on this topic from 1963 to 1970 and found that

> Our general assessment of these findings is as follows: while the results probably do not justify the conclusion that blacks have higher self-esteem than whites, the weight of the evidence certainly does not seem to support the general conclusion that their self-esteem is lower. (1971, p. 8)

Unfortunately, common sense is often hard to defeat even when evidence contradicts it and the belief that African-Americans suffer low self-esteem persists. Thus, Twenge and Crocker (2002) undertook a large meta-analysis of race, ethnicity, and self-esteem. They confirmed the basic finding, but went beyond it to other groups. "From highest to lowest self-esteem scores, the groups are ordered as follows: Blacks, Whites, Hispanics, American Indians, and Asians" (p. 377). Twenge and Crocker went on to address the question of how to understand these major self-esteem findings by considering four different explanations.

The first one is based on the concept of *internalized stigma*. This idea is based on the notion of the "generalized other": In this case, if society as a whole looks down on a group of which I am a member, then I should look down on myself because I internalized that generalized other in constructing my identity. *Stigma as self-protection* is another possible explanation, which holds that self-esteem may be buffered from the effect of discrimination by selective comparison. According to this view an individual who is in the minority may discount failure in a particular domain if this area is one in which his or her minority is perceived as being socially disadvantaged. Instead of attributing failure to internal or personal factors in such situations, it is attributed to external ones such as the social forces of discrimination so that the poor performance does not affect self-esteem.

Next, the *positive racial identity hypothesis* suggests that self-esteem could be higher in a minority group because that group focuses largely on its positive qualities, which elevates its status at least in their own eyes. Finally, the *cultural differences hypothesis* maintains that certain aspects of cultural identity, particularly whether it is based on the individual or the group, could account for the data. In this case, groups that value individualism would be likely to emphasize such things as personal performance, especially success, which would be reflected on measures of self-esteem that detect such a variable. Here, groups that downplay the role of the individual would also tend to de-emphasize personalizing success, which could affect scores on the same measures in a negative direction.

Twenge and Crocker then compared each hypothesis with the data and found that with little question, the cultural difference theory seems to be the only one that is able to account for all the findings. In other words, the central variable that runs through each group in the expected direction is how the individual is emphasized by a particular group. In short, the results appear as they do because, as a group, African-Americans tend to emphasize the role of the individual slightly more than Whites, who in turn, emphasize this quality more than the much more collectively oriented minorities. Although there may be some truth to the other explanations in a particular time or place, they do not seem to be as efficient as this one.

CULTURAL ORIENTATION AND SELF-ESTEEM

Although scarcely dealt with until recently, cross-cultural research on self-esteem is becoming more common. Like much cross-cultural work in general, the dominant theme of this area as it applies to self-esteem concerns comparing individualistic cultures, or those that emphasize independence and the role of the person in social life, and collectivistic cultures, which focus on interdependence and communal social structures (Pettijohn, 1998, p. 67). Recently, it has become reasonably clear that there are at least two schools of thought on this issue and the support for one of them seems to outweigh the other.

On one hand, there are those who maintain that a conception of self-esteem based on either competence or worthiness is a largely Western phenomenon. For example, Hewitt (2002) saw self-esteem as a social construction, something that arises out of contemporary culture to meet contemporary needs, particularly in America. He maintained, for instance, that even the phrase self-esteem is relatively new and then went on to "deconstruct" it as a "linguistic space" that is created to help individuals make sense out of emotional reactions that involve the self. Similarly, Crocker and Park pointed out that self-esteem, or at least pursuing it, is a "particularly American phenomenon, born of the nations' founding ideologies" (2004, p. 405), especially our emphasis on the importance of the individual, the history of the Protestant ethic, and the idea of a meritocracy. Then, they compared this cultural orientation with the Japanese culture's emphasis on the group, an incremental or continuous approach to personal improvement, and the importance of relationships rather than personal achievements. They concluded by supporting the position that culture determines the importance of self-esteem.

On the other hand, Tafarodi and Swann Jr. (1996) investigated the issue of the relationship between self-esteem and culture at some length. They also recognized the possibility that self-esteem may only be a Western concept or phenomenon, which would mean that self-esteem is not a basic human need. However, when they reviewed several studies on self-esteem in collectivistic cultures, such as Asian and Filipino society, it was found that when self-esteem is defined in terms of two factors (competence and worth) rather than one, self-esteem seems important in collective cultures as well. They went on to conduct their own study with Chinese participants and concluded that self-esteem, when defined this way, is present there, too. Tafarodi and Swann Jr. concluded that the problem of individualistic versus collectivistic self-esteem can be accounted for by what they named a "cultural trade off."

The trade, of course, occurs in terms of whether a culture emphasizes competence or worth (or as they said it, "self-competence" and "self-liking"). What appears to happen cross-culturally from this perspective is that both factors are always present, but a culture may load self-evaluation in one direction or the other. Such a trade-off would be consistent with the individual focus of one culture and the communal values of the others. Thus, in a highly individualistic culture such as ours, we would expect to see people evaluating themselves in ways that emphasize their competence through their successes and failures and so forth. At the same time, it would also be reasonable to expect people in a culture built on communal and collective structures to focus on the value or worth of their relationships and to diminish the value of a particular person's role in events. Yet, such a trade-off is never complete: It is not possible to say that self-esteem is mainly dependent on one factor in one culture and the other in a different one. Americans, for instance, do recognize the value and importance of conducting oneself in a worthy fashion interpersonally and Asians know about the importance of trying to do one's best. When seen from a two-factor perspective, what appears to be dichotomous turns out to be matter of emphasis, not exclusion. Accordingly, the evidence seems to favor the direction of seeing self-esteem as a basic human phenomenon. In fact, we will see later in this chapter that there is good reason to suggest that self-esteem is an important basic human need that is cross-cultural in nature (Sheldon, Elliot, Kim & Kasser, 2001).

THE SOURCES OF SELF-ESTEEM

Coopersmith (1967) was one of the first to study the sources of self-esteem and found that there are four: power (the ability to influence or control others), significance (being valued by others as shown by their acceptance), virtue (the adherence to moral standards), and competence (a successful performance in regard to a goal). More recently, Epstein (1979) pointed out that if success is involved in self-esteem, then the possibility of failure must be active, too. Hence, he describes four similar sources, but does so more dynamically: Achievement is balanced by loss, power is offset by powerlessness, acceptance is coupled with the possibility of rejection, and moral self-acceptance must also include the possibility of shame or guilt. There is so much convergence between these two independent lines of work that the results stand out as a basic finding according to the criteria we are using and also provide an excellent framework to demonstrate their worth.

Acceptance versus Rejection

Although it can vary with age, acceptance (or conversely, rejection) affects our self-feeling through our relationships with parents or caregivers, siblings, peers, friends, spouses or partners, co-workers or colleagues, and so on throughout our lives. Of course, there are other terms to describe this source of self-esteem. For example, Harter (1999) made the same observation but used the term "relational self-worth" in her work. I prefer the words "being valued" in my clinical work because that phrase describes the significance of what goes on in an accepting relationship or positive social interaction and how dynamic or active that process can be. In any case, acceptance is a source of self-esteem because it is connected to worthiness. It means that significant others value us in that fashion, whether it takes the expression of attention, respect, or even love.

It is also important to realize that there are many ways that acceptance and rejection can be alive in relation to the development and maintenance of self-esteem. For instance, care, nurturance, and attraction are important features of acceptance, but respect, fondness, and admiration are often more common or appropriate in a professional relationship. Similarly, there are several modes of being rejected, such as being ignored, devalued, used, mistreated, or abandoned, which may negatively affect self-esteem. In all cases, we are dealing with interpersonal events concerning whether one is valued by others. Even as adults, who has not experienced the increase in self-esteem that comes with a new positive relationship such as love or the decrease that usually accompanies a loss in this regard, especially when it occurs through betrayal or abandonment?

Virtue versus Guilt

Coopersmith's (1967) definition of virtue, which is the adherence to moral and ethical standards, is close to Epstein's "moral self-acceptance" and O'Brien and Epstein's (1983, 1988) notion of "moral self-approval." I tend to use the phrase "acting on beliefs" but I do not wish to just add terms to the field when plenty of good ones are already available. We will use Coopersmith's term "virtue" because it implies that there are higher values or standards of behavior to follow to be a worthy person, rather than simply measuring up to some culturally relativistic code of conduct.

Similarly, guilt, particularly what existentialists call "authentic guilt," may be understood as the failure to live up to more than just personal standards or those of a particular reference group. The connection between being virtuous and self-esteem was identified earlier when we examined the findings about values and self-esteem in certain types of self-esteem moments: Each time we *act* virtuously, or in a way that is recognized as adhering to a reasonable standard concerning what is desirable, healthy, or "good," we also find ourselves *as* worthy because our actions express ourselves in these situations. Of course, each time we fail to do so affects self-esteem in a correspondingly negative way, too. Kernis (2003b) examines this relationship further in terms of "authenticity," a theme that we shall explore in some detail later in Chapter 5.

Influence versus Powerlessness

"Power" is the term that both Coopersmith (1967) and Epstein (1979) used to describe one's ability to manage or direct one's environment. However, in this case, I will use the word "influence" to describe this source of self-esteem and break with tradition for two reasons. First, power over one's environment may capture something of how this kind of behavior is actually lived, but other people can be a part of one's environment, too. It is difficult to embrace the idea that a person who acts on their environment to their own ends while affecting others negatively is actually tapping into a genuine source of self-esteem. More to the empirical point, although power can be used to describe a way of relating to others, it may be too strong a word to describe the more subtle aspects of interacting with others effectively. For example, gentle persuasion can be just as effective as more direct assertions of power in some situations and the word "power" may not be able to capture this source of self-esteem.

Second, there may be a gender-based problem with the term "power" in that it may be too "masculine" to be genuinely descriptive, at least for some people. For instance, I have found in working with both academic and clinical self-esteem enhancement groups that women often object to this term. When asked why, the most commonly offered response is that, for them, power carries too much of a negative connotation, as in "power over someone" or "the abuse of power." When I ask what term they would prefer, the word "influence" is recommended most often, perhaps because it is more gender-free or even maybe because it is simply more descriptive and therefore, more accurate. In any event, the ability to interact with the environment, including others in it, in a way that shapes or directs events is a form of competence in dealing with the challenges of living. Success in this area leads to a sense of having some "say so" in life, which means that this type of power helps us deal with events more effectively. Conversely, too many failures tend to engender a sense of inadequacy, incompetence, helplessness, or perhaps even hopelessness, depending on how frequent and how severe the failures happen to be, all of which bode ill for self-esteem.

Achievements versus Failures

"Achievement" is the term chosen to represent the particular kind of success Coopersmith (1967) had in mind when he used the word "competence" because the latter word is too easily confused with one of the basic components of self-esteem revealed by its general structure. Epstein's (1979) term "success" is not used because it is too general. For example, we can say that it is good for a person's self-esteem to be "successful" in regard to any of the other three sources of self-esteem. The use of the term "achievement" is also more accurate in describing this particular source because it is not just any kind of success that counts. We all know, for example, people who are successful in this or that area of life but who also have obvious problems with self-esteem. Moreover, achievement carries with it a much stronger personal connotation than does mere success.

Indeed, starting with William James, a whole string of self-esteem theorists and research point out that success must be in a domain or area that matters to the individual in terms of their identity before it has any value for self-esteem. For example, brushing one's teeth is not a particularly significant act for most of us, but it may be a great personal achievement for an intellectually or physically challenged individual. There also appears to be a set of extraordinary personal achievements that affect self-esteem in an extremely powerful way. The research by Epstein (1979), Jackson (1984), and Mruk (1983) indicates that when we reach a goal that requires dealing effectively with problems or obstacles that also have personal or biographical significance, we demonstrate a higher level of competence at dealing with the challenges of living. Such success is also an achievement in a developmental sense, which makes "achievement" the appropriate term in yet another way.

Competence and Worthiness as the Sources of Self-Esteem

There is one more important point to explore concerning the sources of self-esteem. It concerns what is called "variability" in the literature or how individuals can use these four sources to obtain it. Coopersmith (1967) maintained that individuals may develop healthy levels of self-esteem by being successful in just one or two areas, particularly if these domains of life are approved of by their primary reference group: "We should note that it may be possible for an individual to attain high self-esteem by notable attainment in any of the four areas. This might occur even where attainment in the other areas was mediocre or poor" (p. 38). Writing in an organizational context, Bradshaw (1981) offered an economic analogy that shows this dynamic aspect of the relationship between self-esteem and success. He grouped all the potential experiences that enhance self-esteem in life as a reserve of potential self-esteem "income." The individual, through achieving, having power and influence, being valued, and acting on beliefs, may access this pool of wealth. When activated in this fashion, a "self-esteem income flow" is created, thereby raising self-esteem (p. 7). The strength or frequency of the flow determines the degree or level of our self-esteem. The model also indicates that the four routes to self-esteem can operate alone or in concert with one another. Failures can be seen as detracting from self-esteem, but blocking any one route is not necessarily a problem because others can be used to compensate for it.

However, Crocker and Park's (2003, 2004) poignant research on self-esteem and success powerfully contradicts this position. As they pointed out, the pursuit of self-esteem can lead to unhealthy outcomes when it is driven by a desperate need for success in a particular domain. In fact, this work maintains that most of self-esteem is completely contingent on success and that because the possibility of failure is always present, it may not even be possible to develop a healthy level of self-esteem in the long run. Such a position presents us with a problem. On one hand, it appears as though self-esteem can come from any of the four sources of self-esteem. On the other hand, we just saw that basing self-esteem on only one source is a theoretical and behavioral dead end. How are we to make sense of two such contradictory findings, both of which are accompanied by supportive work?

One way is to understand the various aspects of the problem in the light of the fundamental structure of self-esteem. Success and achievement are clearly tied to competence, but they are not sufficient to create self-esteem: Competence alone, we have seen, only creates a state of contingency that certainly is not helpful for living and does not fit the fundamental structure of self-esteem. Turning to worthiness as a sufficient source of self-esteem is no solution, either. For one thing, acceptance does not give us the skills that are necessary to master the ordinary tasks of life. Also, the fundamental structure of self-esteem shows us that worth is only part of the picture: Otherwise, we would have to include narcissism as genuine or authentic self-esteem. The most efficient way to resolve this situation is to stay with the fundamental structure, which indicates that each basic source of self-esteem is necessary, but not sufficient, to form self-esteem. This position even allows us to understand something of the nature of the relationship between the two components: They seem to balance each other. Worthiness limits the pursuit of competence by providing it with boundaries and direction because it forces the person to strive toward certain forms of behavior and to avoid others. Competence, of course, balances worthiness by requiring more of an individual than simply being loved or appreciated. In other words, it is necessary to access both sources for self-esteem to occur.

PARADOXES REVISITED

In Chapter 2 we saw that there are several research issues that were called self-esteem paradoxes because a certain aspect of self-esteem stands out when viewed from one angle and its opposite emerges when seen from another position. Perhaps another way to understand them is to see them as a "figure-ground" phenomenon, which is more understandable than a paradox. Although not every issue may be resolved in this way, current research offers a higher degree of understanding than in the past.

The "Self" in Self-Esteem Is both Psychological and Sociological

One matter that may have come to some resolution is that there is no longer much debate in the field today about the nature of the self in terms of whether it is a primarily psychological or social phenomenon. Most work now sees the self as resulting from both forces acting together over time, which results in the construction of what is called a "self-theory." Epstein (1985) was one of the first to advance this model in self-esteem work and it is used in many of the more sophisticated theories of self-esteem such as Sociometer Theory (Leary & Downs, 1995) or Self-Determination Theory (Deci & Ryan, 1995). However, Harter may have done the most comprehensive job of describing how people come to have a theory of self and how that understanding moves through the various stages of development in relation to self-esteem.

Harter said, "Our species has been designed to actively create *theories* about our world and to make *meaning* of our experiences, including the construction of a theory of self. Thus, the self is, first and foremost, a *cognitive construction*" (2003, p. 613). Basically, the self-theory starts out as a crude schema that is hardwired into the brain and that becomes modified by experience, much as Piaget suggested with the concepts of schema and adaptation. Over time, patterns are recognized, connections between them are created, and the brain grows in its capacity to organize them into meaningful understandings of the world and experiences within it. At approximately age 18 months, these interactive processes, some of which concern consciousness, create a certain degree of self-awareness. As development continues, basic regularities in self-experience occur, thereby creating a sense of self-sameness or "self." Other developmental and social processes help to stabilize this emerging self in a way that allows identity to form around it. This entire process undergoes continuous growth and modification as the body, personal competencies, and social relationships become more sophisticated and mature. The result is the constellation of integrated biological, psychological, and social processes that we call the self, which is not reducible to any one or two of the components. Hence, in the larger picture, the psychology–sociology distinction no longer makes much sense (Michel & Morf, 2003).

It is easy to see the connection between both psychological and social forces, as well as self-theory and self-esteem, when using the two-factor approach. For example, Gecas and Schwalbe (1983), who worked on self-esteem primarily from a sociological perspective noted that,

> Beyond the looking-glass self is a self that develops out of the autonomous and efficacious actions of the individual. . . . There is a motivational component associated with this locus of self that has been variously conceptualized as self-efficacy, competence motivation, or effectance motivation. This idea (which has become quite prominent within psychological social psychology) stresses that human beings are motivated to experience themselves as causal agents in their environment. . . . In short, human beings derive a sense of self not only from the reflected appraisals of others, but also from the consequences and products of behavior that are attributed to the self as an agent in the environment. (p. 79)

More contemporary work also understands the "self" in self-esteem as both psychological *and* social. Although one aspect of the self may look more important from a particular point of view, it recedes to the horizon from the other. The relationship between the psycho and social contours of the self is one of intimate connection that may be best described in terms of the perceptual metaphor of figure and ground. In this way, not only are they linked, but they actually give rise to and form one another, just like competence and worthiness are needed to form self-esteem.

One possible exception to understanding the self in this way is found in one school of humanistic psychology. The transpersonal branch of this orientation consists of those who hold that the self somehow transcends the individual or that the self is a spiritual, as well as psychosocial, entity. Such an understanding would literally take the concept of worthiness to a "higher plane" because it would mean that certain values stand above all others as they reflect the higher essence of this larger universe.

Unfortunately, there is no way to resolve this issue scientifically, so we only deal with it if necessary. Nevertheless, a comprehensive approach to the research, theory, and practice of self-esteem must make mention of this possibility, whether or not that is comfortable.

Traits and States: Self-Esteem Types and Levels

At one time in the field it was possible to divide self-esteem into three basic levels or types: "high," "low," and on occasion, "medium." Each type or level was characterized by a few basic characteristics, such as a good quality of life or the presence of anxiety or depression. Now we know that much variation occurs even within these basic categories, so simple classification is no longer possible. Let us compile what is said about low and high self-esteem to determine whether it can be organized in a meaningful fashion. We will start with low self-esteem because its heterogeneity is more straightforward than that of high self-esteem.

Low Self-Esteem

We have already seen that low self-esteem is a diagnostic criterion or associated characteristic of nearly two dozen mental disorders, but several individuals summarize the effect of low self-esteem in a way that captures its lived qualities as well.

> Although the relationships are often weak, virtually every clinically recognized variety of emotional and behavioral problem is more common among people with low than high self-esteem. Low self-esteem is associated with dysthymic disorder, major depression, anxiety disorder, eating disorders, sexual dysfunction, pathological shame, suicide attempts, and an array of personality disorders in both children and adults. (Leary & MacDonald, 2003, p. 412)

And after studying self-esteem for over 3 decades, Rosenberg and Owens (2001) also identify the chief characteristics of low self-esteem, especially when compared with their high self-esteem counterparts. They include feelings such as hypersensitivity, instability, self-consciousness, lack of self-confidence, being more concerned with protecting against a threat than actualizing possibilities and enjoying life, lack of risk taking, general depression, pessimism, loneliness, alienation, and so forth.

In addition, there are other situations that often, but not always, become a clinical problem involving self-esteem that do not carry a particular diagnosis. One of them is the effect of trauma. Abuse during childhood is worth spending some time with as an example of more severe levels of low self-esteem. In fact, one of the most impressive studies supporting the position that such abuse does have powerful developmental, behavioral, and clinical implications for a developing person is found in the work of Swanston, Tebbutt, O'Toole, and Oates (1997). An advantage of pointing to this study is that it is one of the few that involves a well-stratified sample of reasonably good size (86 participants), who were compared with control groups that did not experience abuse. Subjects were also followed for a 5-year period, which gives the work longitudinal strength. In addition to confirming the general finding that many sexually abused children suffer increased rates of several types of mental health problems, such as low self-esteem, depression, anxiety, binge eating, and self-injury, this study found that the difficulties continue over time.

Such a finding is important because it supports the idea that sexual abuse can go beyond "just" being a problem: It may create difficulties in other ways as well. For example, the authors went on to indicate that the findings are consistent with Finkelhor and Browne's (1985) model of traumatization. This view identifies four "traumagenic dynamics" that are associated with the "categories of psychological injury experienced by children who have been sexually abused" (p. 605). They are sexual traumatization (learning age-inappropriate sexual behavior), betrayal (feelings of depression, hostility, or isolation associated with the abuse), powerlessness (described as anxiety, a decreased sense of personal efficacy, and an increased risk of victimization in the future), and stigmatization (a sense of self-blame or shame). Note that at least two of these dimensions, power and stigma, are related to competence and worthiness. Thus, it is easy to understand how it is that abuse may take a serious toll on self-esteem and its development.

Of course, it is also important to note that just as with any other childhood difficulty or trauma, which particular problem one develops, or whether one develops any problem at all, depends on such variables as the identity of the abuser, the frequency and severity of abuse, age and level of developmental maturity, the degree of social support present, personality, and, most of all, resilience. Nevertheless, it is clear that one of the most damaging potential effects of childhood abuse is how it may affect self-esteem, which has all kinds of negative possibilities for the future.

Beginning in the late 1980s, people began to notice other characteristics associated with low self-esteem that are far less debilitating and not particularly clinical, although not without consequence. For example, Campbell and Lavallee (1993) found that in contrast to people with high self-esteem,

> Low self-esteem people utilize self-protective strategies, characterized
> by unwillingness to take risks, focusing on avoiding their bad qualities,

avoidance of strategic ploys, and reluctance to call attention to the self. In other words, the self-presentational styles of people with low self-esteem are not self-derogatory, but self-protective, cautious, and conservative. (p. 14)

Campbell also found that such individuals often demonstrate a lack of clarity concerning their identity and are sensitive to self-relevant social cues. Kernis (2003a) and others pointed out that overgeneralization is a thinking pattern that is common among people with low self-esteem. Others, such as Tennen and Affleck (1993); Tice (1993); and Wood, Giordano-Beech, Taylor, Michela and Gaus (1994), found that people with low self-esteem use self-handicapping strategies and lower expectations to help protect themselves against further losses in this area. Typically, such individuals do not suffer the degree of pain the clinical group does, because the self-esteem they do have is protected by these devices. Interestingly enough, people who live this second type of low self-esteem seem to be resistant to change, perhaps even more so than clinical populations: Severe pain can act as a motivator for change, where mere discomfort may not. In fact, research shows that those who live this type of low self-esteem tend to reject positive feedback, focus on negative information about themselves, avoid risk, and so forth, in an attempt to maintain this unpleasant but familiar or "safe" state (Campbell, 1999; Epstein, 1979; Epstein & Morling, 1995; Wells & Marwell, 1976). This type of behavior is usually understood in terms of the need for consistency as being stronger than, but not completely replacing, the enhancement motivations of self-esteem. For example, it has also been found that such individuals desire high self-esteem but prefer to attempt to reach it through more indirect methods, such as associating with those who have it (Brown, Collins & Schmidt, 1988).

High Self-Esteem

Not long ago, high self-esteem was almost invariably associated with positive abilities and characteristics that made it a desirable condition. No doubt these positive aspects of high self-esteem played a major role in it becoming an important psychological concept. However, contemporary research on high self-esteem suggests that not all forms of it are positive, which has the effect of generating considerable confusion in the field and outside of it. This aspect of high self-esteem is known as the "heterogeneity" of self-esteem (Baumeister, Campbell, Krueger & Vohs, 2003). It is necessary to understand this mixed picture of high self-esteem, which can be done by breaking down the findings into two groups: those that are, in general, desirable and those that are largely undesirable.

On one hand, most of the positive characteristics traditionally associated with high self-esteem are still affirmed. However, they can also be separated into two general types: those that help maintain the self and those that allow the self to actualize. Recall that these two basic positive functions of self-esteem are traditionally known as the self-maintenance or consistency function of self-esteem and its growth or enhancement function. The maintenance function of self-esteem that has received most empirical support concerns its capacity to act as a buffer. For example, Baumeister and colleagues (2003) found evidence supporting the position that high self-esteem is helpful in dealing with stress and avoiding anxiety in a way that allows a person to continue functioning in the face of stress or even trauma (Baumeister, Campbell, Krueger & Vohs, 2003). In addition, Terror Management Theory offers considerable support for the importance of self-esteem in managing both ordinary and existential anxiety about death (Greenberg, Pyszczynski & Solomon, 1995; Pyszczynski, Greenberg & Goldberg, 2003). In short, the "anxiety buffer hypothesis" about high self-esteem, as it is often called, is largely confirmed.

The enhancement function of self-esteem also has received considerable support because a good body of work reports the positive affective and behavioral benefits of high self-esteem. For example, there is a positive statistical relationship between high self-esteem and happiness (Baumeister, Campbell, Krueger & Vohs, 2003), thereby making high self-esteem generally attractive and desirable. Similarly, the "hedonic" quality of self-esteem is preferable to the absence of such a positive general feeling, which includes many types of negative affects (Leary & MacDonald, 2003): People with high self-esteem simply feel better about themselves, about life, about the future, and so forth than do people with low self-esteem. High self-esteem is also associated with desirable personal and interpersonal characteristics and behavior. For example, such self-esteem appears to help job performance and problem solving under certain circumstances, especially those that require initiative and persistence (Baumeister, Campbell, Krueger & Vohs, 2003; Dubois & Flay, 2004). High self-esteem is also associated with extraversion (Leary & MacDonald, 2003), autonomy (Kernis, 2003a; Leary & MacDonald, 2003), and authenticity (Kernis, 2003b).

In addition, there is empirical support linking high self-esteem to various types of positive interpersonal phenomena. For example, high self-esteem may be related to prosocial behavior, such as upholding high moral or healthy standards, relationship satisfaction (Leary & MacDonald, 2003), and positive group performance, especially in relation to task achievement (Baumeister et al., 2003). A small body of research indicates that there may be a positive relationship between self-esteem and immunocompetence (Strauman, Lemieux & Coe, 1993;

Bartoletti & O'Brien 2003). More rigorous work on self-esteem and the educational setting shows that high self-esteem is of positive value in that context (Harter, Whitesell & Junkin, 1998). Finally, high self-esteem may even have long-term benefits. "Higher levels of self-esteem similarly have been found in other research to prospectively predict growth in socioemotional functioning among younger, preschool-age children . . . and, at the other end of the developmental continuum, decreased likelihood of mortality among older adults" (Dubois & Flay, 2004, p. 416). Clearly, high self-esteem is linked to the good life: At least, it is preferable to low self-esteem, all criticisms notwithstanding.

However, research also indicates that there are less than positive and even distinctly negative characteristics associated with high self-esteem that must be considered. For example, people with high self-esteem have been shown to place success over well-being and to demonstrate more in-group favoritism than others (Baumeister, Campbell, Krueger & Vohs, 2003; Crocker & Park, 2003). They may blame others for their own shortcomings in relationships or engage in downward social comparisons that put others down personally (Crocker & Park, 2004; Harter, 1999). Some high self-esteeming individuals appear to think more highly of their value to others in relationships than is actually deserved or they tend to overvalue the contributions they make in group situations (Baumeister, Campbell, Krueger & Vohs, 2003). In addition, high self-esteem has been associated with genuinely negative conditions, such as defensiveness (Crocker & Park, 2004; Epstein & Morling, 1995; Greenier, Kernis & Waschull, 1995; Jordan, Spencer, Zanna, Hoshino-Browne & Correll, 2003; Kernis, 2003a), narcissism (Baumeister, Smart & Boden, 1996; Campbell, Rudich & Sedikides, 2002; Crocker & Park, 2003; Sedikides et al., 2004), and some categories of anti-social behavior such as bullying (Baumeister, Smart & Boden, 1996; Salmivalli, Kaukiainen & Lagerspetz, 1999).

In sum, once again, we see that research on self-esteem has expanded considerably and has done so in a way that shows the limitation of thinking in terms of simple types. In this case, the concept of "high self-esteem" has been found to be inadequate in terms of its descriptive power and usefulness because its characteristics may be positive or negative. Later in Chapter 5, we will see if it is possible to deal with this problem by using the fundamental structure of self-esteem to clear up the confusion generated by such heterogeneity.

A Word about "Medium" Self-Esteem

At one time, there was considerable discussion of a type of self-esteem called "medium self-esteem." For example, there are researchers such as

Coopersmith (1959, 1967) who hold that medium self-esteem is simply the result of not having had enough exposure to the developmental factors that lead to high self-esteem, but of also having more than enough exposure to such factors to avoid having low self-esteem. However, others regard medium self-esteem as a distinct type with its own unique characteristics (Block & Thomas, 1955; Cole, Oetting & Hinkle, 1967; Weissman & Ritter, 1970).

For various reasons, the literature concerning medium self-esteem has not grown rapidly. However, this situation may need to change for at least one important reason that is most clearly found in assessing self-esteem. Most measures of it are constructed so that they assess three basic groups: people with low-self-esteem, individuals with high self-esteem, and everyone else. It is important to emphasize the extremes, of course, to help people with low self-esteem and to learn from those who have it in abundance. However, it is also important to realize that the vast majority is found in the middle range. If we genuinely wish to be true to the phenomenon, and if medium self-esteem occurs most often at this level in the life world, then we need to do much more in terms of understanding how it is normatively and normally lived by most people most of the time.

Levels and Types of Self-Esteem

Thinking in terms of types is not only more complicated now, but research is also indicating that the level of self-esteem a person holds within types can change as well. The easiest way to see this phenomenon may be in the difference between global versus situational self-esteem (Harter, 1999). In this case, a person may hold one level of self-esteem in one domain or type of situation and a different level in another. However, levels can also vary in more complex ways. For example, Harter and Whitesell (2003) found that for some people, self-esteem is relatively stable but for others it varies considerably over time or in different situations, or both. Campbell (1999) noted that other factors could affect the level and stability of self-esteem such as what he called the "clarity" of self-concept. Apparently, some individuals with uncertain, weak, or ill-defined self-concepts or identities are much more susceptible to negative feedback or failure. This increased vulnerability may, in turn, affect their level of self-esteem in a way that makes it unstable.

In addition, there is emerging research suggesting that either high or low self-esteem may be lived at two different levels in regard to one's conscious awareness of it. One is called "explicit" self-esteem, which is one's conscious experience of self-esteem, and the other is termed "implicit" self-esteem and is un- or non-conscious (Devos & Banaji, 2003). If so, then additional variations in levels of self-esteem may occur. For example, one person could have high levels of both explicit and implicit self-esteem, whereas another could be high in only one and low in the other. Moreover, these levels may fluctuate in as few as 25 seconds under some conditions (Dijksterhuis, 2004).

The range and variety of research on the levels and types of self-esteem is broad but fascinating because it reveals all kinds of issues and possibilities concerning the dynamics of self-esteem. Although some people may find this work on self-esteem confusing, it may actually reflect progress in the field because we are finally approaching the point of having enough data to allow us to look for underlying patterns. Greenier et al. (1995), Kernis and Goldman (2003), and Kernis (2003a) have done some of the most comprehensive analysis of this material to date.

For example, much of the work done on defensive self-esteem, stability or instability of self-esteem, explicit and implicit self-esteem, and contingent and authentic self-esteem, and so on may be placed in a framework that Kernis (2003a, b) developed. He categorized each type or level of self-esteem according to whether it is "fragile" or vulnerable in at least one obvious fashion or "secure" and relatively steady and healthy. Kernis found that most of the distinctions made between levels or types of self-esteem actually occur in pairs when set in this framework. Thus, we see that defensive high self-esteem is the fragile counterpart to secure self-esteem. Unbalanced explicit/implicit forms of self-esteem, where one aspect is markedly different from the other, occurs in contrast to high explicit/high implicit self-esteem. Contingent self-esteem is set against true self-esteem. Unstable high self-esteem stands opposite of stable high self-esteem. In each case the term that comes first represents a particular form of fragile self-esteem and the second one in the pair describes the more solid self-esteem counterpart. Going one step further, Kernis realized that "optimal" self-esteem could be characterized by combining the self-esteem qualities found on the secure side of the pairs. Thus, optimal self-esteem is seen as being secure, high both explicitly and implicitly, true, and stable, all of which seem to be apparent when people are being "authentic."

Interestingly, authenticity has been a part of existentialism and humanistic psychology since their beginnings (Tageson, 1982). However, until now it has not received much in the way of empirical support, mainly because accessing experiential dimensions of personal well-being is problematic. Fortunately, progress is being made in investigating human phenomena such as authenticity. For example, Koole and Kuhl noted that,

> In more recent years, however, a number of researchers have found ways of rendering the authentic self open to empirical scrutiny. . . . Although this work is still preliminary, sufficient findings have accumulated to conclude that the functioning of the authentic self can be

systematically observed and studied through experimental means. . . . Because Kernis identifies various ways of operationalizing secure self-esteem, his analysis offers researchers some attractive new tools in the study of the authentic self. Indeed, research using these tools has been able to verify that high self-esteem that is genuine, true, stable, and congruent with implicit self-esteem is linked to various indicators of authentic functioning, which include self-insight, unbiased processing, autonomous goal striving, and an open way of relating to others. (2003, p. 43)

Although authors vary somewhat on what actually constitutes authenticity, the most basic definition involves a particular combination of awareness and action. The more the individual is aware of his or her intrinsic motivation, for instance, the more likely the person is to engage in autonomous, authentic, and satisfying action. Self-Determination Theory builds much of its position on research that supports a link between functioning in these ways and psychological well-being (Ryan & Deci, 2003) and we have already seen some correspondence between self-esteem moments and authenticity in Mruk (1983) and Jackson (1984). Indeed, experimentally oriented research on existential themes, such as authenticity, autonomy, and self-esteem, is beginning to emerge to the point where it justified the need for a handbook (Greenberg, Koole & Pyszczynski, 2004).

There are also other formulations of self-esteem levels and types that are worth considering. For example, Tafarodi, Tam, and Milne (2001) noted that when self-esteem is defined in terms of competence and worthiness (self-competence and self-liking, as they named it), they found that another type of discrepancy could occur. In this case, individuals may vary on one component of self-esteem when compared with the other. Thus, some people may be competent, but feel unworthy and vice versa, a condition they called "paradoxical" self-esteem. This approach may actually turn out to be more appealing than thinking in terms of explicit and implicit levels self-esteem because, as they pointed out, accepting a distinction between implicit and explicit levels of self-esteem requires taking another step: Thinking in terms of explicit and implicit selves, which risks adding a new, and perhaps unnecessary, dimension of complexity (Tafarodi, Tam & Milne, 2001; Tafarodi & Ho, 2003).

We shall see in Chapter 5 that the two-factor tradition makes two important points in terms of levels and types of self-esteem. First, this approach will show that it is quite possible to make good sense of what is too often dismissed as the mere heterogeneity of high self-esteem. When defined in terms of competence and worthiness, for instance, it becomes clear that such a definition makes it possible to separate high self-esteem into two specific types: one that is "dark" in ways that others have described and one that is quite healthy or "light." Second, this perspective might be able to make inroads to understanding the complexities of self-esteem in ways that have not been possible before. For example, defining self-esteem in terms of competence and worthiness may allow us to make some progress in terms of integrating levels of self-esteem as well.

Self-Esteem Functions as a Motivational Need and a Call

As was said in the introduction to this self-esteem paradox in Chapter 2, the connection between self-esteem and behavior is probably most often talked about in terms of needs. For instance, Gecas pointed out that, "The motivation to maintain and enhance a positive conception of oneself has been thought to be pervasive, even universal" (1982, p. 20). The same position can be found among those who represent an evolutionary point of view. For example, Leary and Downs noted that "In a discipline with few universally accepted principles, the proposition that people are motivated to maintain and enhance their self-esteem has achieved the rare status of an axiom" (1995, p. 123). Even those who are critical of self-esteem admit that, at least in social psychology, understanding self-esteem as a need is axiomatic (Crocker & Park, 2003).

Perhaps the chief advantage in understanding self-esteem as a need is that needs are capable of giving rise to, and accounting for, large domains of behavior. But saying something is not the same as demonstrating it, so it is fortunate that some research also went on to look for such basic human needs. Sheldon, Elliot, Kim, and Kasser (2001) began by examining the major needs theories, which included developing a list of the 10 most frequently mentioned needs. They are autonomy, competence, relatedness, physical thriving, security, self-esteem, self-actualization, pleasure-stimulation, money-luxury, and popularity-influence. Then, they asked people to identify experiences that were satisfying for them to see if any of the needs were more universal than others at the lived or empirical level rather than in the world of theory alone. Interestingly, "self-esteem, relatedness, and autonomy emerged in a three-way tie at the top of the list" (p. 329). One of the most fascinating aspects of this study is that this finding appeared to occur across cultures, even in a highly individualistic one such as American culture, as well as more collectivistic ones, such as Korean culture, *just as should be the case if we are looking at a basic human need.*

Except for those who see self-esteem strictly as a result rather than a cause of behavior, the need for self-esteem is usually talked about in terms of motivation, which can be understood in two ways. Gecas said, "As aspects of the self-esteem motive, self-enhancement emphasizes growth, expansion, and increasing one's self-esteem, while self-maintenance focuses on *not* losing what one has. The two engender different behavioral strategies" (1982, p. 21). Thus, on one hand, some researchers and clinicians (e.g., Bednar, Wells & Peterson, 1989; Leary & Downs, 1995; Mecca, Smelser & Vasconcellos, 1989; Wells & Marwell, 1976) will talk about self-esteem in relation to the maintenance of the self, which is often done in terms of self-consistency theory. In this case, self-esteem helps to maintain a steady state of inner experience in both active and passive ways. For example, self-esteem appears to act as a shield against the slings and arrows of life, especially when one is under stress. Even Baumeister and colleagues described this aspect of self-esteem as providing "a stock of positive feelings that can be a valuable resource under some conditions" (2003, p. 37). Sometimes, however, that resource is inadequate or becomes exhausted. When that happens, one experiences a drop in self-esteem. If it is a need, then this development should result in a state of deprivation, which, in turn, motivates the person to take action aimed at restoring self-esteem. Others within this camp suggest that the regulatory function of self-esteem is more social in nature. For example, Leary's work (2004a) supporting Sociometer Theory indicates that people experience a drop in self-esteem when they engage in behavior that is likely to result in social rejection or exclusion. The feelings associated with such a drop not only help us avoid social rejection in the first place but also prompt us to engage in restorative behaviors when we have strayed too far off the social path, thereby regulating interpersonal as well as intrapersonal behavior.

On the other hand, another group understands self-esteem in relation to a need for personal growth and development or self-enhancement. Here, self-esteem is seen as a growth motive instead of a deficiency motive to paraphrase Maslow (1968). Such a motivational picture of self-esteem was seen in psychodynamic literature in terms of White's work on competence mentioned earlier. However, it is also found in developmental approaches to self-esteem (Harter, 1999) as well as in humanistic theory, particularly that of Maslow and Rogers who definitely understood self-esteem as a basic human need. In this case, self-esteem is seen as propelling the individual toward taking risks as a way of increasing competence and worthiness instead of just maintaining it. As such, self-esteem becomes connected to authenticity: Instead of moving backward or taking the easy way out, self-esteem pushes people toward the future in a more creative, open, or actualizing way.

It is easy to see how both sides of this paradox are of value, so it should not be surprising to find that people have worked on integrating them in a coherent fashion. For example, White (1959, 1963) attempted to do that under the notion of "effectance," which is an inborn motivation to enhance the experience of mastery and that eventually gives rise to self-esteem. The effectance motive does not conflict with the more defensive regulatory functions of the self because effectance only arises in a "conflict-free" state. Thus, when threat passes, the maintenance function of self-esteem recedes, and the enhancement function has the opportunity to motivate behavior.

Epstein (1980, 1985) brought the two functions together in the formation of a hierarchy. The maintenance function of self-esteem is primary because it helps to keep stable one's theories of the world, others, and self. Threats at this level generate anxiety or even pain, both of which are buffered by self-esteem. Rather than becoming destabilized when threatened in these ways, self-esteem allows us to maintain a sense of worth that is stabilizing. Such constancy helps allow the individual to take countermeasures or to suffer through the situation relatively undamaged. At the same time, the self is driven by the need to expand our abilities and understandings, which, when successfully done, is pleasurable and rewarding and results in an increase in self-esteem. Thus, self-esteem is important for both maintenance and for growth, which suggests that it is a fundamental need. More recently, Self-Determination Theory psychology tied self-esteem to both functions because that would be the most adaptive combination (Greenberg, Pyszczynski & Solomon, 1995). However, the point is that much research on self-esteem supports the idea that it is capable of functioning as a need and a call, which means that both aspects of self-esteem must be incorporated into any integrated theory.

Self-Esteem as a Developmental Product and Process

As Trzesniewski, Robins, Roberts, and Caspi (2004) noted, self-esteem work is characterized by the same "state" versus "trait" issue found in personality psychology. Because the Big Five theory of personality seems to make progress in resolving this issue in that field, perhaps the long-term study of self-esteem could help clarify self-esteem in this one. Accordingly, they conducted a meta-analysis that examined the rank-order stability of self-esteem using 50 articles that involved nearly 30,000 subjects.

> Overall, the findings support the view that self-esteem is a stable individual-difference construct. Test-retest correlations are moderate in magnitude and comparable to those for personality traits; across all age groups, the mediation correlation (unadjusted for measurement error) was 0.47.
>
> In contrast to personality, which showed an increasing linear trend, the rank-order stability of self-esteem showed a robust curvilinear trend. (2004, p. 167)

They also found that the developmental course of self-esteem was fairly predictable. This work suggests that self-esteem is more of a trait than state, just as with many personality characteristics.

Harter has studied the development of self-esteem longer and in more depth than any other researcher of whom I am aware. For example, Harter (1999) traced the development of the self and self-esteem through Piaget's entire developmental structure. At each step of the way, she obtained empirical measures of self-esteem using aged-based assessment scales she and her colleagues developed. Harter found that although each of us goes through the stages in an individual fashion, a general trend emerges. First, early forms of self-esteem develop to fairly high levels in most children, perhaps because of the child's inability to see much beyond their own point of view. Then, self-esteem levels off or drops somewhat as children move into middle childhood, probably because their cognitive development makes possible more realistic comparisons and appraisals. Next, most people experience a significant drop in early adolescence, which may reflect adjustments to puberty and the structure of schools. Self-esteem then seems to increase steadily throughout late adolescence and the 20s. Finally, self-esteem appears to remain fairly high and stable for the next several decades and then eventually tends to decline with age. Thus, self-esteem can be seen as a product that is created by the outcome of various developmental forces associated with age.

Yet, there are also two ways of making a convincing argument for understanding self-esteem as an ongoing process as well. One is that the particular areas that we tend to evaluate ourselves on change somewhat over time. For example, although Harter (1999) tracked self-esteem over most of the life cycle, she found that it was necessary to modify the domains of self-esteem her scales assessed, depending on age. Scholastic competence is relevant up through the early college years, for instance, but becomes replaced by job competence, which reflects a change in priorities and opportunities. Other domains were dropped and some were added, showing that self-esteem does have some variability over time. Interestingly enough, she found that physical appearance was the only domain of self-esteem that ran throughout the life cycle. For the most part, then, this aspect of self-esteem means that (1) people are bound to have new opportunities to increase self-esteem in life (or decrease it, as the case may be); and (2) no one can predict how a particular person will act or react in response to the specific challenges that each domain brings.

Another indication of change occurs in clinical work, an area that I feel is often understudied in scholarly and academically oriented material on self-esteem. However, it has been examined in relation to treating such problems as substance abuse, anxiety, depression, and so forth (O'Brien

& Epstein, 1983, 1988). Other work supporting the process nature of self-esteem can be found in programs that are aimed at modifying it (Bednar & Peterson, 1995; Frey et al., 1992; Hakim-Larson & Mruk, 1997; Pope, McHale & Craighead, 1988). In addition, we also saw that self-esteem is flexible enough to undergo development naturally such as in the case of particularly powerful self-esteem moments that can alter self-esteem quite suddenly. In sum, we may say that self-esteem is a process early in life and then becomes a fairly stable developmental product. Even so, there are times when its character as a process becomes figural again such as when we make transitions between major times of life or when it challenges us in particularly powerful ways.

Self-Esteem as a Variable?

From the 1970s through most of the 1980s, the link between self-esteem and behavior was so widely assumed that people did not pay much attention to it: They "knew" self-esteem was an important if not crucial variable in human behavior. The next decade saw people questioning the strength of that relationship and finding it so lacking that the value of the concept itself came into doubt (Baumeister, Smart & Boden, 1996; Emler, 2001; Seligman, 1995b). Now even some of the same researchers point out that one should not be too quick to jump to either conclusion: "In short, care must be taken to avoid either overstating or understating the causal influence of self-esteem" (Baumeister, Campbell, Krueger & Vohs, 2003, p. 9). One reason for this apparent confusion is that much of the research done on the relationship between self-esteem and behavior is on the basis of work that defines self-esteem largely in terms of worthiness. If self-esteem involves two factors instead of one, for instance, such work cannot establish a cause-and-effect relationship or even show strong statistical correlations, *in principle*. A partial definition is bound to generate largely insignificant results because lopsided beginnings usually lead to skewed endings.

Another way to go about understanding how self-esteem can act like an independent variable from one point of view and a dependent variable from another involves the concept of reciprocity. Instead of looking for lineal causality, some people working from this perspective see self-esteem as a type of self-fulfilling prophecy. For example, Coopersmith said, "Although there are undoubtedly variations in the origins of a cycle from self-esteem to anxiety, the model of a cyclical, self-reinforcing, self-propelling sequence seems appropriate once either state has been established" (1967, p. 133). Others use information processing metaphors to explain the self-fulfilling nature of the relationship between self-esteem and behavior. Here, self-esteem is seen as a form of feedback that plays a critical role: It is "a special type of information that can describe, evaluate, or influence performance" (Bednar, Wells & Peterson, 1989, p. 91). This more cognitive view sees self-esteem serving a regulatory function in the self-system. Hence, once we develop a certain type or level of global self-esteem, we tend to operate in ways that are consistent with it to maintain a sense of self-sameness over time.

Harter (1999) took a more developmental track on the mediating character of self-esteem on the basis of her research on depression in adolescence. In this framework, the link between self-esteem and behavior is based on the direction of self-esteem (i.e., whether it functions as a cause or as an effect for a specific individual at a particular time). For example, for one person, a particular failure or a rejection could lead to a drop in self-esteem and that decline could, in turn, make them more vulnerable to depression. For another, the same event could have little or no effect on self-esteem. For yet a third person, the situation could trigger a full-fledged depression, which, in turn, might also lead to a subsequent drop in self-esteem. Harter found that what determines which direction self-esteem will flow toward depends on one key component not often discussed in traditional self-esteem research: meaning.

Jackson (1984) pointed out that experimental work aimed at establishing simple or one-way statistical causality in regard to self-esteem is doomed to failure. Most of the experimental work done in this field, for instance, involves setting up a situation where someone is asked to solve a problem or compete in a contest where some type of treatment is introduced, usually unknown to the subject. In one case, it might be verbal cueing that is manipulated; in another, rigging the contest so that failure is certain; and in a third setting distraction might be added to the situation, and so forth. However, if it is true that a situation must *mean* something to an individual before self-esteem becomes mobilized, then subjects must be personally connected to the situation and its outcomes for the experiment to be relevant to self-esteem. Yet, Epstein showed us in Chapter 1 that it is difficult for experiments to achieve such status in ethical ways. All things considered, then, we must conclude that most of the experimental work done on self-esteem is likely to be inadequate: Much of it involves contrived circumstances, trivial challenges, and little in the way of significant or lasting outcomes. In other words, it is not at all surprising to find so little in the way of statistical significance between self-esteem and behavior based on traditional methods.

In sum, at this point in the development of the field, it is possible to conclude two things about the status of self-esteem as a variable affecting behavior. One is that there are several possibilities to consider, such as a two-factor approach to self-esteem, before making any kind of declaration about its nature as a variable or about its statistical strength.

The other is that meaningful research linking self-esteem and behavior must be just that: based on meaning. Unfortunately, most of the traditionally oriented work done to date is not.

"GOOD" SELF-ESTEEM ASSESSMENT INSTRUMENTS

It was mentioned in Chapter 2 that the state versus trait and product versus process issues were also alive in the assessment of self-esteem. In addition, we saw in the section on research problems associated with measuring self-esteem that most measures are unidimensional, primarily in a way that leans toward simple dictionary definitions of self-esteem or "worthiness." Because such an approach was shown to be inadequate, most work done using such instruments is faulty. Although the more recently developed multidimensional measures still possess what is generally called a "global self-esteem" scale, they also assess various dimensions of self-esteem, which are far more specific. Typically, these domains include such factors as physical appearance, moral self-approval, competence, and so forth. As Harter said,

> It has become increasingly important to the field to distinguish between self-evaluations that represent global characteristics of the individual (e.g., "I am a worthwhile person") and those that reflect the individual's sense of adequacy across particular domains, such as one's cognitive competence (e.g., "I am smart"), social competence (e.g., "I am well liked by peers"), athletic competence (e.g., "I am good at sports"), and so forth. . . . Conceptualizations and instruments that aggregate domain-specific self-evaluations (e.g., Coopersmith, 1967) have been found wanting in that they mask the meaningful distinctions between one's sense of adequacy across domains. (2003, p. 612)

We saw that even Rosenberg came to recognize this "global-situational" problem in measuring self-esteem in his attempt to distinguish between what he called baseline (global) and barometric (situational) self-esteem. He went on to point out that "it is particularly important to distinguish between global and specific self-esteem because the relationships reported in the literature between self-esteem and other variables are often weaker than might be expected" (Rosenberg et al., 1995, p. 143), suggesting that global measures alone were inadequate.

There are dozens, if not hundreds, of self-esteem measures to consider in assessing self-esteem. However, Guindon (2002) indicated that four of them are used most often, based on her review of citations. They are the Self-Esteem Scale (SES) (Rosenberg, 1965), the Self-Esteem Inventory (SEI) (Coopersmith, 1981), the Tennessee Self-Concept Scale

(TSCS) (Roid & Fitts, 1988), and the Piers–Harris Children's Self-Concept Scale (P-HCSCS) (Piers & Harris, 1969). Other frequently used instruments include the Culture Free Self-Esteem Inventory (CFSEI) (Battle, 1992), the Minnesota Multiphasic Personality Inventory's Self-Esteem Scale (MMPI-2) (Hathaway et al., 1989), the Perceived Competence Scale for Children (PCSC) (Harter, 1985), the Adult Self-Perception Scale (ASPS) (Messer & Harter, 1986), the Multidimensional Self-Esteem Inventory (MSEI) (O'Brien & Epstein, 1983, 1988), and the Self-Liking/Self-Competence Scale (SLSC) (Tafarodi & Swann Jr., 1995). We have seen that unidimensional measures are inadequate, which narrows the list down to a handful. Similarly, we understand self-esteem in terms of competence and worthiness, which reduces the list even further. These requirements result in a limited set of instruments: limited, but good ones in that they are "measuring the right thing" as discussed in Chapter 2. They are the SLSC, the MSEI, and the PCSC/ASPS each of which has its own strengths and weaknesses.

The SLSC might be the measure of choice for doing research on self-esteem where large numbers of subjects are involved because of its brevity. The test meets our basic criteria and is easy to administer, take, and score, thereby making it a fairly non-intrusive measure. The MSEI is a multidimensional instrument that measures domains of self-esteem and includes a global self-esteem scale that is independent from them. This instrument also has one more characteristic that sets it apart from others: It includes a defensiveness scale that helps avoid mistaking various types of responses for those that express genuine self-esteem. This indicator is useful in identifying scores that reflect such things as the ceiling effect, social desirability, or "false positives" such as those who are presenting themselves as though they have high self-esteem but who are actually living fragile, unstable, or inauthentic forms of it. The only other self-esteem test of which I am aware that offers this possibility is the one that is included in the MMPI and that test is extremely time consuming to use. Finally, the various versions of the PCSC and ASPS also assess domains of self-esteem as well as including a global measure. In addition, they have the advantage of being normalized for developmental issues and responses for all the basic age groups of the life span.

EFFECTIVE SELF-ESTEEM ENHANCEMENT TECHNIQUES

Because this book aims to move from research through theory to practice, the last task we have in a chapter that focuses on identifying major findings concerning self-esteem is to look for work that concerns enhancing self-esteem at the lived level. This area is one of the newest in the field, but for those of us who are interested in change or working with self-esteem clinically, it is also the most exciting. As before, the findings presented here are qualitative and quantitative but always based on persistence, significance, or both.

The Importance of Being Accepting and Caring

We saw from the findings concerning parental and social factors affecting self-esteem that how we are treated by others may affect its development. Although such factors may diminish somewhat with age, we never lose this capacity to respond: Parents are replaced by others such as friends, spouses, coworkers, and bosses, who accept or reject us in important ways. Being accepted, then, should be a part of any decent self-esteem enhancement program. This technique may be seen as the most basic one because it is tied to the development of self-esteem in the first place and because most systematic attempts to enhance it include acceptance as a part of the process (Bednar, Wells & Peterson, 1989; Coopersmith, 1967; Epstein, 1979; Sappington, 1989). Also, whether envisioned humanistically as providing "unconditional positive regard," psychodynamically as a "working alliance," or cognitive-behaviorally as "building rapport," this technique has been found to be one of common factors essential to the therapeutic process in general (Arkowitz, 1997). In addition, treating the individual suffering from self-esteem problems with such respect and compassion can itself be a powerful therapeutic experience, mainly because he or she is usually more familiar with rejection than acceptance. In this sense, acceptance can be doubly helpful.

Providing Consistent, Positive (Affirming) Feedback

There are good reasons and some supporting evidence to maintain that consistently providing people with positive (affirming) feedback about themselves or their behavior is another way of building self-esteem (Bednar, Wells & Peterson, 1989; Bednar & Peterson, 1995; Bhatti, Derezotes, Kim & Specht, 1989; Frey & Carlock, 1989). As Bhatti, Derezotes, Kim, and Specht (1989) summed it up, "Many experts suggest focusing on positive rather than negative behavior to begin building self-esteem" (p. 54). No matter which standard approach to self-esteem one uses, positive feedback makes a difference at the theoretical level. For example, a symbolic interactionalist steeped in the Cooley–Mead tradition might understand such information in terms of positive "reflected appraisals" that are involved in the development of an individual's view of their own self-worth. The humanistically oriented therapist could gravitate toward providing positive feedback "unconditionally," which occurs in terms of affirming one's worth as a unique human being. And those who advocate a cognitive approach to the self know the value of positive and negative feedback in such a dynamic system.

There are, however, two caveats to be aware of when applying such a technique. First, humanistic psychology states that such feedback must be "authentic," which is to say based in reality and not phony praise. Second, some cognitive research indicates that there might be value in providing positive feedback in a way that is slow but steady rather than fast or sudden. Their understanding for this practice is that the self-system is designed to be and to remain stable, even when its overall character is negative or painful. Trying to change things too quickly is disruptive to the system and it is likely to be resisted through self-handicapping or some other way of discounting the information (Bednar, Wells & Peterson, 1989; Bednar & Peterson, 1995; Epstein, 1985). Consequently, small positive doses of positive feedback are likely to be more effective than larger ones because they are non-threatening enough to slip into the system, thereby gradually altering it over time.

Generating Positive Self-Feedback through Cognitive Restructuring

In addition to others providing us with feedback that affects our identity and esteem, we provide it to ourselves. This process can be understood psychodynamically in terms of narcissistic supplies and ego ideals or humanistically in terms of meaning and choices. However, the cognitive approach offers the most empirically supported method of intervening at this level. This technique involves three basic steps: learning how to identify problematic habits, labeling them as such according to some nomenclature of common errors, and then substituting a more rational or realistic response for each mistake. Several authors provide lists of commonly used terms describing the problematic thinking patterns that cause inaccurate perceptions and unnecessary pain (Burns, 1980, 1993a; Freeman, Pretzer, Fleming & Simon, 1990; Leahy, 2003). These techniques may work on increasing self-esteem in several ways. First, they interrupt the normally smooth-flowing links between thinking, feeling, and acting in negative ways that create and maintain low self-esteem, thereby creating the possibility for something new to happen. Second, being able to demonstrate some control over behavior allows the individual to feel competent, which is conducive to self-esteem. Third, with practice, new habits of perceiving, thinking, experiencing, and acting also set up a more virtuous cycle.

Increasing Self-Esteem by Using Natural Self-Esteem Moments

We saw that some cognitive, phenomenological, and existentially oriented self-esteem researchers investigate how self-esteem is lived in real life. This work has also indicated that self-esteem can change spontaneously, particularly during periods of transition (Epstein, 1979; Harter, 1993) or at certain crucial turning points (Jackson, 1984; Mruk, 1983). A logical extension of both types of findings is to apply them to the task of enhancing self-esteem (Bednar, Wells & Peterson, 1989; Hakim-Larson & Mruk, 1997). In other words, if we can identify these situations as they are occurring or about to occur, then it might be possible to intervene therapeutically and perhaps even turn them into positive self-esteem moments.

One thing that most clinicians advocate in this regard is to help people increase their awareness of the role that self-esteem plays in their lives (Branden, 1983; Frey & Carlock, 1989). Such interventions usually involve raising consciousness, providing support, and facing a challenge as directly as possible at the time that it arises. To help increase awareness, therapists often encourage clients to keep a journal and write about one's self-esteem, as well as what affects it (Epstein, 1979; Fava, 1999; Frey & Carlock, 1989; Hakim-Larson & Mruk, 1997; Sappington, 1989). Additional support is provided in the therapeutic setting (Bednar, Wells & Peterson, 1989) and problem-solving skills are often enhanced to help foster change (Mruk, 1999). Of course, such an intensive technique usually requires the assistance of a professional.

Enhancing Self-Esteem by Assertiveness Training (Empowerment)

Assertiveness training, and perhaps other forms of empowerment, are based on understanding that one has a basic worth as a human being and that certain rights accompany that fact. Such a deep sense of worth and actual behavioral competence at preserving it appears to be helpful in enhancing self-esteem (Bhatti, Derezotes, Kim & Specht, 1989; Frey & Carlock, 1989). For one thing, we know that having the capacity to stand up for oneself and one's values, or being virtuous, is connected with a basic source of self-esteem and success. Also, people who have this skill are usually more competent in terms of getting their individual needs met. In addition to accessing an important source of self-esteem, standing up for oneself can also limit the effect of factors that lessen self-esteem in one's life. Such assertiveness helps us avoid self-esteem–damaging situations, to say "no" to negative treatment from others, or to leave poor relationships more quickly than is otherwise likely. Fortunately, these skills may be acquired at any age (Alberti & Emmons, 1982). However, the process is not simple: The research on assertiveness training indicates that a good program involves several weeks of training, mainly because each skill must be practiced, as well as demonstrated (Rakos, 1990). Even so, this kind of investment seems well worth the effort, especially for people who consistently end up in self-esteem trouble because of deficiencies in this area.

Increasing Self-Esteem through Modeling

It has been more than a century since William James suggested that successes and failures are crucial factors in determining self-esteem. Psychology has learned a good deal about helping people tip the scale to the favorable side since those early days (Bednar, Wells & Peterson, 1989; Pope, McHale & Craighead, 1988; Sappington, 1989). Modern learning theorists, for example, talk about self-efficacy (Bandura, 1997; Maddux & Gosselin, 2003), which concerns a person's beliefs about how he or she is likely to do in a given situation based on a number of variables, such as past performance on similar tasks. The general idea is to help people increase their sense of self-efficacy by learning to become more successful which, in turn, increases self-esteem. Modeling behavior is one standard way of reaching this goal.

In addition to general research on modeling as a therapeutic tool, the best evidence for increasing self-esteem this way comes from Coopersmith (1967) and Bednar, Wells, and Peterson (1989). "Showing by doing" seems to be helpful for two reasons: First, modeling is often useful when trying to learn complex activities. We cannot help but to model our parents, older siblings, peer groups, and teachers, and we learn all kinds of things in doing so. Second, modeling occurs in clinical situations as well. For example, a good facilitator or therapist will demonstrate techniques for handling conflict or other difficult situations in ways that promote self-esteem, that is by attempting to do so in ways that are both competent and worthy or authentic. Many clients with low self-esteem have had few opportunities to model a person who is reasonably competent *and* worthy, so the clinician becomes especially important as a model. Indeed, clients probably learn more from the clinician in this way than the clinician ever realizes.

Enhancing Self-Esteem by Increasing Problem-Solving Skills

Most self-esteem enhancement programs include the idea that self-esteem helps us to cope more effectively with life's challenges, both small and large (Bednar, Wells & Peterson, 1989; Pope, McHale & Craighead, 1988; Sappington, 1989). Above all, coping well means that a person is able to influence the situations of life or to deal with its problems with a reasonable degree of competence. One way to help increase self-esteem, then, is to teach people how to solve problems more effectively and efficiently (Bednar et al., 1989; Pope et al., 1988). This type of work may be done as a structured activity in the therapeutic setting. For instance, it is possible to break up learning this skill into more manageable steps, each of which can be practiced and evaluated until learning occurs (D'Zurilla & Goldfried, 1971; D'Zurilla & Nezu, 2001). These steps typically include learning how to recognize that a problem exists, being able to identify possible responses and their likely outcomes, knowing how to select the best alternative given a particular situation, and having the ability to develop a realistic plan to reach that goal. The process of learning these skills is facilitated by a good teacher, a non-threatening environment, appropriate reinforcement, and supervised practice, all of which are fairly standard practices in problem solving work.

Several positive things can happen for self-esteem once this skill has been acquired. First, knowing how to better solve problems increases an individual's chances of being successful and we saw that certain types of success are a source of self-esteem. Second, the technique is flexible enough to allow us to target a particular area that is especially troublesome to an individual client and to then help the person develop a realistic problem-solving strategy that is based on maximizing the individual's strengths while minimizing their weaknesses. Indeed, "individualizing" (Fischer, 1986) training in problem solving skills may be the ideal way to address specific individuals with particular self-esteem themes. Thus, increasing competence through better problem-solving skills can be done in ways that are sensitive to age, gender, culture, and so on.

Two Types of Formats May Be Used to Enhance Self-Esteem

There is some consensus about what we might call "format factors" that are helpful in enhancing self-esteem. The first concerns a program's operational format and it allows us to have some design flexibility. One approach is to build a program around the traditional one-to-one relationship between client and clinician (Bednar, Wells & Peterson, 1989; Harter, 1999; Mruk, 1995, 1999). A key advantage of this intense self-esteem encounter is that it focuses on identifying and understanding a particular individual's self-esteem themes and problems in considerable detail both behaviorally and developmentally. The therapist and client may then target these issues as central therapeutic projects. Another advantage is that the process can go on for longer periods of time, meaning that it should be possible for both therapist and client to see change, which is always encouraging. Also, more seriously ill patients or clients with more deeply embedded self-esteem problems often require more attention, which is possible in individual work. On the negative side, we know that this intensive, often long-term format requires considerable resources in terms of clinical expertise, time, and money.

The other major design format is to enhance self-esteem through the group setting, which is positive in a number of other ways (Bhatti, Derezotes, Kim & Specht, 1989; Burns, 1993a; Frey & Carlock, 1989; Mruk, 1995, 1999). For one thing, groups may be designed to meet the needs of various populations. For instance, this format may be tailored to a number of clinical audiences. In this case most of the general rules for clinical groups apply such as screening clients carefully before admitting them to such a group (Vinogradov & Yalom, 1989) and using co-therapists of the opposite gender. In addition, groups may be designed to emphasize growth instead of remediation, which means they can be used with general audiences as well. In fact, such psychoeducational groups seem to be common in the field because they can reach a broad range of people and ages (Frey & Carlock, 1989). The basic structure of this form of group work seems to include a leader who acts as a therapist, facilitator, and teacher and a group size of 8–12 participants.

Whether clinically or growth-oriented, the group format offers several interesting advantages. For example, groups are usually more cost effective, which is important when seen in the light of today's mounting health care crisis. Hence, they can be used to address larger numbers of people and people of limited income (Hakim-Larson & Mruk, 1997). Also, groups may seem less threatening to people who are put off by the idea of psychotherapy or to those who are simply interested in bettering themselves and not having someone "dig around in their heads." Most of all, the group format can do some things better than the individual setting (Vinogradov & Yalom, 1989). The rich mixture of perception, experience, and individual style that comes from being around several different people more closely approximates the conditions of real life than does the individual treatment setting. For instance, a group situation usually presents a greater variety of "safe challenges" or here-and-now opportunities to try out new pro–self-esteem behaviors, such as communicating more effectively or being more assertive. Groups also bring in more of the social factors affecting self-esteem such as offering more opportunities for positive feedback, acceptance, and healthy modeling. Finally, they can offer a sense of camaraderie and support that are hard to duplicate in individual formats: Seeing how others suffer from low self-esteem and witnessing their struggle to gain it can be helpful in many different ways.

Enhancing Self-Esteem Requires Practice

The last factor to be included in any self-esteem enhancement format affects all the others, so perhaps it is the most important. In spite of popular books to the contrary, the evidence shows that enhancing self-esteem in a lasting way takes considerable time and work. There is no effective "1-minute to self-esteem" program. There are several reasons for this, of course, but they can be summed up most succinctly by pointing out that self-esteem problems take a long time to develop: They usually involve deeply ingrained habits of perception, experience, and behavior, all of which are well cemented by the time we reach adulthood. These self-esteem habits shape our world in ways that are both subtle and complex, meaning that change requires considerable unlearning as well as new learning, both of which take time. In the final analysis, then, self-esteem is increased through hard work and practice: In the end, there is simply no escaping this basic existential fact.

Integrating the Techniques

It might first appear as though these 10 tools for enhancing self-esteem, which emerge from examining the literature, do not seem like much in the way of results. However, they are actually quite valuable because they are the *most valid* techniques we have available today, suggesting that they can be used with some confidence and clinical credibility. Although there may not be a great wealth of hard experimental evidence to support the efficacy of a few of these techniques, we have seen that it is possible to mount a clear rationale for using all of them in self-esteem work. Indeed, it should be obvious that some of the methods are valuable because they facilitate a sense of worthiness, which grounds them in that part of the structure, whereas others are important because they increase the behavioral skills necessary to become more competent at living. A few techniques even seem to involve both worthiness and competence. This information may be summed up in an information map, such as the one shown in Table 3.1.

Table 3.1   Integrating Self-Esteem Enhancement Techniques

Worthiness-Based Techniques	Competence-Based Techniques
Acceptance	Modeling
Positive feedback	Problem solving
Competence- and Worthiness-Based	**Common Format Factors**
Cognitive restructuring	Group work
Assertiveness training	Individual work
Self-esteem moments	Practice

In sum, there are four basic groups of self-esteem enhancement techniques at our potential disposal. Acceptance and positive feedback are forms of being valued by others as a worthy person, which connects them with that component of self-esteem. Modeling and problem solving increase competence and reflect that source of self-esteem. Three techniques require both competence and worthiness: Cognitive restructuring involves becoming more competent at thinking in worthwhile ways; assertiveness training means becoming more skilled at standing up for one's rights as a worthy human being; and natural self-esteem moments challenge self-esteem on both levels. The last three tools, the group, individual work, and practice, are format factors that can be useful in helping us tailor programs to specific individual and population characteristics. Now that we have made some sense out of the many findings that populate the field, it is possible to go on to see how people have tried to integrate them at the theoretical and practical levels.

CHAPTER 4

Major Self-Esteem Theories and Programs

We are now at the midpoint of this look at self-esteem, which means that it is time to examine the major theoretical approaches to understanding self-esteem and to enhancing it. In addition to simply updating material, examining what might be regarded as the most promising existing work may also provide a sense of what issues are particularly important in organizing our own efforts in these two areas. Understanding the lay of the theoretical landscape, for instance, should create a better footing on which to develop an integrated theory. Similarly, taking the time to appreciate how people have gone about attempting to enhance self-esteem could result in important insights or guidelines for moving from theory to practice.

To have some criteria to select theories and programs for examination, it is necessary to define what "major" means. The criteria of persistence and significance still work here, but so many new developments have taken place in the field since the other editions of this text that I may no longer use the past practice of selecting one theory to represent each of the major perspectives in psychology. Also, some completely new theories have appeared and others have receded to a historical role. Another way to proceed is by appreciating the three oldest positions in the field, which include what might be called the Jamesian, social learning, and humanistic traditions. Then I will examine several contemporary empirically oriented theories from the cognitive, developmental, existential, and evolutionary points of view.

An important word is necessary before beginning this work. Selecting and reviewing theories is always a challenging task in a field that has many of them. It is virtually impossible to present such material without offending someone through an act of omission (leaving someone or something out), commission (saying something with which the author disagrees), or through interpretation (which can never be perfect). I have had the opportunity to experience all of these phenomena as have most of us who try to share ideas publicly. Thus, it is with great care that I struggled to decide which theories to present and how to condense their rich and powerful ideas into a few pages. Nevertheless, let me say that although I have tried my best to select representative work and to present it accurately, I apologize in advance for any inevitable shortcomings.

TRADITIONAL THEORETICAL APPROACHES

The Jamesian Tradition

We have already examined James' basic approach but the fact that it is being cited in the literature (Crocker & Park, 2003; Harter, 1999) now more than previously means that we should deepen our appreciation of it and its influence. In talking about self-esteem he began by pointing out that each person is born into a set of possible social roles or identities created by factors such as history, culture, family, interests, and circumstance. Over time, we find ourselves becoming invested in some of these "selves" more than others, which creates certain priorities. Over the same time, we also develop an overall sense of how well or poorly we have lived up to these expectations, which gives us our self-esteem and an "average feeling tone" (James, 1890/1983 p. 292). Thus, self-esteem is something that involves areas of life that matter to a person in terms of the individual's identity, how well the person has done in them, and the fact that the person must continue to be concerned with them over time. As James said,

> So we have the paradox of a man shamed to death because he is only the second pugilist or the second oarsman in the world. That he is able to beat the whole population of the globe minus one is nothing; he has "pitted" himself to beat that one; and as long as he doesn't do that nothing else counts. He is to his own regard as if he were not, indeed, he *is* not.
>
> Yonder puny fellow, however, whom everyone can beat, suffers no chagrin about it, for he has long ago abandoned the attempt to "carry that line," as the merchants say, of self at all. With no attempt there can be no failure; with no failure no humiliation. So our self-feeling in this world depends entirely on what we *back* ourselves to be and do. (1980/1983, p. 296)

A chief feature of this definition of self-esteem is that it is dynamic. By using such words as "pitted" (pitting), "carry" (carrying), and "back" (backing) James shows that self-esteem is a vital part of human behavior. By making it contingent on success and failure, self-esteem also takes on many characteristics of a basic need. For example, when we are deprived of self-esteem we seek it out and when we have it we must work to keep it. Such a motivational view of self-esteem can also be seen in the psychodynamic approach to it. For example, Adler (1927) understood self-esteem in terms of a drive toward "superiority" that motivated people to reach higher levels of social status and we saw that White (1963) tied self-esteem to mastery through the effectance motive and competence.

The good news of this model is twofold. First, self-esteem motivates us to try to master the challenges of life. As such, it is a crucial developmental and motivational force. Second, if self-esteem is like a ratio that is dependent on our successes or failures, then change is inherently possible. In fact, James even pointed out that there are several ways to alter the ratio in a direction that is favorable for self-esteem: We may increase self-esteem by finding ways to have more successes in areas that matter to us or we may change the areas that matter to us in ways that lighten the burden of self-esteem. The bad news, of course, is that by making self-esteem dependent on success, it also becomes contingent. For some people, the pursuit of self-esteem in this way is more costly than beneficial as Crocker and Park (2003, 2004) and Crocker and Nuer (2003, 2004) pointed out.

The Social Learning Tradition

Morris Rosenberg

In Chapter 2 we saw that another early approach to self-esteem involved emphasizing its interpersonal character through the Cooley–Mead tradition. This approach was further developed by Harry Stack Sullivan (1953) when he applied it to practical problems in his interpersonal approach to psychiatry. The tradition matured in terms of its empirical work in the mid-1960s when Morris Rosenberg began his monumental investigations with more than 5000 subjects. After defining self-esteem as "a positive or negative attitude toward a particular object, namely, the self" (1965, p. 30), he focused his attention on "the bearing of certain social factors on self-esteem and to indicate the influence of self-esteem on socially significant attitudes and behavior" (p. 15).

Rosenberg began by pointing out that understanding self-image or self-esteem as attitudinal phenomena created by social and cultural forces offers many advantages. Foremost among them is that social science has at its ready disposal various means of measuring attitudes and their formation, meaning that it should be possible to apply the same techniques to understanding ourselves. For example, there are many similarities between external attitudes and internal attitudes in terms of such things as content (what the attitude is about), direction (the positive or negative value of the attitude), intensity (the affective strength of an attitude or how strongly it is held), and stability (how durable or long lasting an attitude is). In his words,

> If we can characterize the individual's self-picture in terms of each of these dimensions, then we would have a good, if still incomplete, description of the structure of the self-image. And the same would be true of any other object in the world. (1965, pp. 7–8)

Of course, Rosenberg was also aware that studying self-esteem this way presents its own problems. One is the reflexivity of the self, which means that self-valuations are more complex than evaluations of external objects because the self is involved in evaluating itself, something that might be analogous to the Heisenberg principle of uncertainty in physics. Another problem is that self-attitudes involve a certain motivational quality that constitutes a powerful bias not usually found with attitudes toward other things: We are inclined to have a positive attitude toward ourselves.

Another important dimension of Rosenberg's view of self-esteem is that this attitude concerning one's worthiness as a person is seen as a "pivotal variable" (1965, p. 15) in behavior because it works for or against us in any situation.

> High self-esteem, as reflected in our scale items, expresses the feeling that one is "good enough." The individual simply feels that he is a person of worth; he respects himself for what he is, but does not stand in awe of himself nor expect others to stand in awe of him. . . . Low self-esteem, on the other hand, implies self-rejection, self-dissatisfaction, self-contempt. The individual lacks respect for the self he observes. The picture is disagreeable, and he wishes it were otherwise. (p. 31)

In short, the presence or absence of such perceived worthiness disposes one toward positive or negative experience and behavior.

Rosenberg went on to explore the way in which self-esteem (or the lack of it) is created: It results from a process of comparison involving values and discrepancies. According to this view, individuals have self-esteem to the degree they perceive themselves as matching up to a set of central self-values. These core values concern what individuals have learned to be worthy of emulating or attaining through the process of socialization (Rosenberg & Simmons, 1971). The relationship between ideals, perceptions, evaluations, and degrees of self-esteem runs in the expected directions. The smaller the gap between the so-called ideal self and the current, actual, or "real" self, the higher is self-esteem. Conversely, the greater the gap, the lower the self-esteem, even if one is actually viewed by others in a positive way. Of course, tying self-esteem to values and to the process of socialization also means that this theory of self-esteem is deeply social and sociological.

Stanley Coopersmith

At about the same time as Rosenberg, Stanley Coopersmith was doing work on self-esteem that was also based on worth or worthiness and social learning. However, his concern was more practical in that he aimed to develop "a conceptual framework that might serve as a guide in investigating self-esteem, or a tool for altering it" (1967, p. vii). After doing 8 years of empirically oriented research on the subject, Coopersmith concluded that, "For both psychologists and laymen, 'self-esteem' has great significance—personally, socially, and psychologically. It is therefore disconcerting that so little is known about the conditions and experiences that enhance or lessen self-esteem" (1967, p. 1). Instead of comparing groups and developing norms, Coopersmith turned toward studying how self-esteem is learned, ways in which self-esteem could be nurtured, and what might be done to modify it when necessary. In addition to looking at four different types of self-esteem (high, low, medium, and discrepant self-esteem) and ways of assessing it (the SEI, mentioned in Chapter 3), he also researched its sources. However, his most important contribution may have been to develop the first clear strategy for enhancing self-esteem.

Although Coopersmith did not go farther than offering suggestions for increasing self-esteem, three of them have stood the test of time. He began by advocating a form of assessment consistent with theory and research:

> First, the conceptual analysis . . . posed four major bases of esteem: competence, significance, virtue, and power. That is, persons come to evaluate themselves according to how proficient they are in performing tasks, how well they meet ethical or religious standards, how loved and accepted they are by others, and how much power they exert. We believe that determining the basis or bases a given individual employs in judging his worth may well be a crucial step in determining the source of his difficulties and in guiding therapeutic efforts. (1967, p. 262)

Next, he built on the findings that children with high self-esteem tend to have families that set clear limits and expectations. Therefore, Coopersmith suggested that structured therapeutic situations might be more effective in increasing self-esteem than unstructured techniques. Finally, he strongly advocated modeling as a central therapeutic device.

> A third implication is that the patient may benefit quite markedly by modeling his behavior after an effective, assured, and competent individual. The exact behavior that an individual may require or seek to follow undoubtedly varies with each person, but it may be that the style of response is more critical than the particular action. Thus the individual may observe how an effective individual deals with anxiety, resolves ambiguities, and makes decisions. (1967, p. 263)

Although Coopersmith did not investigate the efficacy of these modes of intervention, they are clear extensions of social learning theory and practice.

Whether conceived of socially or psychologically, the social learning approach to self-esteem emphasizes defining it in terms of worth or worthiness; researching self-esteem empirically instead of just talking about it; and changing self-esteem through altering various social practices such as those concerning childrearing or education as well as by working in the clinical setting. On the positive side of the ledger, these qualities give the social learning perspective on self-esteem considerable appeal because it implies that we can and should do something about raising self-esteem. Thus, in retrospect, it is no surprise that this approach underlies much of the self-esteem movement of the 1980s and 1990s with its focus on enhancing self-esteem in the educational setting. As we saw earlier, however, defining self-esteem largely in terms of worthiness also leads to problems, such as weak results, poor statistical strength, and considerable backlash against the entire field from which it is now just recovering.

The Humanistic Tradition

Self-esteem has been an important theme in the humanistic approach to understanding human behavior from its beginnings. Indeed, both Abraham Maslow and Carl Rogers regarded self-esteem as a basic human need that plays a key role in both development and behavior. For example, Maslow placed self-esteem among the most basic human needs in his famous hierarchy (1954). Rogers (1961) talked about self-esteem in regard to self-acceptance and congruence, both of which are seen as necessary for healthy human functioning.

According to the humanistic perspective, self-esteem emerges naturally in the course of development, providing an individual receives a sufficient degree of "unconditional positive regard" (Rogers, 1951), especially when young. The importance of self-esteem in the humanistic tradition is also seen through its absence. For example, Rogers pointed out that when people have more conditional positive regard than unconditional appreciation, their self-esteem becomes contingent on reaching goals that others set for them or on the approval of others, either of which blunts their development. And Maslow noted that if an individual does not develop adequate self-esteem, then he or she is "stuck" in that stage of the hierarchy. In that case, much of the person's behavior becomes aimed at either reaching this goal or compensating for it in some negative fashion. In general, then, humanistic psychology sees self-esteem as necessary, if not central, for self-actualization, which is seen as the greatest "good" in this approach.

Although not a traditional humanistic psychologist, Branden (1969) carried its themes into his "Objectivist" approach and made self-esteem a popular topic. In this case, self-esteem is seen as a basic human need that is tied to our highest capacities: reason, choice, and responsibility.

> Man experiences his desire for self-esteem as an urgent imperative, as a basic need. Whether he identifies the issue explicitly or not, he cannot escape the feeling that his estimate of himself is of life-and-death importance. No one can be indifferent to the question of how he judges himself; his nature does not allow man this option. (p. 110)

Thus, self-esteem is seen as a need that drives human behavior in two ways. First, Branden stated that we are not born with the knowledge of what fills the need, which means that we must find out about that through trial and error: "Man's need of self-esteem is inherent in his nature. But he is not born with the knowledge of what will satisfy that need, or of the standard by which self-esteem is to be gauged; he must discover it" (Branden, 1969, p. 110). In other words, we learn about competence and worthiness through our highest human faculties: reason, choice, and responsibility. This process, as Branden described it, involves exercising one's conscious ability to assess situations realistically and to respond to them in a way that is consistent with basic or fundamental human values. Living rationally in this way brings certain powerful positive feelings that are right "in principle" (p. 110). Happiness, joy, pleasure, and self-acceptance are seen as natural responses to living such an authentic existence.

Second, like most humanistic psychologists, in addition to motivating us in such a positive, rational, humane, and actualizing direction,

Branden maintained that the need for self-esteem is so great that the lack of it motivates people just as strongly, but in negative ways.

> So intensely does a man feel the need of a positive view of himself, that he may evade, repress, distort his judgment, disintegrate his mind—in order to avoid coming face to face with facts that would affect his self-appraisal adversely. . . . If and to the extent that men lack self-esteem, they feel driven to *fake* it, to create the *illusion* of self-esteem—condemning themselves to chronic psychological fraud—moved by the desperate sense that to face the universe without self-esteem is to stand naked, disarmed, delivered to destruction. (1969, p. 110)

If one is cut off from legitimate sources of self-esteem (or, more properly, if one cuts oneself off from them), then one searches for substitutes. Branden called the result of this deficiency "pseudo self-esteem," which is manifested in all kinds of negative behavior ranging from mild neurosis to acute forms of depravity.

In a later book entitled *Honoring the Self* (1983), Branden clarified the dynamic nature of self-esteem by specifying two conditions. First, he identified four basic "pillars" of positive self-esteem: the degree of an individual's conscious awareness; one's integrity as a person; the willingness to accept responsibility for one's decisions; and self-acceptance or being honest about the kind of choices one makes. Second, he emphasized that we all must struggle to honor the self because it may be challenged at any time. Thus, self-esteem "is often a struggle of heroic proportions" (p. 19).

We see how each pillar supports the others by looking at what happens when one is missing. For instance, the lack of awareness of the need for self-esteem makes it more difficult to understand how important it is for us to make choices that affirm our integrity as a person. A low degree of integrity means that our actions become incongruent and lessen our ability to engage in honest struggle. Failing to take responsibility is a self-deception of the greatest sort because it limits our ability to see, let alone correct, our self-esteem mistakes. Finally, the inability to accept the value of being ourselves leads to the possibility of self-neglect, which may express itself relatively mildly, as in the form of mere insecurity, or may lead to more severe forms of disturbance such as addiction, an exaggerated need for power, or even various forms of cruelty. In later work, Branden (1994) added two more pillars to complete the picture of self-esteem that he drew. They are assertiveness, which involves honoring one's wants and needs, and purposefulness, which pertains to goal setting and efficacy. Although early humanistic theories concerning self-esteem were not accompanied by a significant degree of empirical support, we shall see that this situation is different today.

CONTEMPORARY EMPIRICALLY BASED APPROACHES

Seymour Epstein's Cognitive Experiential Self-Theory

Although cognitive psychology has not been a part of the history of the field for long, it has been instrumental in terms of integrating psychological and social influences as we saw in Chapter 3. Seymour Epstein's Cognitive Experiential Self-Theory (CEST) is one of the first cognitive theories of self-esteem, and it still receives much attention today. It is based on the notions of information (experience), organization (concept formation), representation (a system of concepts arranged hierarchically), and the process of development. This view finds that human beings organize information and experience of the world, self, and others into what Epstein called "personal theories of reality."

> A major assumption of the theory is that the human mind is so constituted that it tends to organize experience into conceptual systems. Human brains make connections between events, and, having made connections, they connect the connections, and so on, until they have developed an organized system of higher- and lower-order constructs that is both differentiated and integrated. Whether we like it or not, each of us, because he has a human brain, forms a theory of reality that brings order into what otherwise would be a chaotic world of experience. We need a theory to make sense out of the world, just as a scientist needs a theory to make sense out of the limited body of information he or she wishes to understand. (1980, p. 102)

These personal theories of reality include both an understanding of the world and others (what Epstein called a "world theory") and an understanding of who we are in relation to them (a "self-theory").

Like all theories, personal theories make sense out of data; in this case, it is the information given to us through our experience, family, culture, and so forth, in addition to what is more sensory in nature. As with any theory, we generalize from a set of concepts in a way that helps us to understand the past, view the present, and anticipate the future. Finally, such personal theories are practical in that they are "prescriptive," which is Epstein's way of saying that they help us to survive and grow. This cognitive device allows us to identify our needs and to find ways of satisfying them that are likely to be successful given the particular time, culture, and circumstances in which we live. In his words, such theories are

> A conceptual tool for fulfilling life's most basic psychological functions, namely, to maintain a favorable pleasure/pain balance over the foreseeable future, to maintain a favorable level of self-esteem, to

assimilate the data of reality within a stable, coherent, conceptual system, and to maintain favorable relationships with significant others. (Epstein, 1985, p. 286)

Epstein went on to define self-esteem as a basic human need to be "loveworthy" (1985, p. 302). As a basic need, it occupies a central role in our lives as a motivational force both consciously and otherwise. For example, if one's level of self-esteem is altered, Epstein indicated that it would affect the entire self-system (1980, p. 106).

However, one crucial aspect of the relation between self-esteem and our theories of the self, world, and others involves a powerful conflict. On one hand, the primary function of these theories is to make sense out of the chaos of life. Once the self and world theories become established, they create a basis for stability, which means that the individual works hard to maintain them. Change is resisted because it can be destabilizing. Altering one part of a system affects many other parts, which can lead to disrupting one's ability to function in general. Thus, feelings, especially painful ones like the loss of self-esteem, become important in this system. They constitute a powerful feedback mechanism that helps to minimize potential disruption by warning us affectively. The anxiety that accompanies a threat to self-esteem, for instance, motivates us to avoid or fight the danger to maintain our sense of worthiness and identity.

On the other hand, a good theory must be able to expand over time to accommodate new information. As our theory of the world expands in a positive way, such growth is pleasurable in that it makes us feel good about ourselves. This pleasure is reinforcing, which means that the individual seeks to change even further. Therefore, instead of just holding things steady and protecting us from disruption, self-esteem also drives us toward, of all things, change. The result of these two natural but opposing forces is a basic self-esteem conflict or paradox with which we must deal.

> As a fundamental preconscious postulate, self-esteem has profound effects on behavior and emotions. Accordingly, the regulation of self-esteem is of critical importance to the individual. However, a person's reaction to events that have the potential to influence self-esteem is determined not only by the person's need for enhancement but also by the person's need to maintain the stability of his or her conceptual system. That is, the combined effects of both variables must be taken into account. (Epstein, 1985, p. 303)

Thus, this theory of self-esteem, which is based on a sense of worth, places self-esteem squarely between the two primary forces that govern the self: self-maintenance and self-enhancement.

Next, we find that Epstein envisioned self-esteem as being structured like a hierarchy with three levels that generate both the trait and state aspects of self-esteem. Like the base of a pyramid, basic self-esteem is the most stable and influential level once it has solidified developmentally. Next, there is an intermediate level of self-esteem. This position on the hierarchy can be thought of as the degree of self-esteem one has in particular domains of experience or activity, including such things as skill levels or competence, general lovability, a sense of moral approval, and so forth. Although all of us are concerned with all of these areas, the degree of interest given to them varies with each individual, which means there is plenty of diversity in self-esteem. The upper portion of the self-esteem hierarchy is the most visible and fluid because it is situation-specific. These everyday fluctuations of self-esteem come and go rapidly as we move through our days and weeks. However, except under unusual circumstances such as self-esteem moments, this level of self-esteem is relatively weak in its ability to affect or modify the other two levels: Instead, they both readily influence this more transitory manifestation of self-esteem so that things return to "normal" fairly quickly.

Epstein has modified his theory of self-esteem so as to give more attention to information processing at different levels, one that is called "rational" and the other that is named "experiential." These two systems, "are not simply different ways of reacting within a single system, but are conceived as two separate systems for adapting to reality" (Epstein & Morling, 1995, p. 10). In terms of self-esteem, then,

> If people have two conceptual systems for adapting to the world, with one based on schemata derived primarily from emotionally significant experiences and the other based on more abstract, verbal beliefs, it follows that people may have different assessments of their self-worth in the two systems. These would consist of an explicit evaluation, directly accessible via verbal report, and an implicit self-assessment that can only be inferred. We shall refer to the two kinds of self-esteem as *explicit* and *implicit* self-esteem. (1995, p. 19)

Consequently, this theory allows for the possibility of different types of self-esteem as well as the more traditional categories of high and low self-esteem. For example, one might have high explicit and high implicit self-esteem or low explicit self-esteem and low implicit self-esteem, either of which would be fairly stable. However, according to this view it is also possible to have high explicit but low implicit self-esteem, which is likely to be more unstable. Finally, in addition to recognizing the differences between global self-esteem, domains of more specific self-esteem, and types of self-esteem, this approach also lends itself to the development of methods of assessing self-esteem multidimensionally. For example, the

MSEI was developed from an earlier version of this theory. Much work on explicit versus implicit self-esteem also involves measuring it in pre- and post-test situations.

Susan Harter's Developmental Approach

It was mentioned earlier that in the field of self-esteem, as elsewhere, the gap between psychological and social views of the self is closing. Susan Harter brought the two together by using modern developmental psychology to show how both behavioral competence (the Jamesian tradition) works with social approval (the Cooley–Mead–Rosenberg tradition) to create self-esteem or self-worth. Of course, it is important to note that, for Harter, the terms "self-esteem" and "self-worth" are "interchangeable" (1999, p. 5). When studying self-esteem in adolescence, then,

> Our findings reveal that both James' and Cooley's formulations, taken together, provide a powerful explanation for the level of self-worth . . . the effects of these two determinants are additive. At each level of social support (representing the average of classmate and parental approval), greater competence in domains of importance leads to higher self-worth. Similarly, at each level of competence in domains of importance, the more support one garners from classmates and parents, the higher one's self-worth. (1999, pp. 182–183)

As can be seen by the previous quotation, Harter's approach to self-esteem depends on competence and social approval (worth), which makes it a two-factor approach. In general, domains of competence that are of particular importance to an individual combine with various sources of social approval to result in a sense of self-worth or self-esteem. The domains in which a person may exhibit competence, of course, vary with developmental readiness or age. The amount of support and approval one experiences also depends on age as this source of worth moves from parents to teachers, peers, friends, spouses or partners, coworkers, and so forth over time. However, the relationship between domain competence and approval or support is always additive, meaning that self-worth or esteem consists of their sum at any given time.

Self-esteem, then, starts out in relation to many domains and reflects those that are most important at a particular time of life. Approval takes a similar developmental course. However, some time during middle childhood an individual's cognitive capacities mature to the point where the person develops an overall evaluation of themselves, which is referred to as global self-esteem, and it constitutes another part of the additive picture. Thus, the model is truly multidimensional: Each dimension of competent or incompetent behavior, positive or negative social feedback, and high or low global self-esteem becomes important to the self cognitively and affectively. What happens in the domains and what occurs in important relationships continues to influence the self and self-esteem. However, the self and self-esteem may also influence what happens in the domains or relationships. This condition results in what Harter called "directionality." Thus, self-esteem is seen as a "phenomenological mediator" (Harter, 1999). In later work, Harter (2003) also noted that this process of mediation is a particularly powerful one in terms of organizing a person's perception, experience, and behavior. Such a view stands in stark contradiction to that of those who see self-esteem as a mere "epiphenomenon" (Seligman, 1990).

What makes Harter's approach distinctly developmental, however, is that she ties the interaction of competence and social support or approval to the processes of cognitive maturation and social growth. In other words, Harter connected her theory of self-esteem directly to the cognitive structures of the self as they unfold according to the stages and steps seen in neo-Piagetian developmental theory. Indeed, she is even able to show how the preoperational cognitive structures of early childhood configure self-esteem in ways that are different from those characteristic of an older, concrete operational child or the formal operational adult, and so forth.

One result of emphasizing social as well as psychological processes is that this two-factor approach enabled Harter to trace the development of self-esteem throughout the entire life cycle, which is an extraordinary achievement. Although all of the processes cannot be presented here, it is important to note that she found that there is predictability to the types of domains of behavior and social feedback that may be most significant for self-esteem at a given age, just as one might expect from a developmental perspective (Harter, 1999, p. 119). For instance, there are only five domains of self-concept that have relevance for the development of self-esteem in early childhood, but there are 12 in late adulthood. Some, such as peer acceptance, drop out of significance by early or middle adulthood, but others, such as concerns about mortality, appear at that time. Indeed, only the domain of physical appearance stays with us throughout the life cycle in regard to self-esteem: Apparently, the fact that we are social creatures means that we can never fully escape the way others respond to how we look. Like it or not, the reaction of the other always matters to us at some fundamental level, probably in terms of our social desirability or worth as a person.

Harter also made it clear that there is a tremendous degree of individual variation in this process. For example, academic competence can be achieved in writing, math, social science, physical science, shop class, and so forth, or in any combination of such domains. Social support or approval from parents is especially important in childhood, but other sources become important, too, such as grandparents, teachers, and peers. The result is that there are myriad developmental possibilities for each individual and all of us must make our own unique way through them. Among other things, this condition is important for both assessing and for enhancing self-esteem. For example, such multidimensional processes and possibilities mean that it is necessary to assess self-esteem that way, too. For Harter, then, assessment begins with understanding the various domains of life that are developmentally tied to the stages of growth such as childhood, adolescence, and so forth. Then, it is necessary to construct an instrument capable of assessing self-evaluation in each relevant domain, together with a scale that assesses the general evaluation of oneself (global self-esteem). The final step requires creating a large enough sample of subjects to determine what is normative at each major time in life.

The fact that she and her colleagues have developed such instruments for childhood, adolescence, adulthood, and late adulthood stands as a tribute to the range of this approach. However, it also has power. For example, this model of self-esteem and its measures have been used to research problems with self-esteem and depression in adolescents (Harter & Whitesell, 2003). In addition, we shall see that the approach even lends itself to the practical world of specifically clinical work such as in the treatment of conditions and problems that involve or affect self-esteem in childhood (Shirk & Harter, 1996).

An Existential View: Terror Management Theory

Terror Management Theory (TMT), based on the work of Ernst Becker, places self-esteem at the intersection of two primary human motivations, which gives self-esteem great importance for understanding human behavior. One motivation is an irreducible, biologically based desire to live, to expand, and, if conditions are right, to even flourish. The second motivation is having to live with the awareness of the fact that we must all die. These processes are simply lived out for most organisms. The development of consciousness, however, changes this natural condition by creating a paradox unique to human beings: The same characteristic that distinguishes our species as unique also creates a specific and terrible awareness of death. If left unchecked, consciousness of the inevitability of death is thought to be so overwhelming that it could only result in paralytic fear. Thus, human beings require something that will buffer them from existential dread in a way that allows them to live to the fullest while also facing reality: That something is self-esteem.

According to this view, human beings contend with the terror of death through the same capacities that created the problem in the first place: our abilities to think, to organize, to communicate, and to do all of that in a social context. With culture came the possibility of developing systems of meaning that transcend the death of an individual, thereby avoiding the paralytic terror that awareness of death would otherwise create.

> Our species "solved" the problem posed by the prospect of existential terror by using the same sophisticated cognitive capacities that gave rise to the awareness of death to create cultural worldviews: humanly constructed shared symbolic conceptions of reality that give meaning, order, and permanence to existence; provide a set of standards for what is valuable; and promise some form of either literal or symbolic immortality to those who believe in the cultural worldview and live up to its standards of value. (Pyszczynski et al., 2004a, p. 436)

Being connected to a group, family, or community is helpful in warding off terror, but only some form of immortality is capable of triumphing over death, so belief systems that include such a possibility hold great attraction. From the beginning, then, cultural belief systems, such as religion, and their related practices evolved to organize behavior in a way that gives it meaning, *especially in the face of death*.

For the system to hold together, however, the individual must sustain it through beliefs and actions that affirm the values and standards of a particular transcendent worldview, otherwise the entire system crumbles and terror reigns. TMT maintains that the way to regulate behavior so that it supports a given worldview and allows the individual to feel protected from terror is through the development of self-esteem.

> TMT posits that self-esteem is a sense of personal value that is obtained by believing (a) in the validity of one's cultural worldview and (b) that one is living up to the standards that are part of that worldview. It is the feeling that one is a valuable contributor to a meaningful universe—a sense the one's life has both meaning and value. (Pyszczynski et al., 2004a, pp. 436–437)

In other words, self-esteem evolved to help the individual transcend the terror of death by living with others in a shared community of morals, beliefs, and practices that are thought to extend beyond that dark door. This sense of connection and protection occurs by internalizing the various standards of a "sacred canopy" (Berger, 1967) that gives the world the appearance of being comprehensible, orderly, and meaningful instead of chaotic, brutal, and short.

At the same time, these standards act as the pathway to self-esteem: They are, in fact, *the* contingencies for self-worth. The social standards concerning what is good, desirable, and worthy act as an internal measure for how one is faring in his or her journey toward immortality. The more that a particular individual regulates his or her behavior in accordance with a given religious or cultural belief system, the more meaningful the person's life becomes and the better they feel about themselves, both of which push the terror of death farther away from consciousness.

Of course, if self-esteem is useful in regulating pro-social, desirable, or worthy behavior in this way, it is also useful in controlling negative forms of behavior, especially those that might disrupt the order. When individuals behave in ways that threaten the worldview of a particular group or culture, existential anxiety resurfaces and lowers self-esteem. This anxiety may be reduced by the restoration of self-esteem, which is done through re-engaging in socially sanctioned, worthy behaviors. Thus, culture provides protection against the terror of death by showing us how to transcend it and self-esteem helps to regulate behavior in a way that sustains such worldviews. The result of these two forces, belief and regulation, is a self-sustaining process that carries the individual and group into the future in a meaningful way. As TMT states,

> TMT proposes that people need self-esteem because self-esteem provides a shield against a deeply rooted fear of death inherent in the human condition. . . . When self-esteem is strong, this anxiety is mitigated and the person is able to go about his or her daily affairs and act effectively in the world. When self-esteem is weak or challenged, this threatens a "leakage" of this core anxiety, which instigates various forms of defensive behavior aimed at shoring up whatever aspect of one's worldview or self-evaluation has come under threat or at more generally bolstering self-worth through compensatory efforts. (Pyszczynski et al., 2004a, p. 437)

The authors of TMT and others have conducted or reviewed dozens of studies concerning this "anxiety-buffering" function of self-esteem. Typically, they show how increasing an individual's awareness of mortality also increases the person's anxiety in ways that the theory predicts, thereby generating considerable empirical support (Pyszczynski et al., 2004a).

However, adherents also acknowledge that there are biologically based motives and drives in many organisms that contradict the need to reduce tension, anxiety, or terror, especially in human beings. These drives are manifested though such behavior as curiosity, exploration, experimentation, risk taking, and the like. Such motives cannot be dismissed because they have survival value. For example, they sometimes result in important discoveries, play a key role in creativity, and may even be instrumental in the development of new ideas, skills, and so forth, all of which may give an individual or group an adaptational advantage. Yet, some motivations, such as risk taking or exploration, actually take us into closer proximity to the possibility of dying, which seems to contradict the entire theory.

TMT attempts to solve this problem by offering a "dual role" or function of self-esteem:

> From an evolutionary perspective, an organismic growth/enrichment motivational system makes a great deal of sense. In order to survive long enough to reproduce and pass on its genes, an animal must be driven to explore, take in new information, and integrate that information with its existing conception of the world. . . . Thus, it seems likely that a superordinate drive toward growth and enrichment would be just as important and basic as a drive toward self-preservation through defensive processes. (Greenberg et al., 1995, pp. 82–83)

In some sense, this modification of the theory may be seen as contradicting it (Ryan & Deci, 2004). After all, if the function of self-esteem is to avoid death, then how could it encourage individuals to risk their lives for new and exciting possibilities? For TMT, the key lies in the idea that both motives and needs are biologically based. Growth and enrichment motives do not necessarily contradict the need for security and survival, providing that the risk-taking behavior results in the acquisition of skills and behaviors that affirm or enrich the individual or the culture. In addition to playing a role in helping the individual to master the basic tasks of human development, such a motivation can also lead to new discoveries or skills not seen before. If they happen to be valuable for a particular society at a particular time, then they increase the likelihood of survival for the entire group. The individual, of course, is also rewarded through material gain or status, which boosts self-esteem in ways that are meaningful, too. Thus, in the end, TMT goes on to conclude that, "The pursuit of self-esteem is thus neither a good thing nor a bad thing but rather, a part of the system that human beings use to both regulate their behavior and to cope with their existential situation" (Pyszczynski et al., 2004b, p. 464).

The Evolutionary Approach: Sociometer Theory

Evolutionary work in the social sciences has become quite popular in the past decade. Although TMT may certainly be characterized in that fashion, its existential tone distinguishes it from another, strictly evolutionary approach to self-esteem that is becoming significant called

Sociometer Theory. As Heatherton and Wyland pointed out, this theory begins with the assumption that human beings "have a fundamental need to belong that is rooted in our evolutionary history" (2003, p. 39). Indeed, as a species our early ancestors had little of the usual types of biological equipment to assist in survival. For example, by comparison with other animals, our teeth are dull, our sense of smell is poor, our claws are fragile, our night vision is pathetic, and we only have two legs: When push comes to shove under these conditions, it is a wonder that we survived at all.

The one thing we did have, however, was our ability to work together in groups, a characteristic that facilitated such things as the development of language, tools, culture, collective knowledge, technology, and so forth. Especially in our early days, groups were the key to survival both for individuals and as a species. One of the most threatening things for a human being, then, was to be cut off from the group. Not only could this condition mean death, but even worse in an evolutionary sense, it could mean the loss of the opportunity to pass on genetic material, which is the basic biological imperative of all life. In other words, not only are groups necessary for human survival, but their significance far outweighs that of the individual.

According to Sociometer Theory, then, there is considerable evolutionary survival value in minimizing the threat of becoming lost, abandoned, isolated, or excluded by the group. To adapt to this situation, biological specialization evolved to help regulate behavior in a way that reduced the risk of being cut off from others.

> Thus, given the vital importance of social acceptance and the disastrous consequences of rejection throughout human evolution, human beings developed a psychological system for regulating their relationships with other people—a psychological module that monitors and responds to events that are relevant to interpersonal acceptance and rejection. (Leary, 2004a, p. 374)

This particular evolutionary module, termed the "sociometer," is concerned with social status, social relationships, and other indexes of social behavior that may signal the possibility of rejection or exclusion.

There are other social modules that have evolved to fulfill special functions, such as the attachment–separation modules of infancy, a bonding module associated with parenthood, and so forth, but all of them are designed to fulfill three functions (Leary & Downs, 1995). First, they evolve in a way that searches the environment for relevant cues, especially threatening ones. For the most part, such monitoring is a background process, much like our ears may be listening to a conversation while we drive an automobile: We listen to the words, but our ears are still attuned to the sound around us, such as traffic noise, and they alert us to them when necessary. Next, when threat is detected the module is tied to enough other brain-based processing agencies and modules to evoke a strong sympathetic nervous system or affective response such as suddenly being alarmed by a siren. Finally, the detection of threatening stimuli and a strong response to it leads to changes in behavior designed to deal with the emergency effectively: In this example, stopping conversation to look for the emergency vehicle and becoming prepared to move to the side of the road if necessary.

> In brief, people appear to possess a psychological mechanism (a sociometer) that monitors their interpersonal worlds for information relevant to relational value, alerts them through unpleasant emotions and lowered state self-esteem when their relationship value is lower than desired or declining, and motivates behavior that helps to enhance relational value (and, hence, self-esteem). (Leary, 2004a, p. 379)

Thus, the sociometer "scans" the environment for signs of trouble and alerts us to possible threats or opportunities by evoking our feelings about ourselves in pleasant or unpleasant ways. When self-esteem is threatened or drops, it motivates the individual to regulate behavior so that it does not result in rejection or so that it may even increase chances of affiliation. In this way, self-esteem helps to avoid behavior that is likely to get us into trouble and enhances socially desirable behavior that could improve our chances of getting important needs met, even such basic ones as food and the opportunity to pass along genes.

Unlike other theories, then, self-esteem is not a free-standing motive that gives rise to its own needs or that is intrinsic to our nature. Rather, Sociometer Theory contends that "most behaviors that have been attributed to the need to maintain self-esteem may be parsimoniously explained in terms of the motive to avoid social exclusion" (Leary & Downs, 1995, p. 129). Because it is a module that is carried with us, the sociometer may even regulate behavior in the absence of other people. For example, in situations where others are not present, the sociometer becomes generalized enough for us to consider what others would do if they saw our behaviors at these times, which in turn, helps us regulate our behaviors in socially acceptable ways.

So far, this understanding of self-esteem may seem largely directed at self-esteem as a state rather than as a trait because it is designed to be sensitive to current situations in any number of domains of social life. However, the theory compares the sociometer with a gauge to illustrate how it also functions as a trait.

In addition, what is commonly called trait self-esteem—a person's typical or chronic level of self-esteem—is also relevant to the workings of the sociometer and interpersonal self-regulation. If we think of the sociometer as a meter or gauge that assesses relational value, trait self-esteem may be conceptualized as the resting position of the sociometer in the absence of incoming interpersonal feedback. (Leary, 2004a, p. 381)

This aspect of Sociometer Theory is also used to account for types and degrees of self-esteem and differences in behavior associated with them. For example, people for whom the "resting point" of the gauge is high because of their developmental history are able to afford a wide range of behavior before the gauge will reach the danger zone. Such individuals may be reasonably confident, fairly spontaneous, relatively open, and able to take risks more freely than others, all of which are advantageous and often associated with high self-esteem. People whose needle is already set to a lower point to begin with, however, must be more cautious lest it fall farther. In this case, they would tend to monitor social situations more critically, hold back on initiative, or be more anxious than their counterparts who are higher on the sociometer.

In addition, the metaphor of a gauge allows Sociometer Theory to account for various self-esteem problems in this way. For example, Leary (2004a) noted that one common type of "miscalibration" occurs when the sociometer is set too low. In this case, the individual is likely to be overly sensitive, seek out negative social cues, brood about them longer than necessary, and perhaps even become depressed. Conversely, the resting point of the sociometer can also be too high, which means that people may act as though they have more social value than they actually do. Here, the person is likely to run afoul of social mores or damage relationships before they take notice of what is happening. Still other meters may be hypersensitive, which could result in frequent wide swings from medium to low and back or from one end of the scale to the other.

If hypersensitivity is possible, then so is hyposensitivity. People with hyposensitive sociometers, which is to say sociometers that are "stuck," as Leary described it, do not experience much in the way of fluctuations and are not likely to see the need to change behavior quickly. It is even possible to think of several personality disorders in terms of having defective sociometers, such as the schizoid or anti-social types. The metaphor of a gauge can also be applied to normal interpersonal situations and human relationships, such as a sexual one. In this case, mutual attraction can be seen as moving the needle to higher regions of self-esteem, thereby promoting social risk taking; or the interaction may move the pointer down, such as after an argument, thereby encouraging the development of better communication skills in the future.

In addition to theoretical potential, then, this approach to self-esteem has practical applications that may be helpful in understanding a wide range of human behavior that includes groups, relationships, and even clinical phenomena. In short, although the evolutionary approach is the newest major perspective on self-esteem, it certainly brings much to the theoretical table in the field of self-esteem work, just as it does elsewhere in the social sciences.

Summary of Findings about Theories

There are many other theories concerning self-esteem that are worth considering. For example, Self-Determination Theory (SDT) offers important insights and considerable research on self-esteem. In Chapter 5, we will see that the work this approach has generated on what is called "intrinsic motivation" is essential to understanding how self-esteem is tied to authenticity. However, the approach itself focuses on autonomy, competence, and relatedness as central motivations and not self-esteem. Instead, SDT understands self-esteem as being contingent on them. Therefore, rather than exhausting all the standing theoretical views of self-esteem, we must ask the more phenomenological question: What do the general theories of self-esteem show us about developing a good theory about it?

Several "findings" emerge in this regard. First, major perspectives in the social sciences offer unique ways of seeing self-esteem. For example, we saw that the psychodynamic, social learning, humanistic, existential, and evolutionary perspectives all offer at least one major theory of self-esteem, which suggests that the topic is a viable one today. This point is important because we will see in Chapter 7 that some of the newer psychological points of view, such as the new positive psychology, do not seem to understand self-esteem this way. Second, there seems to be a fairly consistent set of specific self-esteem themes or issues that are addressed in these theories. They include understanding self-esteem as a developmental phenomenon; showing how there can be types of self-esteem; and appreciating that self-esteem is tied to motivation, which links it to behavior in several ways. Finally, although each general theory of self-esteem starts out at the abstract level, they all open up implicit or explicit pathways to changing self-esteem at the practical level much as good theories should.

MAJOR SELF-ESTEEM ENHANCEMENT PROGRAMS

Most of the major theories of self-esteem presented in this chapter emphasize theory and often include research support, but they tend to be weak in terms of practice. In the late 1980s, several applied programs designed to enhance self-esteem began to appear. Yet, many of them seem short on theory or thin on research, which suggests that there are few genuinely comprehensive approaches in the field. Nevertheless, it is possible to examine work on enhancing self-esteem, something that may be done by relying on the same criteria of persistence and significance that were used with theory and research. In gathering data, then, I looked for self-esteem enhancement programs that seemed to focus explicitly on enhancing self-esteem instead of more general therapeutic goals and examined them in terms of their persistence and significance as defined earlier. The result is a brief presentation of the basic self-esteem ideas on which a particular program builds, as well as a discussion of the techniques each one uses to enhance self-esteem. The goal of this work is to find what is required to make a good (i.e., theoretically sound, practically oriented, empirically supported) self-esteem enhancement program.

Frey and Carlock: Eclectic Variations on a Humanistic Theme

Basic Ideas

Diane Frey and C. Jesse Carlock are two clinicians who introduce their work by saying, "Many books on self-esteem focus either on theory or practice. This book takes theory of self-esteem and translates it for the reader into practice. In this way it stands alone among all other books on self-esteem" (1989, p. vii). The definition of self-esteem that they develop is remarkably similar to Branden's, "Self-esteem has two interrelated components: the feeling that one is competent to live and the feeling that one is worthy of living" (1989, p. 7). The major mechanism for regulating personal experience is found in the humanistic concept of "organismic self-regulation." The main body of this program consists of a large collection of experientially oriented human growth and development activities. Frey and Carlock offer an eclectic approach that uses many ideas from other perspectives. For instance, the development of the self-concept is presented in terms of social learning factors, particularly negative environmental influences (or "psychological pathogens," as they say) that contribute to self-esteem problems. Also, they use the cognitive concepts of "self-talk" and self-fulfilling prophecies as central routes to changing self-esteem.

System and Techniques

The most outstanding characteristic of this approach to enhancing self-esteem may be that the program is systematic. Although Frey and Carlock bring an incredibly divergent mix of theoretical concepts and experiential exercises into play in their approach to enhancing self-esteem, all of these ideas and activities are organized into a clear four-stage process or framework. Moreover, the authors stress that although each phase is a distinct step on the path to enhancing self-esteem, they actually constitute a system in which the whole process is greater than the sum of its parts. Hence, following it sequentially provides the maximum benefit.

This process of enhancing self-esteem begins with the "identity phase." This part of the process is the least well defined of the steps, probably because it involves the question of identity, which, as we saw in Chapter 2, is a much larger one than self-esteem. However, the authors do offer a clear rationale for beginning here: "Initially in intervention, an individual with low self-esteem needs to discover his/her own identity. Because of distorted perceptions, such persons rarely have a clear understanding of who they really are" (Frey & Carlock, 1989, p. 181). In addition to learning about oneself in some basic ways, this step allows for the fact that there are often obstacles that block awareness or self-experience that must be worked through to know about ourselves and our self-esteem. Accordingly, Frey and Carlock offer several standard exercises to help individuals engage in self-discovery such as values clarification activities and the like.

Although the search for identity can probably be expanded indefinitely, at some point it is necessary to shift into the second stage, which focuses on developing an "awareness of strengths and weaknesses." This stage concerns helping clients to develop an appreciation of their assets and liabilities as persons. These activities generally focus on identifying strengths in a way that makes them meaningful to participants, although weaknesses are looked at too. This part of the work is necessary because individuals with low self-esteem are usually practiced at ignoring their assets and are good at focusing on their liabilities. Indeed, such resistance is a constant problem in moving to higher levels of self-esteem, especially in the beginning. Two kinds of work characterize this stage. First, the facilitator consistently offers positive feedback each time such an opportunity presents itself. Of course, this feedback must be done on the basis of sincerity (it must be true) and concreteness (it should be clear and specific). The second kind of intervention involves altering how people filter information to help them take in information more accurately. This technique requires people to acknowledge the positive, as well as the negative, and to not exaggerate the significance of the latter or minimize the importance of the former. Several activities are offered to assist in this process, especially providing a supportive group environment and offering positive feedback experiences.

The third stage, called the "nurturance phase," is the most complex. The preceding step has the effect of developing a more positive sense of self-esteem by focusing on strengths rather than weaknesses. However, this part of the process only plants the seeds for lasting change. The analogy is quite appropriate because it implies a beginning but one that is fragile and in need of further attention. Thus, "The first two phases in themselves are not sufficient as newly acquired positive self-esteem can be lost if it is not nurtured. Teaching nurturing helps the person to enhance strengths and use them to minimize weaknesses" (Frey & Carlock, 1989, p. 197). The aim of the nurturing phase, then, is to help the new pro–self-esteem behaviors to take root, so to speak. It is especially important to foster the ability to help people transfer their newly developed awareness of the importance of positive self-esteem to environments outside the supportive but limited atmosphere of the therapist's office or group room. Moreover, Frey and Carlock recognize that this project is difficult under even the best of circumstances. For instance, they point out that some people suffer from home or work environments that are "toxic" (a richly descriptive term) to self-esteem. The deepest or most intensive work of the program is done during this phase.

The major thrust of the activities involves dealing with the self-fulfilling dynamics that Frey and Carlock place at the heart of perpetuating low self-esteem. In particular, the negative thinking and behaving patterns that sustain low self-esteem must be overcome and replaced with more positive ones. Accordingly, they offer a number of exercises and activities to facilitate this development. For instance, teaching individuals to identify their self-esteem needs and to get them met in appropriate ways are steps in the right direction. Similarly, participants are asked to affirm their own positive qualities, as well as those of others, in a supportive group setting. Likewise, the importance of individuals developing their own self-esteem support systems is stressed.

In the final stage, this approach focuses on the importance of maintaining self-esteem after the program is over. In this fourth or "maintenance" phase, "One needs to learn how to maintain adequate self-esteem just as it is necessary to maintain a car, house, or an interpersonal relationship if it is to grow and flourish" (Frey & Carlock, 1989, p. 205). There are several important reasons for building such a step into a self-esteem enhancement program. First, Frey and Carlock see increasing self-esteem as an evolving process, so the work that goes on in therapy is just the beginning. As people or their circumstances change, the ways they get their self-esteem needs met may change too. Thus, "During the maintenance phase, individuals are taught to turn experiences into learning situations, practice facilitative risk taking, set appropriate goals, forecast desired personal outcomes, and publicly affirm goals" (p. 206). The exercises and activities used to further these aims include learning how to set realistic goals and how to develop appropriate risk-taking strategies.

In addition to developing a systematic approach to enhancing self-esteem, Frey and Carlock note that there are at least three significant practical issues to consider that are almost always present in helping people change. The first is called resistance and it concerns dealing with the usual technical problems associated with change in general as well as those explicitly associated with changing self-esteem. Next, they focus on the role of, and need for, assessment in changing self-esteem. They note, for instance, that self-esteem issues vary considerably from person to person, which means the clinician must become attuned to differences in participants and make appropriate adjustments, a process that is facilitated by accurate assessment. Finally, Frey and Carlock recognize that changing self-esteem is a difficult, long-term project: "The change process, like much of human learning, is erratic. Improvement can be followed by a slight regression, which is in turn, followed by improvement. This process repeats itself until some stabilization of changed behavior occurs" (p. 213). Ultimately, then, the entire system is based on persistence and hard work.

Summary

One outstanding feature of this approach to enhancing self-esteem is that the program is broken into clearly defined steps, each one of which includes specific objectives and concrete activities. Moreover, these steps progress in an extremely logical fashion and the exercises are based on fairly common therapeutic or growth-oriented activities. Finally, it is important to note that this program is flexible, which means that it may be applied in a number of clinical and growth settings.

Increasing Self-Esteem Behaviorally: Pope, McHale, and Craighead

Basic Ideas

Alice Pope, Susan McHale, and W. Edward Craighead's approach actually focuses on working with children and adolescents, even those who excel academically but still have low self-esteem. It also addresses the needs of various challenged populations. However, this system is based on social learning theory, which means that change occurs on the basis of general and specific learning principles that apply to all ages. This approach begins by defining self-esteem as "an *evaluation* of the information contained in the self-concept, and is derived from a child's feelings about *all* the things he is" (p. 2).

Like most social and learning approaches to self-esteem, this way of understanding it is based on a discrepancy notion: the difference between the individual's ideal self-concept (what one thinks one should be) and the perceived or actual self-concept (how one currently sees oneself). Self-esteem problems are seen as resulting from a significant difference between these perceptions, which creates the possibility of two basic self-esteem problems. The first one occurs when the ideal self-concept is too high or unrealistic given the individual and his or her circumstances. The resulting gap between what is desired and what is actually seen creates low self-esteem: the greater the difference, the greater the self-esteem problems. This type of low self-esteem is associated, for instance, with overachieving children who do well in school or elsewhere but who still feel unworthy because they fail to meet their expectations, however unrealistic they may be. The second type of self-esteem problem occurs when the ideals and expectations are appropriate for a particular person, but the individual fails to live up to them in realistic ways. For instance, an underachieving individual can suffer a sense of worthlessness that comes with failing to meet reasonable expectations of performance given their actual abilities.

In either case, this enhancement program focuses on working with five domains affected by self-esteem: global (overall) self-esteem, social self-esteem (how the child evaluates himself or herself in relation to others), academic self-esteem (the child's school performance and abilities), how the child sees himself or herself as a valued (or unvalued) family member, and the quality of the child's body image (how a child sees his or her physical appearance and abilities). The goal is to identify areas where self-esteem problems are especially strong, then design cognitive-behavioral activities to either increase skills to bring performance up to reasonable standards or to reduce exaggerated standards to allow a reasonable degree of skill or success to be and feel satisfactory.

Because learning is the engine that powers this approach, it is not surprising to find that general learning principles are used to effect change, especially positive reinforcement and modeling, among others. Indeed, even the role of the therapist is couched in a learning framework. For instance, the authors indicate that the clinician must be a warm and caring *teacher,* as well as a skilled practitioner. Modern social learning theory also recognizes the importance of certain cognitive processes as crucial components of behavior and behavioral change. One of them, problem solving, is a pivotal element in this approach: "One of the basic findings of cognitive psychology is that humans possess problem solving skills. The potential discrepancy between our ideal and perceived self-concepts can be viewed as a problem to be solved" (Pope et al., 1988, p. 11).

In addition to presenting a general strategy for change based on such an orientation, Pope and colleagues are also concerned with the developmental context of self-esteem. Their program recognizes that there are relatively specific, age-related, developmental factors in the five areas mentioned earlier that affect self-esteem. This realization means that it is necessary to tailor intervention strategies toward the cognitive and behavioral skill level of the client. At the same time, it is recognized that each individual is unique. Children and adolescents (as well as adults) have personal preferences, different environments, and individual talents or deficits that must be considered in creating an effective self-esteem enhancement program. In other words, the program depends heavily on rigorous psychological assessment.

System and Techniques

The program begins with a detailed assessment process aimed at identifying an individual's particular self-esteem problems, needs, and potentials. Interviews with the child and significant others, actual observations of the client in his or her natural environments while engaged in everyday activities, and psychological tests are all methods of gathering information that are recommended by the authors. The assessment process aims at identifying which basic type of self-esteem problem appears to be present and determining how serious it is, both of which involve a person's global self-esteem. The other four areas (social esteem, academic esteem, how one is esteemed as a family member, and one's feelings about body image) are evaluated as well, making the assessment comprehensive.

Pope and colleagues recommend using standard tests, such as the Piers–Harris (1969), to assess general self-esteem problems and issues. They also recognize that assessing specific areas like those mentioned earlier are more difficult, mainly because that involves creating specific age-based norms for each domain, and because human development can vary considerably in any one of them. The authors are also sensitive to such factors as gender and self-esteem, as well as cultural diversity (although that term is not used) and self-esteem. Hence, they strongly recommend talking to others involved in the child's life: Such sources of information, especially that which is obtained from family and schoolteachers, can reveal important things about how a child lives out academic, social, familial, and physical issues that may not be apparent in the therapy hour.

In addition to identifying self-esteem problems, a good assessment includes understanding the individual's particular strengths (Fischer, 1986). This part of the process is important because it is easier to design activities or experiences that are more likely to be successful and rewarding if we work with existing skills. Finally, the authors suggest that the clinician should assess and understand the individual's cognitive and self-evaluative styles. In other words, the therapist should develop a sense of the subject's "private speech" or habitual thinking patterns, especially those that concern the standards by which the person judges his or her behavior. In short, the assessment process is a crucial one for this enhancement approach. Not only does it let the therapist know with whom he or she is dealing so that the program can be individualized for the client, but accurate assessment also gives ideas about what is realistically possible.

This enhancement program aims to increase self-esteem by teaching the individual new, age-appropriate skills designed to help him or her handle the demands and problems of life more effectively. Pope and colleagues recommend that the clinician share this intent with the client in language that he or she will understand so the individual can be a partner in this process. The clinician and client contract to meet together on a regular basis to do this kind of learning. One or two 30-minute sessions per week are recommended for younger children, and one or two 60-minute sessions per week for older clients. Pope and colleagues also point out that the program may be offered in group or individual settings. In either case, the therapeutic activity is structured in two ways. First, the process is broken up into eight segments, each of which focuses on a certain kind of behavioral, cognitive, or social skill related to self-esteem. These skill areas are learning to solve social problems, developing positive self-statements, using a realistic attributional style, increasing self-control, setting appropriate standards, developing social understanding and social skills, increasing communication skills, and improving body image. The authors make it clear that the eight skill areas are arranged in a particular order and that following this sequence is a crucial part of the program (Pope et al., 1988, p. 41). So important is this point that it is stressed in the introduction to the program and then again as the major point of the book's afterword.

Second, the format for all the activities associated with any of the areas is structured in a consistent way. In other words, each area becomes a program module. These modules always begin with an assessment of the individual's skills, abilities, and potential in each particular area so that the therapist knows what is needed and what is possible. Once the particular skills that are needed are identified, they are taught by following specific exercises. Then, the "homework" is assigned to the client, a technique that reinforces the new material and helps transfer it to the real world.

Although all the modules are structured in the same way, an individual may need less time in one area and more in another until a satisfactory degree of progress occurs, so help is individualized. Note that this program relies heavily on what behavioral therapists call "homework," which means that problems are identified, clients are given new alternatives to try, they receive feedback about their attempts, and clients apply the new alternatives to real life until the new skills become habitual. Such techniques make good theoretical and practical sense in a learning-based program because skill acquisition takes time and practice. Including real-life experiences into treatment means that learning may occur even after the program ends. In fact, "booster" sessions are recommended to "meet with the child to reassess his ability to use his new skills in a way which enhances his self-esteem" (Pope et al., 1988, p. 139).

Summary

There is also much to be said for this self-esteem enhancement system. First and foremost is what computer programmers call its "transparency." The steps and procedures are extraordinarily systematic in that there is a clear, logical connection between the recommended exercises or activities and well-respected cognitive-behavioral therapeutic techniques, such as using positive reinforcement, teaching problem solving, and modifying self-talk. In addition, the program is structured in a stepwise fashion. This process makes it possible to track progress by comparing initial base ratings with final outcomes. A final strength of this approach is that it is designed to intervene in childhood, which could make it more effective in the long run because of the potential for prevention as well as treatment.

Bednar, Wells, and Peterson: Enhancing Self-Esteem Cognitively

Basic Ideas

The self-esteem enhancement system found in *Self-Esteem: Paradoxes and Innovations in Clinical Theory and Practice* (1989) by Bednar and colleagues is based on two perspectives. The first consists of concepts found in modern information-processing psychology, which makes it a cognitive approach. The second set of ideas concerns a theory of psychopathology and its treatment that is based on a combination of cognitive and existential thought. After defining self-esteem as a feeling of self-approval, Bednar and colleagues go on to say that it is a dynamic phenomenon that develops as a result of the cognitive processes of feedback, circularity, and self-regulation.

> Our model of self-esteem is based on four underlying assumptions, each of which involves *feedback* about personal and interpersonal acceptability. . . . In brief, feedback is a special type of information that can describe, evaluate, or influence performance: in our case, human behavior. (1989, p. 91)

Two types of feedback seem to be most important in relation to the development of self-esteem. Information about our behavior and selves that comes from others (or the social environment in general) is called external or interpersonal feedback. This type of information includes many of the social factors affecting self-esteem we found in reviewing self-esteem research such as gender and cultural influences. The other form, called internal feedback, comes from our own experience, especially from the evaluations we make of our own behavior and of ourselves.

Both types of information play a role in regulating our actions, but internal feedback is more important because it is affective, stronger, more direct, and difficult to dismiss. Bednar and colleagues also maintain that the sad reality is that most of us face more negative sources of feedback about ourselves than positive ones. Because it is less frequent, they maintain that positive feedback is more important than negative. This internal/external, positive/negative feedback system is constantly operating and continually provides information to us about ourselves and what we are like. At some point in the developmental process, however, these feedback systems become self-regulating and, therefore, relatively stable. At that point, we achieve a degree of positive or negative self-esteem and seek to maintain it, much as others suggest.

The other major process affecting the development of self-esteem is the individual's "response style" or how a person characteristically responds to psychological threat or conflict. According to this view, such stress (or what other theories call "anxiety") is an inevitable part of life. Although they can vary in terms of intensity and frequency, there are two opposing ways to deal with these stressors: People can respond to psychological threat by attempting to avoid or to cope with it and each alternative has powerful consequences for self-esteem. Avoidance, for instance, is a form of denial, which makes it an immature, defensive response when compared with coping, which is mature and realistic. Probably because it seems to promise less pain initially, avoidance is the path of least resistance in dealing with threat and anxiety. But avoiding conflict is more costly in the long run because doing so cuts us off from valuable information concerning ourselves and the world around us.

> It is as though we try to say to ourselves that this is too unpleasant to be true and then proceed to act as though it were not. However, there must be some recognition of the possibility of truth; otherwise there would be no threat that would mobilize the defenses. . . . Obviously, the prospects for personal growth are virtually non-existent when the individual's response to threat is *to deny that which it has already glimpsed to be true.* (Bednar, Wells & Peterson, 1989, p. 74)

Avoidance makes it difficult to make realistic and effective decisions about what needs to be done, let alone take advantage of important possibilities for growth.

In addition, excessive avoidance leads to chronic defensiveness, which creates its own burden: In turning away from the truth, we are trapped by it because now we must manage both the conflict and the false solution we offer it. Ultimately, habitual avoidance results in a phenomenon the authors call "impression management," which means having to maintain a facade as well as continuing to avoid the threat that gave rise to it. This stance toward the world and others requires a massive expenditure of perceptual, psychological, and behavioral energies. The more we choose avoiding over coping, the more likely serious distortions and unrealistic behaviors are to occur. The development of positive self-esteem becomes extremely difficult under such conditions. If impression management continues long enough, then low self-esteem develops and with it comes an increased sensitivity to threats or even the possibility of threats. Eventually, this self-fulfilling prophecy leads to more serious difficulties, including the development of abnormal or pathological behavior.

Bednar and colleagues maintain that although human beings both cope with and avoid conflict, they tend to develop a response style that favors one or the other over time through the process of "reciprocal determinism," which is a form of the self-fulfilling prophecy. Of course, the healthy way to deal with conflict is to cope with it, which, according to Bednar and colleagues, requires considerable effort, even courage. Coping means facing the problem honestly, tolerating discomfort and uncertainty while doing so, taking psychological risks associated with being open to self-awareness about shortcomings, and, above all, accepting responsibility for one's actions. These are the existential components of self-esteem. However, this response style is not typical of those who live with low self-esteem or problems associated with it.

From this position, changing self-esteem must be based on the laws governing feedback, circularity, and self-regulation. The authors point out, for instance, that to survive, systems can never really be completely closed; they must always maintain the ability to adapt to changes in the environment because change is an environmental fact. Hence, new kinds of feedback can affect old patterns. If this influence becomes strong enough, relatively significant changes may occur. It is even possible for new homeostatic balance to be reached. In regard to self-esteem, then, if we can change the coping versus avoiding ratio in a favorable direction, there should be a corresponding change in the quality of self-evaluations. If this new and positive information occurs frequently or powerfully enough, then the self-fulfilling nature of the system should lead to higher levels of self-esteem, which, in turn, should generate healthier, more rewarding functioning. Instead of a vicious cycle, the same dynamics of feedback, circularity, and self-regulation set up a virtuous one.

System and Techniques

The central task in enhancing self-esteem is to reduce the degree to which a person engages in behavior (including thoughts and feelings) that promotes avoiding problems and to simultaneously strengthen the individual's capacity to cope with them. Because Bednar and colleagues recognize that there are affective, behavioral, and cognitive factors that make up experience, they structure clinical activities so that intervention occurs on all three levels: "The easiest way to do this is to deal with psychological events as they occur in the 'here-and-now,' which allows immediate access to the thoughts and feelings that accompany behavior as it occurs" (Bednar, Wells & Peterson, 1989, p. 173). This present-centered focus is characteristic of existential encounters.

In short, the therapeutic methods used to enhance self-esteem in this approach emphasize "experiential" learning, which means that the therapy focuses on how the client actually avoids conflicts and problems, especially as they arise in the actual therapy session,

> Experiential learning, then, is the crucial consideration in helping clients come to a fuller realization of their self-defeating patterns of avoidance. We are continually looking for opportunities during the therapy hour to "catch" the client fully engaged in a "Catch-22," or paradox. Our assumption is that when personal learning takes place simultaneously at a cognitive, behavioral, and affective level, it has more psychological impact than when these domains are insulated from each other. (Bednar, Wells & Peterson, 1989, p. 174)

The process of change this program offers involves mastering four reasonably specific, indispensable steps. First, it is necessary to identify the client's dominant avoidance patterns of dealing with conflict, anxiety, or psychological threat. The therapist attempts to do so by observing how the client engages in avoidance here-and-now in the sessions. The aim is to have the client come to see these patterns for what they are, which involves pointing out the avoidant pattern of behavior. The therapist asks the client to name or label the way he or she closes off dealing with conflict honestly. Each such pattern is identified in this way so that the client develops a sense of ownership for his or her own ways of avoiding dealing with conflict. Second, the therapist moves the client toward identifying and labeling all the thoughts and feelings that accompany these avoidance patterns. This is done by having the client describe in as great detail as possible such things as the actual behavior involved in a particular way of avoiding, what he or she feels when engaging in avoiding, and the kind of thinking that goes on at these times. Even though painful, this step is also best done in the here-and-now with the therapist because the material is psychologically fresh.

The third and critical phase is to help the person face the avoidance patterns he or she characteristically uses and confront the negative self-evaluations that accompany them. In other words, the client is asked to face underlying fear, cowardice, or self-loathing head on. Once again, this is done most effectively *in vivo* or with real conflicts that emerge in the actual sessions. The aim is for the client to encounter his or her own modes of avoidance as they are actually being lived. The act of making this realization and accepting responsibility for it often occurs as a painful event, but this pain is seen as a necessary first step toward coping. This new and honest behavioral response is also pointed out and focused on. The client must describe in as great detail as possible what it is like to finally face the problem and to try and cope with it. The therapist takes care to have the individual identify, explore, and label positive responses and self-evaluations, because doing so is reinforcing and because it helps break old cognitive and behavioral patterns. The final step is one of continued learning or "gradually learning to cope with personal conflicts" (Bednar, Wells & Peterson, 1989, p. 140). This step may be done *in vivo* and by using events from life outside the session. It involves continuing to identify, label, and experience the positive nature of coping over avoiding whenever it occurs until coping becomes the primary response style. The authors conclude by pointing out that such learning is a process and takes time.

Bednar and colleagues offer specific technical suggestions concerning timing and methods of facilitating this process at each step of the way. In addition, they divide therapeutic work into two basic kinds of activity. The first, called "remediation," constitutes the bulk of the program and is aimed at breaking the negative avoiding patterns. The other work involves strengthening what they call the client's "disposition to cope," a process that is "different from and more pleasant for the client than describing avoidance behaviors because it does not involve attempts to alter the personality in such fundamental ways" (1989, p. 209). Thus, self-esteem can be enhanced by conflict-free learning as well as by intensive work on problematic areas. In fact, sometimes it is necessary to focus on positive behaviors to balance the hard work of dealing with negative material.

It is important to appreciate that Bednar and colleagues specify that their program requires skilled assessment and that they identify two types of essential assessment activities. The first is called "process evaluation," which aims at determining "the client's capacity for a candid and realistic conversation about the meaning and significance of personal problems with a nonpunitive, reasonably astute professional person" (1989, p. 188). Because the therapist is looking for limits as well as ability, he or she is active in this assessment. For instance, the therapist makes it clear that it may be necessary to actually push the client toward sensitive or painful material. In such work, the focus is on what makes *this* particular person defensive, the degree to which the patterns of avoidance are ingrained, and how well the individual can tolerate looking honestly at himself or herself. Process evaluation, which assesses how well the client is able to take advantage of the therapeutic process, is done throughout the program. It is especially important to pay attention to this dimension of the work at its beginning, lest the program moves too fast or too slow for an individual. The other form of assessment focuses on what the authors refer to as an evaluation of "content and substance." This type of evaluation focuses more on understanding the specific patterns of coping and avoiding that a person characteristically uses. For instance, it includes assessing what specific issues trigger these responses in an individual's unique personality and life and which behaviors he or she uses to avoid facing the conflicts involved in his or her responses.

Finally, Bednar and colleagues unequivocally indicate that the role of the therapist and the abilities of the person in that role are vital to this self-esteem enhancement program. In fact, it may be said that the entire process hinges on the ability of the therapist because he or she actively seeks to "make things happen" in the therapeutic encounter. Such an orientation also means that the responsibility of making sure that things do not happen too quickly or too intensely also falls to the therapist, because either of these two possibilities could be harmful to the client. For it to work, this approach to enhancing self-esteem depends on an intense personal encounter right in the office and on client risk-taking both in and out of the session. Obviously, such an orientation is not a "soft" path to self-esteem. Indeed, the authors say that, "Psychological anguish induced in treatment is the first sign of personal change in the direction of coping" (1989, p. 134). Experiencing the full effect of one's own negative self-evaluations, then, is a necessary but tricky part of treatment. Accordingly, Bednar and colleagues clearly emphasize the need for the program to be offered by a highly skilled, experienced therapist.

Summary

Perhaps the most important and distinguishing feature of this approach is that it is an explicitly clinical program. This highly individualized approach requires professional assessment and intervention by a well-trained individual who is capable of handling an intensive treatment process that involves risk-taking by the client both in and out of sessions. Another advantage the program offers is that it is capable of addressing the more serious self-esteem problems: The combination of intensive individual work coupled with a high degree of clinician expertise allows other conditions, such as clinically significant depression or character pathology, to be treated at the same time as work is done on self-esteem.

Harter's Developmental Approach

Basic Ideas

It will be remembered that Harter (1999) offered an approach to understanding self-esteem based on two factors or types of developmental forces that work together in an additive fashion. These two "general antecedents" (p. 313) of self-worth are competence and what she calls social approval, which I refer to as "worth" or "worthiness." Competence in the domains of life that are important to individuals personally plays an important role in fostering self-esteem and reflects the Jamesian approach to understanding self-esteem. Approval from others, particularly significant others, also feeds into the self-esteem picture and is emphasized by the social learning tradition we saw earlier. Typically, the two forces and sources interact with each other to produce a normal or healthy level of self-esteem that follows the usual developmental patterns for various age groups. Like all developmental phenomena, however, multidimensional developmental processes also mean that individual variation is the rule rather than the exception: In this sense, we all have to "find" our own way to self-esteem in a manner that reflects individual temperament and circumstances. Typically, the result is a fairly healthy match among personality, skill acquisition in desired domains, and adequate social support over time, all of which usually leads to normal, reasonably healthy levels of self-esteem.

Sometimes, however, the road through development is not smooth, which means that various types of difficulties may occur. In general, they include such possibilities as insufficient success in important domains, a lack of social approval at particularly significant times, and unfortunate mismatches between domains that are important to a particular person and the degree of approval that is received in relation to them. Such events can affect an individual in a negative way, depending on the meaning the domains hold at the personal level. When that happens, self-esteem problems occur. Depending on the directionality of the interaction of self-esteem and behavior for a given individual, the difficulties may then play a role in such phenomena as insecurity, anxiety, depression, and a whole host of DSM-IV problems mentioned earlier that are connected to self-esteem. According to Harter's theory, if the lack of competence or worthiness is related to such difficulties, then it should be possible to work on them in corrective ways and thereby alleviate many self-esteem–related problems.

System and Techniques

Harter begins by noting that, historically, there are two general approaches to enhancing self-esteem. One is to focus on increasing a sense of worth as a person, which is characteristic of the self-enhancement approach that we saw the self-esteem movement embrace. In this case, the aim is to make the person feel better about themselves so that they will be more interested in functioning effectively. This approach was especially common among educators and, as we have seen, led to harsh criticisms of the field. The other approach, called "skills enhancement," focuses on helping people to acquire the skills that are necessary to be effective in life, which, in theory, leads to degrees of competence. Pope and colleagues took this approach, and it seems to be drawing more adherents today, especially in educational settings. Harter also takes this path and builds her program around three things: assessing the individual, tailoring interventions to behavioral domains that are important to the particular person, and using various cognitive and social techniques to enhance competence and worth or self-esteem.

Assessment plays a key role in this approach for reasons that are similar to those that influenced Pope and colleagues' program. If self-esteem is understood as being connected to various domains of living, then it is necessary to have an idea of how a particular individual is functioning in them to spot areas of difficulty. It is also important to identify areas in which the individual is doing well because in this approach working with strengths is just as important as working on weaknesses. Similarly, if self-esteem is seen as being influenced by social forces and significant others, then it is helpful to know the major characters in a person's life, especially who is helpful and who is not. In short, a multidimensional model of self-esteem that is tied to development requires a multidimensional assessment of the individual that is based on norms for each major stage of life. Once assessment is complete, areas of concern are identified and potential strengths are clarified. Then, this information is used to develop a treatment strategy that is tailored to the person's specific needs. The clinician may select from a number of treatment techniques depending on what assessment reveals, but they can generally be divided into two categories that reflect the basic structure of self-esteem.

The first set of techniques is termed "Intervention Strategies Directed at Cognitive Determinants" (Harter, 1999, p. 316). The general strategy is to reduce major discrepancies between the ideal and real self or, in Jamesian terms, one's "pretensions" in comparison to one's "successes." One way to accomplish this goal is to identify areas of life that are important to the individual but in which they are not doing well. Then, it is possible to direct work at increasing skills that are necessary for success in those areas. As success increases, the discrepancy should decrease, thereby making self-esteem rise. If that route is not possible, one may also focus on the importance of each area and reduce the significance of the ones in which an individual has little chance to succeed. If such a tactic proves to be less than helpful, then it is always possible to increase the importance of another area that is more promising. Other more cognitively oriented techniques include encouraging the development of a more realistic image of the self, which allows one to use a host of techniques from attribution theory, narrative therapy, and so forth. All variations of this technique should reduce the discrepancy, thereby altering the self-esteem picture in a positive way.

The other set of interventions, of course, is more social in nature. This approach requires an accurate sense of the client's social world, who is in it, and what roles they play in terms of offering positive or negative social support or influence. Once this information is established, it may be used to develop realistic intervention strategies that increase social support and, therefore, the individual's sense of social worth. For example, it might be possible to help a child see the support that is being given to him or her more clearly, which could help them feel less isolated. In another case, it might be helpful to encourage the individual's significant others to be more supportive or to at least reduce negative interactions. In still other situations, it may even be necessary to help find new social sources of approval from which to internalize positive identifications. Finally, of course, Harter makes it clear that both cognitive and social interventions can and should be used together to create an optimal plan. She termed her approach the "case-formulation method" (Shrik & Harter, 1996) and concluded that aged-based assessment is the key to the process of designing appropriate interventions.

Summary

What is especially remarkable in Harter's approach is that she is one of the few individuals who has done major work in all three areas (theory, research, and practice), thereby giving her approach a high degree of consistency. The theory is powerful because it is based on two factors of self-esteem rather than one, which means that can draw from both the Jamesian and social learning traditions. The approach is also highly developmental in character, which means that it has the potential to apply to a wide range of people. It is even possible to see this program as a life span approach to self-esteem. Though not normed against large numbers of subjects, Harter has also developed assessment instruments that are both multidimensional and that span the entire life cycle. Finally, she has combined theory with assessment to offer an approach to enhancing self-esteem in the clinical setting that is extremely individualized to the needs of the client.

A Note on Burns' *Ten Days to Self-Esteem*

Although it is often referred to as a self-help program and does not offer a theory of self-esteem as the foundation for its use, there are two reasons David Burns' cognitively oriented *Ten Days to Self-Esteem* (1993a) and its companion *Ten Days to Self-Esteem: The Leader's Manual* (1993b) deserve attention. First, the program is a systematic approach to dealing with problems related to self-esteem, especially excessive anxiety and depression. Burns defines self-esteem in terms of worthiness and then presents 10 sessions or steps aimed at enhancing self-esteem. These steps are arranged in a sequential order and are worked in a self-help or a group setting. They are "The Price of Happiness" (which involves introducing the program, assessing problem areas, and finding out what one has to do to change), "You FEEL the Way You THINK" (an introduction to cognitive principles of behavior and how to change it), "You Can CHANGE the Way You FEEL" (emphasizes learning about the difference between healthy and unhealthy feelings and emotional responses), "How to Break Out of a Bad Mood" (cognitive techniques to alter negative feelings and moods), "The Acceptance Paradox" (contrasting Western and Eastern approaches to and techniques of change), "Getting Down to Root Causes" (identifying one's own self-defeating attitudes and beliefs), "Self-Esteem—What Is It? How Do I Get It?" (understanding and developing conditional and unconditional self-esteem), "The Perfectionist's Script for Self-Defeat" (ways of dealing with a major set of self-esteem problems common in our society today), "A Prescription for Procrastinators" (how to increase personal responsibility), and "Practice, Practice, Practice!" (the need to work the steps to benefit from them). Each step involves specific activities, including assessment and enhancement techniques, that help prepare the individual for the next level.

This program is highly structured through the use of a manual that includes specific guidelines for practitioners and clients. This "manualized" approach increases the program's reliability when compared with the others, which also means that it is relatively easy to research its effectiveness. Also, his program seems to be more thoroughly tested than others: It has been used with various populations, including those who are severely mentally ill and has been the focus of a longer term research project (1993a, 1993b) aimed at testing its efficacy, something that is very rare in this field.

Second, the approach also brings up a self-esteem issue that most scientific research and practice tend to avoid. We encountered this question in Chapter 3 when we looked at the humanistic approach to defining self-esteem, particularly in regard to the spiritual possibilities associated with its transpersonal school. Crocker and Park (2003, 2004) and Crocker and Nuer (2003, 2004) also made mention of this dimension of self-esteem when they showed how contingent self-esteem that is based on competence alone leads to a psychological dead end. Burns talked about this issue using the metaphor of a ladder.

> If you feel worthless and inferior, you may start out on the ground because you have very little self-esteem. On the first rung of the ladder you develop conditional self-esteem. . . . Once you have conditional self-esteem, you can climb up to the next rung on the ladder. On this step you develop unconditional self-esteem. You realize that self-esteem is a gift that you and all human beings receive at birth. . . . On the next step, you can adopt the even more radical position that there is no such thing as self-esteem, just as there is no such thing as a worthwhile person or a worthless person. . . . This solution to the problem of self-esteem is in the Buddhist tradition because self-esteem is rejected as a useless illusion. . . . The death of your pride and your ego can lead to new life and to a more profound vision. (1993a, pp. 186–188)

Note that I am not necessarily agreeing with the position that "egolessness" is the ultimate goal of a search for self-esteem. However, such a concern does raise some important self-esteem questions such as how one understands it in relation to approaches that de-emphasize the importance of the self or even see it as an obstacle to reaching "higher" levels of functioning. Harter (1999) and others also notice this issue in relation to Zen. Having done some work in that area (Mruk & Hartzell, 2003), I think some insight may be gained by exploring the relationship among virtue, self-esteem, and selflessness. The connection is that acting virtuously often involves behaving in ways that transcend the self, particularly the ego. However, that line of thought is highly speculative at best and certainly beyond the scope of our work.

Summary of Findings about Enhancement Programs

At this point the phenomenologically significant question becomes what do these major self-esteem programs show us about how to design a good program? In other words, is there a general structure that underlies scientific approaches to increasing self-esteem? Knowing about the essential components of such a process is important in two ways: This type of information may be helpful in developing a phenomenological or meaning-based program and such findings may help us to evaluate the quality of a program with regard to existing standards of practice. First, data indicate that there is *theoretical consistency* between the major approaches to enhancing self-esteem and the general theories of self-esteem that they represent or on which they are founded. For example, Frey and Carlock's approach is based on a definition of self-esteem that is compatible with Branden's humanistic formulation and many, if not most, of their growth-oriented techniques are humanistic. Pope and colleagues clearly build on social learning theory and practice, which is seen in Rosenberg's and Coopersmith's theories. Harter's work has its roots in both traditions, which means that it reflects the two-factor school. Bednar and associates identify their program as being cognitive and existential, and the techniques they suggest for enhancing self-esteem seem to be compatible with both points of view. The point is that major self-esteem enhancement programs tend to have logical, identifiable ties to general theories of self-esteem, which, in turn, are connected to even larger theoretical perspectives in social science. A good self-esteem enhancement program is, then, set within *the context of a general theory of human behavior.*

Second, an examination of data presented in this chapter suggests that *self-esteem enhancement programs are systematic.* Good programs are structured in a programmatic or stepwise fashion. In each case, the program is organized according to clearly defined stages. Furthermore, these steps are always arranged sequentially to produce a cumulative effect when executed properly. Moreover, each phase is organized in a particular way: Any given step in any particular program aims at a reasonably clear goal and includes a specific set of therapeutic activities designed to help the client reach it. Additionally, major programs involve common processes. The more notable ones include increasing awareness of the importance of self-esteem, dealing with defensiveness and resistance to change, changing self-defeating behaviors, and acquiring new competencies. When seen phenomenologically, each program stands as a path toward self-esteem that, if followed properly, will eventually lead people to higher levels of competence and worthiness. In short, enhancing self-esteem can be a specific, perhaps even specialized, therapeutic enterprise.

Third, each major self-esteem enhancement program recognizes the *importance of assessment.* This component can be included as an informal process as in Frey and Carlock or in Bednar and colleagues, or as a formal one as seen in Pope and colleagues or in Harter. Moreover, assessment usually works hand in hand with therapeutic work so that they strengthen each other. Identifying how significant a person's self-esteem issues are, knowing what type of self-esteem problems are being presented, and being able to adjust the pace and intensity of techniques to the needs of a particular person, all involve assessment procedures and skills. In short, assessment is an important part of enhancing self-esteem in two ways: It tells us what is needed for a given individual and prevents us from harming people.

Fourth, self-esteem enhancement programs do not rely on theory and technique alone. They all recognize the *importance of the role of the therapist or facilitator and his or her presence as a person* in enhancing self-esteem. I doubt that any of the programs could be run successfully by just walking through the steps mechanically. Moreover, much of the process and outcome depends on the usual therapeutic intangibles, such as being reasonably caring, providing a certain degree of nurturing or warmth and acceptance, and being able to listen well, as well as other common factors (Arkowitz, 1997; Seligman, 1995a) in the therapeutic process. However, each program also requires learning various skills, so the role of the clinician or facilitator in enhancing self-esteem is also that of teacher, coach, and champion, as the case may be. This dimension of enhancing self-esteem means that setting clear goals, providing workable steps to reach them, offering encouragement when necessary, and above all, being sensitive to the "teachable moment" (Havighurst, 1972) are involved in the work. Enhancing self-esteem, then, seems more active than many traditional therapies.

The fifth and final finding about self-esteem enhancement programs is that there is a useful degree of *clinical diversity* present among these systems. For instance, Frey and Carlock's program is extremely flexible. It may be used with many kinds of individuals providing they are basically healthy and may be done in group or individual formats. Pope and colleagues and Harter offer ways to set up highly structured programs, which are helpful in dealing with special populations such as children or specially challenged individuals. And Bednar and colleagues clear a path to dealing with more serious self-esteem problems that require intensive and lengthy treatment. In short, it is clear that certain key elements run throughout almost all of this work, suggesting that solid programs are ones that are built on a type of fundamental structure that is helpful for enhancing self-esteem. Now, let us see how this search through the research and theory of self-esteem takes us to a more integrated position.

CHAPTER 5

A Meaning-Based,
Two-Factor Theory
of Self-Esteem

The investigation of major definitions and theories in this field found that a good theory of self-esteem is likely to be characterized by a number of key features. The first one, of course, is that such a broad view is based on one of the three standard definitions of self-esteem that have emerged over time. In addition, a solid theory tends to be firmly grounded in one of the major scientific perspectives that characterize this field. Third, a major theory is capable of accounting for important self-esteem findings such as types of self-esteem and how self-esteem is connected to behavior. We have already seen that a phenomenological perspective on self-esteem meets two of these criteria: Self-esteem is understood as consisting of competence, worthiness, and the relationship between them, and such a view is consistent with one of the established theoretical perspectives of the field, namely, the humanistic position. Now we must turn to the third requirement and show how a phenomenologically oriented meaning-based approach can deal with major self-esteem findings and integrate them in a unified, comprehensive fashion.

THE FUNCTION OF SELF-ESTEEM
AS MEANING MAKING

We begin by understanding self-esteem in terms of a matrix—a matrix of meaning based on the two factors of competence and worthiness as represented in Figure 5.1.

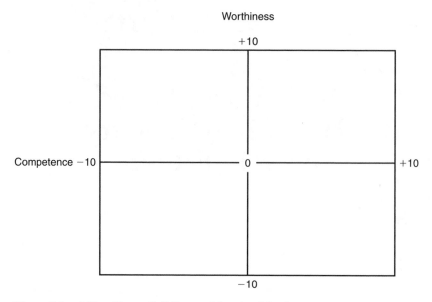

Figure 5.1   A Two-Factor Self-Esteem Meaning Matrix.

This diagram shows how competence and worthiness interact with each other to create self-esteem. Like Tafarodi's and Vu's (1997) metaphor of a rectangle, the relationship is such that the two factors work together to create a matrix or source of self-esteem. Competence is placed on the horizontal axis because this dimension of self-esteem usually involves some form of behavior. Behavior, of course, is easier to observe than an internal state such as worthiness and individual abilities are well disposed to being described in terms of a standard distribution. Thus, this aspect of self-esteem can be well represented with a horizontal line that runs from negative to positive with the midpoint acting as the central tendency or norm. Such a line depicts the positive advantages of competence as well as the negative implications of being deficient in any domain of behavior relevant to self-esteem. For instance, superior or good performance at a particular task, skill, or activity is represented numerically with a positive value from 0 to 10, which is found on the right side of the line. Inferior performance is placed on the other side, starting with 0 and extending to −10, which represents the poorest performance possible. The result is a continuum of competence ranging from low, through average, to high. Global or general competence would be represented in the same fashion.

There is also good reason to represent the other factor, worthiness, with the vertical axis of the matrix. For example, we have seen that worthiness involves values such as general social values concerning what is desirable, feelings of being valued in a relationship, and individual self-values. It would be difficult to use the horizontal axis to represent values because that axis is usually used to rank order more observable phenomena and because values are typically arranged in terms of ascending importance or desirability. Thus, it is more descriptive to think of worthiness and unworthiness as spanning a hierarchical range which, of course, is best illustrated with a vertical axis. Those who are well accepted and virtuous, for instance, would be found at the upper end, which is represented by the number 10. Those who live in a chronic state of self-loathing would be in the lower region, perhaps near the extreme of −10. Most of us would be somewhere between the two extremes, presumably somewhat higher than the 0 point.

Note that one problem with the rectangle metaphor is that it provides no way of telling which factor should be height and which one should be length. In addition, the figure of a rectangle is capable of taking so many different forms that it does not express the relationship between competence and worthiness well. These aspects of the analogy are problematic because the fundamental structure of self-esteem, as well as the literature on the two factors, indicates that competence and worthiness stand in a particular relationship with one another to create self-esteem, and that this interaction is such that it is balanced. The only four-sided figure that corresponds to these conditions is, of course, a square. Thus, it may not be coincidental that when the horizontal axis of competence is bisected by the vertical line of worthiness, and vice versa, the figure that emerges is that of this particular rectangle.

THE BASIC TYPES OF SELF-ESTEEM

In Chapter 3 we saw that there are several types and levels of self-esteem such as fragile, secure, high, low, stable, unstable, defensive, true, paradoxical, optimal, and so forth. An effective theory of self-esteem must not only account for such findings but should also demonstrate how they are even possible in the first place. Therefore, an integrated understanding of self-esteem must show how a relationship between the two factors of competence and worthiness is able to generate types of self-esteem and do so in a way that is reasonably consistent with the research on them. Figure 5.2 shows that when competence and worthiness are placed in dynamic relation to one another, as required by the fundamental structure of self-esteem, the result is the formation of four quadrants, each of which is qualitatively and quantitatively distinct from the others.

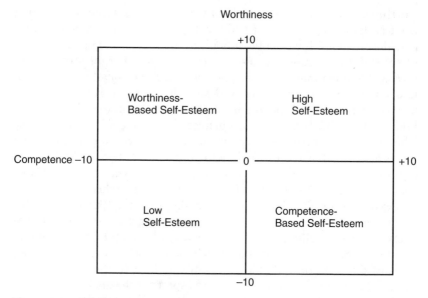

Figure 5.2   Self-Esteem Meaning Matrix with Basic Types of Self-Esteem.

As the diagram indicates, it is not accidental that we encountered research on different types of self-esteem: They are inherent to its fundamental structure. Indeed, that the relationship between competence and worthiness spontaneously generates four possibilities means that there *must* be types of self-esteem. Otherwise, something is wrong with our understanding of the fundamental structure. Fortunately, a phenomenological analysis not only incorporates one of the most important self-esteem findings in the field but actually predicts it. The next step is to examine whether the characteristics associated with the four types of self-esteem necessitated by the fundamental structure are consistent with major research findings in the field.

Low Self-Esteem

According to the two-factor theory, low self-esteem involves living both a lack of competence and a lack of worthiness. Such a configuration only occurs in the lower left quadrant of the matrix. It is easy to imagine how the combination of reduced coping skills and a shrunken reservoir of positive self-feeling would make people vulnerable in this fashion. For example, they would not have much protection from the shield that self-esteem offers against the slings and arrows of life, and they would be ill-equipped to mount campaigns aimed at obtaining the kinds of successes that would lead to a sense of competence. Of course, low self-esteem ranges in terms of degree, which is reflected in the severity of the problem that it generates for individuals. Even so, the phrase "low self-esteem" is usually associated with such things as caution, timidity, lack of initiative, conflict avoidance, insecurity, anxiety, depression, and so forth, as we saw again and again in the literature. All of these qualities are consistent with this configuration of self-esteem and the diagram.

High Self-Esteem

According to the meaning matrix generated by the fundamental structure, people with high self-esteem typically exhibit a positive degree of both competence and worthiness. This configuration is only found in the upper right-hand quadrant. It is easy to see how much of the literature we reviewed on high self-esteem is consistent with this quadrant of the matrix. For example, we would expect people who experience a high degree of worthiness to feel good about themselves in general, to be relatively open to new experiences, to feel accepted and acceptable, to be pleasant to be around, and so forth. People who are also high in competence, which is characteristic of this quadrant, would also be likely to have the skills that are necessary to succeed in life. Both sets of characteristics are found in the literature we saw indicating a relationship between self-esteem and happiness, initiative, openness, spontaneity, a secure identity, and, of course, a general absence of psychopathology.

So far, so good. However, unless we can account for it in other ways, it would be difficult for us to understand how other characteristics associated with high self-esteem could be placed in this quadrant without contradicting the way that competence and worthiness have been said to work together. These characteristics are the ones that have been referred to as the dark side of self-esteem and that have caused considerable negative fallout on the field in general. People with high degrees of narcissism, egotism, and even antisocial traits often feel good about themselves and they may score high on self-esteem tests. People with other characteristics may be mistaken for having high self-esteem when they do not, such as those whose self-esteem is contingent upon success. For example, as long as overachievers are competent enough to continue to be successful in whatever way is important to them, they are also likely to test positively on measures of self-esteem. However, having such self-esteem may not offer them much to fall back on in the face of failure or setbacks, which may result in negative self-experience or expression that is not generally associated with genuinely high self-esteem. Fortunately, the matrix offers a new way of understanding such "false positives" and other difficulties caused by the heterogeneity of self-esteem that is not otherwise possible.

Worthiness-Based and Competence-Based Self-Esteem

To understand how a two-factor approach to self-esteem that is founded on its fundamental structure can make sense of this situation, it is first necessary to remember that the research shows us there are several types of high self-esteem. Some of them are characterized by individuals acting as though they have high self-esteem when, in fact, they are actually suffering from a substantial lack of it (Deci & Ryan, 1995; Greenier, Kernis & Waschull, 1995; Jordan et al., 2003; Kernis, 2003a; Tafarodi, Tam & Milne, 2001). Over many years, this aspect of the self-esteem picture has been called by various names including discrepant, pseudo, defensive, unstable, paradoxical, and fragile self-esteem, each of which has its own advocates and supportive literature. To be sure, there are interesting distinctions between these terms, but in general they all share one common feature: Sometimes such individuals look like they have genuine self-esteem and even test that way on simple assessment instruments when, in fact, they do not possess it.

The fundamental structure of self-esteem allows for two distinct ways in which such a phenomenon could occur, and both of them involve using one factor in an attempt to compensate for deficiencies in the other. First, it is possible to have a high sense of worthiness that is not accompanied by correspondingly appropriate competent behavior. The only quadrant that is characterized by such a self-esteem configuration is the one on the upper left, which is why it is called worthiness-based self-esteem. This type involves attempting to make up for the lack of competence in desired domains through a number of mechanisms such as minimizing failures, denying shortcomings, surrounding oneself with accepting others, or believing that one merits high self-esteem just because one feels good about oneself as a person.

The other major type of problematic high self-esteem is a mirror image of worthiness-based self-esteem. This configuration is found in the opposite or bottom right quadrant where it is possible to demonstrate high degrees of competence while lacking a sense of worthiness. In this case, such individuals attempt to compensate for low feelings of self-worth by focusing on their competence, particularly in domains that are important to them. Individuals with competence-based self-esteem tend to focus outwardly instead of inwardly because competence involves actual manifestation of abilities or successes. Focusing on one's activities also makes it possible to avoid seeing or experiencing one's lack of a sense of self-worth, as long as one is nearing success or on the way to the next success.

Under many conditions, either worthiness-based or competency-based self-esteem can look like high self-esteem: Individuals may test that way, they do possess some realistically positive qualities, and they certainly do not give the appearance of having low self-esteem. However, they are not to be confused with people who have secure or authentic self-esteem because the fundamental structure of self-esteem, as described by the matrix, shows that both competence-based and worthiness-based self-esteem are inherently unstable. In each case, one factor is deficient enough to create a state of imbalance, instability, or "fragility" (Kernis, 2003a). Indeed, each of the four major types of fragile self-esteem that Kernis describes in his review of the literature is accommodated in these two quadrants of the matrix terms, because each one of them is structurally imbalanced in principle.

In the case of defensive high self-esteem, for instance, it is quite conceivable that some people consciously behave as though they feel positive about themselves when they actually do not. For example, if an individual possesses enough competence so that it compensates for negative feelings concerning worthiness, or vice versa, then it is possible to focus on the positive quality and thereby ignore the deficit at least some of the time. Thus, the matrix accommodates research concerning self-esteem that is contingent on either competence or on worthiness. Similarly, high explicit self-esteem coupled with low implicit self-esteem could occur in either the upper left or lower right quadrants. However, such individuals need not be aware of such an imbalance, which would account for forms of paradoxical self-esteem.

Depending on the severity of an individual's doubts about his or her worthiness, he or she may also demonstrate defensiveness, instability, or general fragility in the face of loss, setbacks, failure, and so forth, because the person does not have a reservoir of positive worth to fall back on during those times. Those who have reservations about their competence may look and feel quite well when things go their way, but rejection, criticism, isolation, or abandonment are more threatening to them. They must react to such threats defensively because they lack the sense of competence necessary to engage in behavior that would earn them a sense of worthiness on their own. Those with paradoxical self-esteem are likely to exhibit similar symptoms of distress because they arise from a state of imbalance between competence and worthiness. However, in these cases such individuals may lack more insight as to why they are responding in these ways than other groups typically suffer.

Finally, we can see how the matrix accommodates the research on unstable self-esteem. This type of self-esteem typically involves dramatic short-term fluctuations. The condition is likely to occur for individuals who have an imbalance of competence and worthiness, but who have not achieved quasi-stability by emphasizing one over the other in a reliable fashion as those who live competence or worthiness-based self-esteem seem to do. Such an unstable foundation makes one vulnerable to situational events affecting one's competence or worthiness. Thus, this type of self-esteem tends to rise or fall on short notice just as the research found (Kernis, 2003a, b). Such uncompensated gaps between competence and worthiness are most likely to be found in the upper left and lower right quadrants of the matrix, as low self-esteem tends to be more steady because it is balanced, although in a negative direction.

Readers of the previous editions will note that I have used different terms to describe two types of self-esteem. In this edition the labels of "Defensive Self-Esteem I" and "Defensive Self-Esteem II" have been changed to "Worthiness-based Self-Esteem" and "Competence-based Self-Esteem," respectively, for two reasons. First, although the term "defensive" certainly is descriptive clinically, the numerals *I* and *II* do not say much about how they are different from each other. Second, the new terms presented in this edition are not only more descriptive, but they also reveal their connections to the fundamental structure of self-esteem more clearly. Although the names have changed, the dynamics and characteristics associated with each type of self-esteem remain the same. In any case, the point is that when looking at the fundamental structure of self-esteem, it is not surprising that research shows that when it is based on incomplete definitions, high self-esteem is associated with narcissism, egotism, defensiveness, aggression, success, approval, and so forth. Once again, it is the imbalance of the two factors that creates the problem of the heterogeneity of self-esteem, much of which is cleared up when self-esteem is defined in terms of competence and worthiness.

REFINING THE TYPES: INTEGRATING LEVELS OF SELF-ESTEEM

So far, we have seen that it is possible for the matrix to accommodate four basic types of self-esteem, as well as paradoxical and unstable forms of it, all of which are found in the research on self-esteem. Although part of the picture, this basic typology does not integrate other research that we encountered in Chapter 3 concerning levels of self-esteem. For example, it will be recalled that some work indicated that low self-esteem is associated with clinical problems whereas other work describes it in more neutral terms.

A similar issue was encountered in the development of the fourth edition of the Diagnostic and Statistical Manual of Mental Disorders system (DSM-IV-TR or simply DSM) (American Psychiatric Association,

2000). Perhaps the prototypical method used there may be helpful here. According to this approach, one way of classifying human behavior diagnostically is to develop qualitatively distinct categories that are clearly distinguishable from one another. Such a categorical system is helpful in dealing with phenomena that are substantially distinct in ways that are easy to determine, such as an infection versus a broken bone. But human behavior is also dimensional, which means that it is necessary to consider a range of symptoms or behaviors. For example, anxiety is often useful when one is preparing for an important exam, looking out for danger in a combat situation, and so forth, but it may also become a clinical problem. The same is true with many other emotions. Depression, for example, ranges from mild to severe. Also, many personality characteristics vary in this way. For instance, conscientiousness ranges from a positive personal quality to the compulsive personality disorder.

The DSM uses a combination of categorical and dimensional features, called a "prototypical" system (American Psychiatric Association, 2000), to distinguish between types and levels of clinical conditions. For example, anticipating an exam, feeling sad, acting conscientiously, and being cautious are at one end of various dimensions of behavior, while agoraphobia, severe depression, compulsiveness, and paranoia are at the other end, respectively. Although the ends of such continua are connected in terms of forming a range, they also differ qualitatively. No one knows exactly where the difference between non-clinical and clinical significance lies. However, it is possible to differentiate between such conditions on the basis of a prototype, which is the point at which one becomes "clinically significant." This distinction is reached when one exhibits a preponderance of clear symptoms or other indications that have been found to be problematic enough to warrant professional attention when they come together in a particular fashion. Thus, each major diagnostic group is first characterized by a central theme, such as anxiety, dissociation, mood, and so forth. Then, it is possible to break disorders into subtypes that reflect the central features of a particular condition but with enough variation to be recognizably different.

Perhaps the study of self-esteem can be approached in the same way. For example, each quadrant may be seen as a group of related self-esteem characteristics that are qualitatively distinct enough to be distinguished from one another, much like the major diagnostic groups. Yet, for each basic self-esteem group, it is possible to see different levels or degrees of competence or worthiness. This aspect of self-esteem is represented by an *imaginary* diagonal line that runs through the middle of each quadrant. High self-esteem, then, ranges from the coordinate 0 to the coordinates of +10, +10, while low self-esteem drops along the range that runs from 0 to −10, −10. Worthiness-based self-esteem varies from 0 to +10, −10 and its competence-based counterpart travels from 0 to −10, +10 on the diagram.

In addition, it is likely that there are significant qualitative distinctions between the end points of each range. Thus, if we use the halfway point in any quadrant, which is identified by a +5 or a −5, then we can follow the form of the DSM one step further and speak in terms of two different subtypes or levels within each quadrant. Finally, it is important to note that this further differentiation of the variety of ways in which self-esteem is lived is consistent with the general structure of the phenomenon. As such, we should be able to place levels of self-esteem in the matrix, as well as basic types, which is accomplished in Figure 5.3. I have included all the major possibilities in one diagram instead of showing one quadrant at a time to demonstrate the consistency of the model

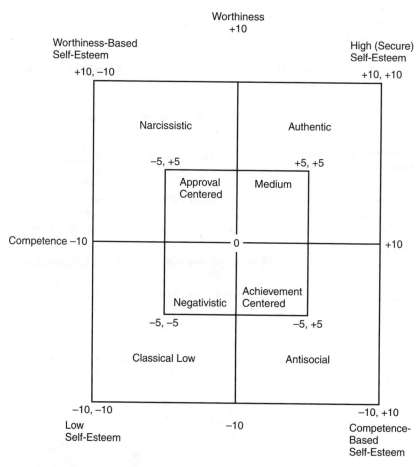

Figure 5.3   Self-Esteem Meaning Matrix with Basic Types and Levels.

in a single gestalt. However, it is also necessary to "unpack" each section to get a closer look at how self-esteem is layered.

Levels of Low Self-Esteem

While examining the research on low self-esteem in Chapter 3, we saw that it is possible to think about two subtypes or levels of low self-esteem. Rosenberg and Owens (2001) offered one clue to this phenomenon when they pointed out that many of the characteristics that have been attributed to low self-esteem actually exist as a continuum or range of experiential and behavioral possibilities. That low self-esteem varies in terms of degree suggests that it is dimensional. One part of this continuum, the 0 to −5, −5 range on the imaginary diagonal in the quadrant, would pertain to mild problems of this type. The outermost remaining half would then be used to represent clinically significant problems associated with a low sense of competence and worth, or low self-esteem. In other words, we differentiate between types and levels of self-esteem, just as is done in the DSM.

Negativistic Low Self-Esteem

Dividing the quadrants up in this fashion allows us to name two constellations of characteristics or symptoms and separate them by degree as well as by core features. For example, we saw in Chapter 3 that not all people who live low self-esteem reach the level of clinical significance, so more than one term is needed to describe the ways in which low self-esteem is lived. Some authors use the phrase "neutral" self-esteem to describe milder levels of low self-esteem (Tice, 1993). However, the condition is still clearly negative because it limits possibilities and diminishes a sense of well-being or happiness. The phrase "negativistic" captures the lived character more accurately, so this type is called "negativistic self-esteem," suggesting that it does constitute a certain problematic lifestyle but not more.

This descriptor also touches on certain personality characteristics common to members of this group such as their generally negative outlook concerning their chances of success and failure or good and bad fortune in life. In general, the research on this level of low self-esteem shows that it is not necessarily a terrible thing to have or to live, contrary to popular opinion (Brockner et al., 1993; Snyder, 1989; Tice, 1993). The research in Chapter 3 showed that people with low self-esteem want the same kinds of things as people with high self-esteem. However, those with low self-esteem are also more concerned with conserving this valuable psychological resource than risking it. Therefore, they employ a number of methods to avoid losses such as holding to a lower sense of expectations, using self-handicapping strategies, and avoiding risk. Such a condition does not warrant a diagnosis; however, it is costly in terms of missing out on many opportunities in life. Thus, negativistic self-esteem constitutes a genuine self-esteem problem of living, but not one that is clinically significant much like the "V-Codes" of the DSM systems.

Classical Low Self-Esteem

We also saw in Chapter 1 that some 24 clinical conditions are associated with low self-esteem in the DSM. The point of clinical significance can be represented by the coordinate −5, −5 in the diagram and below simply because it divides the quadrant into less severe and more severe areas. Depression is most commonly associated with low self-esteem diagnostically, but it plays a major role in other DSM diagnoses as well, such as anxiety disorders, eating disorders, attention deficit disorder, and so forth. All of these conditions are well documented as involving low self-esteem in one way or another. Although desirable, it is not possible to discuss in this book how self-esteem plays a role in all of these conditions because we must stay focused on the central topic. Fortunately, much of the literature on those disorders covers that material, so the main point for our purposes is quite clear:

> Prospective studies conducted with children, adolescents, and young adults, for example, suggest that low self-esteem increases their susceptibility to a wide range of problematic outcomes and experiences such as depression, eating disorders, teenage pregnancy, victimization, difficulty sustaining and forming close relationships, involvement in antisocial behavior, substance use, and suicide ideation and attempts. (DuBois & Flay, 2004, pp. 415–416)

Also note that new research is beginning to show the importance of dealing with low self-esteem in relation to the effective management of various serious chronic mental disorders, such as schizophrenia (McReynolds, Ward & Singer, 2002; Silverstone & Salsali, 2003).

Levels of Worthiness-Based Self-Esteem

As should be expected if the matrix is correct, it should be possible to differentiate between the two imbalanced types of self-esteem that are often confused with genuinely high self-esteem. Such an off-centered foundation is not the basis on which to build an edifice for living because this condition requires constant attention, including a readiness to defend against internal, as well as external, threats. However, there is much variation in both worthiness-based and competence-based self-esteem, just as in the case of low self-esteem. Therefore, it is necessary to imagine diagonal lines dividing them as well.

Approval-Centered Worthiness-Based Self-Esteem

Worthiness-based self-esteem is a type of imbalance that is dependent on worth, especially the type of worth that comes with acceptance or the approval of others. Such a self-esteem problem may take the form of meeting a parent's or partner's idea of perfection; living up to an external social or religious standard that is not necessarily a part of one's own value system; maintaining a high social status at all costs; or soliciting love and attention through dependency, subservience, or sexuality, and so forth. However, in all cases this way of feeling worthy is largely contingent on only one source of self-esteem. When characterizing self-esteem in this way, however, it is important to remember that we are talking about a matter of degrees. Thus, to say a person lives worthiness-based self-esteem does not necessarily mean that they have no competence. In fact, such individuals are quite competent in a variety of ways, but not in ones that matter to them in terms of being approved of or of feeling accepted.

We have all known people who could be placed in the non-clinical portion of this quadrant. They are, for example, people who seek the approval of others as a way of making themselves feel good. For people who live this level of self-esteem, the incongruence of having a sense of worth but not of demonstrating a corresponding degree of competence, must be avoided. Consequently, these individuals tend to become sensitive to criticism when the issue does arise. In addition, they may underachieve in the workplace and rationalize their performance by avoiding confrontations, making excuses, blaming others, and the like. Other approval-oriented individuals exhibit their fragility in more obvious ways such as by constantly soliciting positive interpersonal feedback, which is done in myriad ways. Still others even believe their exaggerated sense of self-importance, deny their shortcomings, and act in a way that ordinary language would label as being stuck up, snobbish, or conceited. However, the underlying self-esteem dynamic is the same.

Such self-centered people are often inconvenient or annoying if, for instance, one has to work or live with them, but they are not diagnosable because the behavior in this part of the quadrant does not reach clinical significance. Because approval and acceptance are indications of worth, which is one of the primary sources of self-esteem, the phrase "approval seeking" is used to describe this non-clinical but still fragile or unstable form of self-esteem. Some literature seems to refer to this type of self-esteem as "normal narcissism," which appears to have certain benefits upon first glance, such as spontaneity, lack of social anxiety, and the like. However, it has been shown that when narcissism is factored out, any positive qualities that remain are attributable to whatever amount of genuine self-esteem the person happens to possess, and not the narcissism (Sedikides et al., 2004). In other words, normal narcissism does not correlate positively with genuine self-esteem.

Narcissistic Worthiness-Based Self-Esteem

If such behavior is enduring, inflexible, and a source of impairment—which are three main indicators of a personality disorder according to the DSM IV-TR system—then the area of clinical significance has been reached. On the matrix, this configuration of self-esteem is represented by the −5, +5 position and beyond on the diagonal of the worthiness-based quadrant. At this point, the individual crosses the line to well-known clinical self-esteem problems (Crocker & Park, 2004; Deci & Ryan, 1995). People who demonstrate a greatly exaggerated sense of their own importance, those who seem to expect others to automatically recognize their special character or abilities, and those who react far too strongly when someone questions his or her contributions or accomplishments, may be demonstrating self-esteem problems severe enough to warrant the diagnosis of a narcissistic personality disorder (Raskin, Novacek & Hogan, 1991). In addition, it is possible to also place delusional grandiosity and even mania here (Epstein, 1980).

The particular imbalance between competence and worthiness associated with this quadrant can be so severe that the individual becomes quite vulnerable to relatively mild challenges, to ordinary social slights, or even to imagined injury. This vulnerability often means becoming vigilant with regard to perceiving potential threats and maintaining a constant readiness to defend against them. Indeed, if the self-esteem structure of such an individual becomes even more unstable or fragile, then a threat to his or her narcissism could lead to a strong negative reaction. After all, a fall from a high place is a frightening possibility and people react strongly when in danger. In addition, when emotions are flaring strongly, it is easier to give in to the impulses such as wanting to destroy a threat rather than facing it. Thus, verbal aggression may be used to protect the self from further injury or collapse. Such an individual might even be so fragile or unstable that he or she resorts to something like reactive aggression (e.g., revenge) to soothe a narcissistic injury. This level of this worthiness-based self-esteem seems to account for a significant portion of the literature linking the so-called dark side of self-esteem with psychopathology and aggression. Similarly, this understanding helps us to comprehend how it can be said that increasing self-esteem is necessary in the treatment of such conditions as narcissism or borderline personality disorders (Levin, 1993). Otherwise, helping such individuals think even more of themselves might seem inappropriate.

Levels of Competence-Based Self-Esteem

Although loaded in the opposite direction, the dimensional versus categorical characteristic of competence-based self-esteem runs parallel to its counterpart. This time the lack of a sense of worth emerges from one's developmental history, but instead of dealing with it, the other component of self-esteem (i.e., competence) is pressed into service. Thus, an individual attempts to compensate by exaggerating the importance of success and of being successful. When someone is staked in this direction, their self-esteem is just as contingent as in the other case. Similarly, this type of self-esteem also is a matter of degrees and combinations that range from minor or non-clinically significant to major or clinically significant, with the −5, +5 position on the diagram as the cut-off for either one.

Achievement-Oriented Competence-Based Self-Esteem

As we saw in Chapter 3, a collectivistic society pushes people toward the worthiness dimension of self-esteem, whereas individualistic societies pressure individuals toward valuing personal achievements more highly. Thus, it is not surprising to find that many people in our culture live out self-esteem issues in terms of successes and failures. The less such a focus is balanced by an abiding sense of worthiness, the more likely a person's self-esteem is to become fragile or unstable. Again, the result of such imbalance is the creation of a certain vulnerability and readiness to respond defensively. At lower levels, success-oriented competence-based self-esteem is seductive, mainly because success feels good and our society places such a high value on it. As long as we continue to be successful, we receive valued acknowledgments and rewards that can easily mask an underlying sense of deficiency.

The problem occurs, of course, when things do not go well, as in the case of Crocker's and Park's (2004) work on high-achieving college students who suddenly find themselves unable to get into a highly ranked graduate program. Often, individuals who live this type of self-esteem at this level are highly motivated, work hard, and sometimes even become extraordinarily accomplished in any given areas. In essence, they become overachievers and as long as they continue to achieve, they look good to people in general. Likewise, they tend to score high on tests given to measure self-esteem. Because of the inherent imbalance in this configuration of competence and worthiness, however, the picture can change quite dramatically under certain conditions. For example, having their abilities questioned, their work seriously criticized, or their project fail is destabilizing enough to evoke defensive reactions, just as we saw with the opposite set of self-esteem dynamics. Depending on degree and circumstance, these reactions are minor ones, such as making downward social comparisons or deriding detractors (Crocker & Park, 2003). But at other times the degree of fragility is great enough to shatter the veneer of high self-esteem and evoke more aggressive reactions in an attempt to get what one wants or to push a sense of failure away. Baumeister and colleagues (1996) examined this dark aspect of high self-esteem and even discussed it in relation to aggression.

Perfectionism could also fall under this quadrant insofar as anything less than perfection is seen as a failure, which, in turn, can generate a high degree of self-criticism. In this case, each flaw and every failure can become a threat, which is a painful, but not necessarily clinical, condition. However, as we near the midpoint of this quadrant, such perfectionism becomes clinically severe, as with certain eating disorders that have been found to be connected to problems with self-esteem (Baumeister, Campbell, Krueger & Vohs, 2003; American Psychiatric Association, 2000; Harter, 1999; Rosenberg & Owen, 2001). For example, if the lack of experiencing oneself as a worthy individual is coupled with other unfortunate factors, such as high self-expectations, critical parents, a certain biological vulnerability, being young, being a female in a society obsessed with weight, being thin, and dieting, then anorexia and related conditions become high risks. The same dynamic could apply to the perfectionistic demands of the compulsive personality.

Antisocial Competence-Based Self-Esteem

At the extreme end of the high-competence low-worthiness range, success becomes increasingly tied to one's sense of value or worth. Depending on how clever, creative, or talented one is, an individual may even become very good at being successful in any given area. Sometimes such individuals are quite aggressive, but in socially "acceptable" ways. Examples of such behavior includes business men and women who uncaringly destroy the careers of others to get to the top, corporate moguls who succeed at any cost, and power-driven politicians who make unsavory deals or worse to get their way. When such behavior is exhibited in ways that conflict with society's rules, individuals are said to be acting in an "antisocial" fashion, which is why this term is used to describe the extreme end of this quadrant. Not only does it describe the behavior, but the term is also meant in the clinical sense. Individuals who deliberately, consciously, and consistently violate the rights of others to get what they want do not seem to be particularly interested in feeling worthy as the term applies to self-esteem. In its most extreme form, antisocial competence-based self-esteem is helpful in understanding human brutality such as that demonstrated by the absolute ruthlessness of various dictators around the world. Thus, competence-based self-esteem accounts for another portion of the negative behavior and aggression that is said to reflect self-esteem's dark side.

Levels of High or Secure Self-Esteem

Now that the pseudo forms of high self-esteem that create the problem of heterogeneity have been placed in their proper locations, it is possible to look at the remaining quadrant, which consists of positive competence and positive worthiness or genuinely high self-esteem. Because the clutter caused by the heterogeneity of self-esteem has been significantly reduced, let us first consider the upper-most end of this continuum, which begins at the +5, +5 level of the matrix.

Authentic Self-Esteem

This first thing to notice about the quadrant in which genuinely high self-esteem is located is that it is the only one that consists of a positive relationship between self-esteem's two factors. It is reasonable to assume that such self-esteem is more secure or stable than other forms because of this balanced state and one should be able to place research on high positive self-esteem in this area. According to Kernis's (2003a, p. 23) analysis, the highest form of self-esteem is characterized by four main qualities. In general, high self-esteem is *secure* enough to allow the individual to perceive and admit faults or limitations; *consistent* across conscious (explicit) and non-conscious (implicit) levels; *true* in that it does not require continual validation of either worthiness or competence; and *stable,* which is to say that it is largely balanced over time. These characteristics certainly warrant being placed in the upper right quadrant. However, one should not confuse such "optimal" self-esteem, as Kernis referred to it, with lived realities. In real life, we could expect the individual with this kind of self-esteem to be *usually* secure, as people always have bad days; *mostly* uniform, because learning about oneself always takes time; *generally* true, as we all encounter challenges of living from time to time and cannot be expected to handle all of them perfectly; and *largely* stable because we all undergo periods of uncertainty in life.

Next, there is the question of what to call this type of high self-esteem. In some ways, it is unfortunate that we can no longer use the classical term "high self-esteem" because that most closely describes what we are discussing. However, the work on the heterogeneity of self-esteem shows us that there are several forms of high self-esteem and most of them are not genuinely high at all. Instead, it is important to identify exactly what one means by high self-esteem, lest confusion occur. Various terms have been used to help identify this form of self-esteem in the last decade and this book mentions them in a number of places. They include "healthy," "optimal," "genuine," "true," "real," and "authentic" self-esteem, among others. Of the options, "authentic self-esteem" might be the most representative for three important reasons.

First, it was mentioned in Chapter 3 that the term "authentic self-esteem" is now being used in qualitative and quantitative research. Indeed, there is even a growing body of literature based on using the experimental method to research authenticity, which marks a huge turning point in this area (Greenberg, Koole & Pyszczynski, 2004). Although self-esteem is not seen quite the way it is presented here, Self-Determination Theory, for instance, differentiates between the protective functions of self-esteem and its enhancement functions based on experimental research concerning intrinsic motivation and authenticity (Ryan & Deci, 2004). In addition, Kernis (2003a, b) finds support for the relationship between self-esteem and what I have called "self-esteem moments." Thus, this term has behind it a body of supportive work that appears more solid than that which accompanies other terms.

Second, the phrase "authentic self-esteem" also helps us make clear clarifications in areas in which they are needed. For example, the authentic–inauthentic distinction can be applied to all of the types of high self-esteem we have encountered so far. In addition to seeing what makes secure self-esteem authentic, for instance, all the varieties of what Kernis (2003a) called "fragile" self-esteem can be understood as being inauthentic by the same token. In other words, self-esteem that is defensive, paradoxical (differing at the explicit and implicit levels), contingent, or unstable, cannot be authentic high self-esteem because they all involve an imbalance of competence and worthiness, which makes them inauthentic in *essence,* as well as by contrast.

Finally, the word "authentic" has strong existential connotations— connotations that take us back to the "life world" where self-esteem is actually lived. For instance, to be authentic or inauthentic as a person is a fundamental existential question that each one of us faces. How well or poorly we do that certainly ought to matter in terms of self-esteem because it reflects our ability to meet the challenges of living in a worthy way over time. Once again, we find ourselves right back at the fundamental structure of self-esteem.

Medium Self-Esteem

It would be a sad comment on human affairs if the types and levels of self-esteem identified so far constituted the entire self-esteem picture. For instance, if it is true that authentic self-esteem is at the high end of that quadrant then, like all extremes, including those of the other quadrants, its occurrence in the population is likely to be the exception rather than the norm. If not, then it would be likely that most of us would have to be in pretty poor psychological shape and that does not actually seem to be the case, at least in terms of clinical significance. Does that mean we should expect equal distributions in the four non-clinical areas? Although there are many people who live worthiness-based, competence-based, and low self-esteem, there is good reason to believe that they do not constitute the majority of the population even if they are combined. For one thing, such a condition would make testing self-esteem quite difficult because there would be little in the way of a normal range against which to compare the others. For another, the major self-esteem instruments do seem to indicate that most people are found well between the extremes, which is to say normal and normative.

Fortunately, there is one more level of self-esteem to consider that addresses this final part of the self-esteem picture. Medium self-esteem is a part of the self-esteem literature, albeit a small one. The dominant view on the character of medium self-esteem is represented by Coopersmith (1959, 1967) and Rosenberg (1965). This perspective holds the position that medium self-esteem results from enough exposure to positive experiences to avoid problems in this area, but not enough to reach a genuinely high state. In this view, higher self-esteem is always seen as more desirable, even though it may involve some social costs such as the envy of other people. Also, the testing literature makes considerable use of the medium range of self-esteem, although the exact measure of the central tendency varies somewhat from group to group or culture to culture.

Of course, medium self-esteem is also anticipated by the matrix. Possessing some, but not an unusually large degree of competence, and solid, but not overwhelming worthiness, definitely places such people in the upper right-hand quadrant. However, they cannot be located as far up its diagonal as are those individuals with authentic self-esteem; otherwise there is no way to distinguish between the two groups and we know that such a difference exists. We accommodate this condition by simply dividing the quadrant into two levels of self-esteem as we have done with others, which in this case, would be at the +5, +5 position in the diagram. This location means that medium self-esteem is reasonably stable, secure, or balanced, but capable of moving up to the higher, more authentic level of self-esteem found in this quadrant. Last but not least, it is important to remember that many human characteristics occur in terms of a standard distribution, the center of which is normal, average, and adequate for living. Verbal ability, spatial reasoning, language skills, IQ, athletic ability, and many developmental phenomena are distributed in this way. Why should self-esteem be any different? This type of self-esteem can be accurately placed on the diagram if we remember that most of us would be found in this level of the positive quadrant. Finally, all of the information on types and levels of self-esteem is represented in tabular form to summarize it in a single gestalt, as indicated by Figure 5.4.

Worthiness-Based Self-Esteem	High Self-Esteem
1. General Type: Unstable or fragile self-esteem characterized by a low sense of competence compensated for by focusing on worthiness.	1. General Type: Relatively stable self-esteem characterized by varying degrees of openness to experience, optimism, and lack of defensiveness.
2. Levels	2. Levels
a. Approval seeking: Contingent on approval from others, sensitive to criticism and rejection.	a. Medium: Stable sense of adequacy in terms of competence and worthiness, interested in more.
b. Narcissistic: Exaggerated sense of worthiness regardless of competence level and reactive to criticism. Vulnerable to defensive acting out.	b. Authentic: General sense of realistic competence and solid worthiness. Actively concerned with living out positive, intrinsic values.
Low Self-Esteem	Competence-Based Self-Esteem
1. General Type: Reduced level of self-esteem characterized by a concern to avoid further loss of competence or worthiness.	1. General Type: Unstable or fragile self-esteem characterized by low sense of worthiness compensated for by focusing on competence.
2. Levels	2. Levels
a. Negativistic: Generally cautious style of self-regulation, focuses on protecting current level of self-esteem rather than losing it.	a. Success seeking: Contingent on garnering successes or achievements and anxious about and sensitive to failure.
b. Classical: Impaired functioning due to low sense of ability and worth. Vulnerable to depression, giving up.	b. Antisocial: Exaggerated need for success or power. Vulnerable to aggressive acting out.

Figure 5.4   Integrating Types and Levels of Self-Esteem.

THE DEVELOPMENT OF SELF-ESTEEM

As discussed earlier, self-esteem must be understood as a developmental phenomenon and much work has been done in this area (Coopersmith, 1967; Rosenberg, 1965; White, 1959). However, no one seems to have done as much work on the development of self-esteem as Harter (1999, 2003). Not only has she tied the development of self-esteem to cognitive and social growth, but she has also extended this framework from childhood, through adolescence, and all the way to late adulthood as well. Harter's multidimensional approach is compatible with a two-factor definition of self-esteem; the various dimensions of the theory can be roughly equally divided between social factors associated with approval or worth and behavioral factors associated with competence in various domains of life. Most of Harter's efforts are dedicated to understanding the development of self-esteem in childhood or adolescence and stands as a classic in the field. However, it is necessary to discuss some aspects concerning the development of self-esteem in adulthood. In particular, new research on authenticity and self-esteem in adulthood needs to be integrated here. Also, the clinical focus of this book is enhancing self-esteem in adulthood, which makes this area more important for our purposes.

Childhood "Precursors" of Self-Esteem

Erikson pointed out that identity is the central task of adolescence and Piaget found that this time is also when formal operational thinking begins. Both identity and advanced cognitive abilities are needed when it comes to talking about the "self" in self-esteem, so I am reluctant to use that term in regard to childhood. However, worthiness and competence are components of self-esteem that are important while growing up, so it is necessary to make some observations on what might be seen as the "precursors" of self-esteem and the relationship that occurs between the components over time. The only thing that is necessary to keep in mind is that considerable time must pass before individuals come to the point at which they consciously "have" self-esteem in such a way that also means they alone are responsible for managing it.

Although both traits are connected to each other throughout development, it is likely that the worthiness dimension of self-esteem precedes competence. For example, even before an infant is born, he or she is already surrounded by a value-laden environment that structures what is perceived as good or bad, desirable or undesirable, attractive or unattractive, or worthy and unworthy in general. The infant is also more passive than active at this time of life as being exposed to values requires much less effort than actively exploring them. Although each perspective understands the development of worthiness from a different angle, it is usually emphasized early in the process of growth. For example, White (1959) talked about "loveworthiness" and identification with parental figures or objects. Coopersmith (1967) connected worthiness to various patterns of parenting. Rosenberg (1965) spoke of "reflected appraisals," humanists focused on being accepted "unconditionally" (Rogers, 1961) as having a major impact on our worthiness, and so on. In a certain sense, then, the first source of worthiness we encounter, and perhaps also the first source of self-esteem, is being valued by others. Also, later on in life it is important to accept ourselves to achieve authentic self-esteem, but even that task is made easier if we have had "good enough" (Winnicott, 1953) acceptance in the first place.

Middle Childhood and the Emergence of Self-Esteem in Adolescence

Competence is also a part of infancy, but it usually takes much longer to develop. Although parents and families are typically accepting of children and their abilities in the early years of life, the world of middle childhood is an unforgiving place by comparison. It is filled with evaluations of motor, social, intellectual, personality, and behavior characteristics. The classroom, the playground, and many peer-related activities are arenas for a comparison of abilities and traits according to the external and usually less accepting standards of teachers and peers. After all, who has not experienced the effect of being picked first for a team, or last? The latency period (ages 7–11) is the most crucial stage for the development of self-esteem because this is when children discover, become known by, and eventually identify with, their abilities and characteristics. No wonder self-esteem work with children often involves evaluating their functioning in the social, athletic, and cognitive domains (Harter, 1999; Harter & Whitesell, 2003; Pope, McHale & Craighead, 1988). These trials of "industry versus inferiority" (Erikson, 1983) set the foundations for the other factor that is necessary for self-esteem, which is the development of competence.

Age seems to be especially important during this period in the development of self-esteem. Each year seems to bring with it a range of new challenges at living and more sophisticated standards in play, with friends, at school, and so on. During this extended developmental time, the child has many successes and failures both great and small. Eventually, certain patterns develop and the child finds that he or she is relatively competent in certain kinds of tasks or areas and less so in others. Some of these skills are valued as being more worthy than others, which means that there is also plenty of individual variation in what could otherwise seem like a regimented process. By the end of this stage of self-esteem development, the individual comes to have what the literature refers to as a basic or global level of self-esteem. Over all, then, the relationship between competence and worthiness is that of equal partners in the self-esteem: It is the "additive" result that Harter (1999) and the two-factor school in general talk about in regard to self-esteem and in measuring it.

By now, the developing child is well on the way to acquiring his or her own self-esteem type and level. The material we considered on the development of self-esteem indicates that an individual can run into three kinds of problems in this stage of self-esteem formation. First, a child may already have encountered major obstacles or problems in the early development of worthiness or competence. For example, such factors as early childhood behavioral problems, learning disabilities, unsupportive or abusive parenting, and social-economic deprivation may affect the development of self-esteem in ways that impede its movement toward a positive direction (Harter, Whitehall & Junkin, 1998). Second, the child's natural competencies may not be relevant to the skills required for success in a given environment or the opportunities for developing such skills may be limited, either of which could create a situation in which the child's chances for failure outweigh the possibilities of success. Third, the developing individual may encounter a conflict of values. Those experiences that involve intrinsic or internalized values are helpful to the development of self-esteem but contingent or external values are not. When the individual faces a conflict between such values or value choices, much more is at stake than may meet the eye (Deci & Ryan, 1995; Ryan & Deci, 2003).

Various factors that help or hurt the developmental process include genetic predispositions (Neiss, Stevenson & Sedikides, 2003), the nature of the gene/environment fit between a child and the world into which he or she is born, how observant the parent is, how caring or rejecting a teacher happens to be at a critical time, how supportive or rejecting other children are, whether the child's culture emphasizes individualistic or collective values, and so on. Those who find circumstances favorable because of one positive factor or another move forward in their growth more easily, whereas those who do not, acquire the beginnings of a problematic self-esteem theme. In either case, this phase of the development of self-esteem appears to solidify during adolescence which, in turn, adds the final ingredients of identity and self-awareness. Although self-esteem does seem to be somewhat open to fluctuations at the beginning of this process, the level and type of self-esteem acquired by the end of this period seem to be the basic sense of competence and worthiness with which the individual must begin to face the challenges of living on their own.

Self-Esteem in Adulthood

We see how dynamic the development of self-esteem is early in life. Even so, it is largely reactive in the first two stages because of the biological and cognitive constraints of childhood and early adolescence. However, the research on self-esteem moments show us that it can become quite conscious and thematic in adulthood. In addition to continuing to master new types of social relationships and acquiring the competencies that are necessary for adulthood, for instance, we know that there are special times when our self-esteem is challenged directly. The major change between how self-esteem is lived early in the life span compared with how it is alive in adulthood is captured by thinking of the former in terms of *developing* self-esteem and the latter in terms of *managing* it. Of course, although self-esteem can be increased in adult life, it is also possible to lose it. Moreover, a good deal of what happens to this vital psychosocial resource for living depends on the way we face the challenges of living over time.

As indicated earlier in Chapter 3, Epstein has probably done the broadest work on the full range of self-esteem moments in adult life. Perhaps the most dramatic example of his research occurred when he took advantage of the "natural laboratory" of life and asked participants to keep a record or journal of the events that they experienced in a given period of time and to monitor themselves for fluctuations in their self-esteem (1979). The data were then analyzed according to certain parameters of experience, such as the type of situation that triggered the response, the kinds of emotions experienced during the event, their relative intensity, and behavioral manifestations of the experience. As already noted, Epstein found that two such experiences seemed to affect self-esteem most directly: ones involving "success–failure" and "acceptance–rejection." These situations affected self-esteem in the expected directions. However, Epstein also found that 10 dimensions describing feeling states were significantly associated with changes in self-esteem.

> When self-esteem was raised, high levels were reported for happiness, security, affection, energy availability, alertness, calmness, clear-mindedness, singleness of purpose, lack of restraint, and spontaneity. When self-esteem was lowered, high levels were reported for unhappiness, anger, feelings of threat, weariness, withdrawal, nervousness, disorganization, conflict, feelings of restraint, and self-consciousness. (1979, p. 62)

It is important to note that Epstein's findings are consistent and quite compatible with our more phenomenological framework. If we examine his findings in terms of the self-esteem meaning matrix, for instance, it is clear that the success–failure experiences are competence based and therefore can be located on the horizontal axis. Successes range, then, from small (which would be represented by a +1) to large (+10). Failure would range in the opposite direction. We would expect varying degrees of positive affective states to accompany increases and negative ones to be associated with decreases because of the pleasure associated with mastery and the pain associated with failure. Likewise, the way acceptance–rejection affects self-esteem is compatible with the worthiness–unworthiness dimension of the matrix in the same fashion. The beginning and ending of a love relationship, for example, could be an example of such a situation and their significance for self-esteem could be placed higher or lower on the vertical axis of the matrix, respectively.

Finally, the meaning matrix integrates other important dimensions of self-esteem that we have seen, such as in the research on gender and culture. It is possible to understand these phenomena in terms of the fundamental structure of self-esteem and place such findings in the matrix as well. In this case, one would say that, just as society influences other values, the forces of socialization can influence which component of self-esteem is *most* important for a given group. Indeed, the work that we covered on culture and self-esteem shows that entire societies exhibit similar patterns, with one culture emphasizing competence more than worthiness and vice versa. At the same time, it is important to note that such variations are always a matter of degree, not structure. Harter (1999), Epstein (1979), and Tafarodi and Swann Jr. (1996) clearly remind us that both genders and all cultures value and need competence *and* worthiness to develop and maintain self-esteem.

Significant life events can also affect self-esteem. For instance, several self-esteem researchers have examined self-esteem–related events that seem to occur primarily in adulthood. Epstein (1979), Mruk (1983), and Jackson (1984) examined particularly intense self-esteem moments that can be understood in terms of the fundamental structure of self-esteem represented by the matrix. These experiences seem to involve a uniquely powerful kind of self-esteem moment that occurs only in situations with two key characteristics. First, these self-esteem moments begin with a fairly ordinary conflict in the everyday world of a given individual. Second, these conflicts quickly and deeply mobilize problematic self-esteem themes, which seem to follow one into adulthood. When both types of conflict become active at the same time, self-esteem appears to be put "at stake" in a way that means it can be either won or lost. Jackson (1984) likened these self-esteem conflicts to Freud's notion of the repetition compulsion, meaning that we are doomed to repeat them until we get them right. We can also understand such situations phenomenologically in terms of the meaning-making function of self-esteem and its relation to authenticity. This approach has the additional value of opening up a whole line of supportive research.

As mentioned in Chapter 1, I investigated the phenomenon of problematic self-esteem themes using 20 subjects who represent a fairly stratified sample of American adults (Mruk, 1983). Let me briefly elaborate on that work to help us understand the importance of these naturally occurring moments for self-esteem in adulthood. The participants were asked to describe two experiences in detail: a time when they were pleased with themselves in a biographically crucial way, and a time when they were displeased with themselves in this fashion. The experiences spontaneously chosen by all the subjects can be described as breaking through a personal difficulty or limitation (which resulted in being pleased) and failing to do so (which resulted in being displeased). Three of the subjects were then extensively interviewed about their descriptions, a procedure that resulted in six research protocols (three instances of both types). The transcripts were subjected to a phenomenological analysis based on Giorgi's (1975) version of the method described in Chapter 2 for two reasons: This technique is probably the most representative or standard format in American phenomenological psychology and it is a step-by-step process, which means that independent researchers can use the method to verify or disprove the findings. The complete set of data, which is called extended narratives, was then examined in terms of meaning units (meaningful transitions in the narrative data) depicted in the subjects' stories of their experiences. These units, in turn, were analyzed for similarities across the subjects, and the resulting empirical regularities were then used to identify essential components of the phenomenon or its "constitutive" elements. Such findings became the building blocks for developing the underlying general structures of each type of experience and eventually led to my first articulation of the fundamental structure of self-esteem (Mruk, 1983).

Examples of the men and women dealing with certain self-esteem–related problems in their lives were presented in Chapter 1. These examples showed how certain situations challenge an individual's current configuration of competence and worthiness, or self-esteem, in a way that reopens the individual's history concerning one or more unresolved biographic self-esteem themes. Another example, not mentioned earlier, concerns a person who is desperately afraid of leaving the safety of the first floor in a building and will not go to higher floors under *any* circumstances. One day this individual's best friend suddenly comes down with a particularly life-threatening illness and is being treated on the 38th floor of a large medical facility. The person describes driving around the hospital for hours before making a decision about whether to "do the right thing."

The problem is a challenge because making the visit also required facing traumatic childhood experiences associated with sudden deaths, something that is tied to what gave rise to the phobia in the first place. The friend may be dying, too. The suffering soul drives and drives and drives until a decision is made. I do not identify the outcome of this self-esteem moment, the person's age, gender, or even cultural background because I want to emphasize that these conflicts are painful to people regardless of such variables. It could be you, me, or anyone at all. These are human dilemmas in that we have a strong desire to do that which is worthy, but we also seem to lack the competence to do so. Or they involve situations where we are capable of doing the worthy thing, but are tempted to choose not to do it. In one way or another we all "drive around" these problems, not knowing what the outcome will be until we actually enact our decision and face the challenge of living authentically or inauthentically.

The identifying characteristic of these self-esteem moments is their dual nature: A situation that requires competence and worthiness in the present (the surface conflict) opens up an unresolved conflict from the past (the source conflict). In addition, both conflicts seem to involve a single solution that is clearly "better," that is, more healthy, mature, competent, and worthy at both levels of the experience. For example, it is usually better to stand up for one's rights, overcome a fear, treat one's body with respect, face loneliness, or be there for your loved one than it is to avoid these things. Yet the underlying source conflict goes beyond the immediate situation in that it means doing precisely what one has become skilled at avoiding due to a historically painful lack of competence or worthiness. In other words, the individual finds himself or herself at a crossroads of self-esteem. He or she sees an uncertain, less taken, pro-self-esteem path leading in one direction and a secure, well-known, safe, but ultimately anti-self-esteem road leading in another. All the while, the surface conflict relentlessly demands making a decision, right now.

The study found that there are six steps or stages that a person must live through to resolve such self-esteem dilemmas. The first three stages that a person goes through in becoming pleased or displeased with himself or herself are the same, so I only describe them once. The last three stages are different for each experience, so I describe them separately. Being pleased or displeased with oneself begins when a person comes to a situation that can be called a biographical *fork in the road*. Typically, it begins when life forces the individual to choose between two alternatives. One of them is clearly worthy but requires a certain degree of competence. The other is less worthy or even unworthy but does not involve demonstrating higher or new forms of competence. The person hesitates to make the decision because, in addition to the fact that one alternative is more difficult to execute than the other, the individual now faces a personally troublesome, historically significant self-esteem theme concerning competence and worthiness that has been awakened by the situation. Notice here that because the person's history is involved, the surface nature of the problem need not be terribly difficult. Most people, for instance, can speak in public even if they are nervous about it, and visiting a sick friend in a hospital is usually experienced as a caring moment rather than a terrifying one. The second stage is a particular kind of *choice and conflict*. Here the individual becomes acutely, but not necessarily fully, aware that he or she *must* make a choice and that the decision is a much larger one than it appears to be on the surface.

The third stage is one of *struggling, movement, and action*. It is by far the most complex part of the process, primarily because the individual now finds himself or herself engaged in two conflicts: one of which is situational and one that is biographically significant. Moreover, the alternatives creating the conflict have competing motivational structures. One solution is positive and worthy: It calls the individual forward both in terms of handling the immediate situation competently and in terms of wanting to actualize by going beyond merely repeating the unworthy and incompetent patterns of the past. These forces are counterbalanced by those associated with the other alternative, which is negative in that it encourages protective, repetitive, avoidant, or inauthentic behavior. Here the individual is "pulled" back toward historically familiar but ultimately constricting domains of incompetent behavior and unworthy experience. As the individual struggles between the options, he or she becomes more inclined toward one choice, one that is made in the context of what is going on at this point in the individual's life, the unique characteristics of the situation itself, and some degree of choice. Although gradual shifts occur during the process of struggling with the self-esteem challenge, the outcome could go either way until the last moment at which time the individual begins to act and starts to live one reality over the other.

Although either outcome occurs after a painful struggle, coming to the more positive resolution seems to be associated with how long and how deeply the individual engages in the process of struggling. It seems that the more the person understands what is actually at stake at both levels of the conflict, the more he or she is motivated to take the pro-self-esteem path. Although other factors are at play, such as how much social or environmental support the person has at the time, we shall see that this stage also presents important possibilities for therapeutic interventions.

The fourth stage in becoming pleased involves moving into what I describe as *release, relaxation, and being pleased*. It is characterized by the individual's immediate feelings of release (the affective response), relaxation (a more bodily reaction), and a conscious sense of being satisfied (a cognitive response) with his or her performance in the face of this particular challenge of living. This step gradually gives way to the fifth stage, called *meaning and affirmation,* where the individual experiences the consequences of the way in which he or she resolved the conflict and the meaning of his or her behavior. The surface level of acceptance usually involves a sense of taking responsibility for the task at hand, but the source or historical level is experienced as a shift in the competence and worthiness of the self-esteem meaning matrix. The result is that the individual comes to appreciate that he or she is *already* being more competent at living and is *already* more worthy as an individual, because both have been actualized situationally (in the here-and-now) and biographically (in terms of the person's life history).

Finally, a *learning and a settling* occurs in the sixth stage when life moves on and the entire situation begins to become a part of the person's history in a way that alters the story of the individual's problematic self-esteem theme in a positive direction. Although personal history can never be erased, it can be modified or sometimes even transformed, and thereby lived in a more positive fashion in the future. The self-esteem matrix is thus affected by the meaning of this event and this kind of behavior is "added" to the individual's position in terms of competence and worthiness. The experience also stands as a landmark, reminding the person how important it is to face such conflicts in a pro-self-esteem way in the future.

In contrast to becoming pleased, the fourth stage of an individual becoming displeased with himself or herself in a biographically crucial way begins when a person ends the struggling, makes their decision, and acts in the unworthy mode of avoidance: Self-consistency is chosen over self-actualization. The result is *relief, tension, and being displeased,* which means that instead of being released from the conflict and free of it for "good," the individual only experiences a temporary sense of relief from having escaped the need to face the underlying conflict, this time. Rather than the relaxation and openness to life that accompanies being pleased, the person encounters the tension and constriction associated with failure and missed opportunity in regard to both the surface and source levels of the situation. Often, this painful state is met with more defensive measures, so such displeasure is buried, suppressed, denied, or acted out, none of which is to any avail in the long run and some of which can even make things worse.

As the individual moves toward the fifth stage of becoming displeased, which is one of *meaning and disaffirmation,* he or she begins to reengage the ordinary tasks of living. This particular situation and its challenge to self-esteem begin to fade, but in doing so they become a part of the problematic self-esteem story and even strengthen or deepen it through reinforcement. Once it is psychologically safe, however, the individual tends to report genuine remorse, guilt, or at least regret over missed opportunity. Eventually, time moves on and the sixth stage of this negative self-esteem moment also becomes one of *learning and settling*. This final transition in the process is similar to its counterpart in that the event also stands as a self-esteem landmark, which is why the title of the stage is the same in both experiences. However, an important difference does occur: The event and experience recede from awareness, but they can remain alive as a signpost or reminder of how important it is to act differently—the next time. Therefore, although this increased consciousness may be helpful as a reminder in dealing with such challenges more effectively in the future, there is no corresponding modification of the self-esteem matrix. In fact, self-esteem may even be lost.

The reader familiar with the research on authenticity and autonomy mentioned in Chapter 3 will notice certain similarities between the findings about self-esteem moments garnered through qualitative analysis, such as described above, and more experimentally oriented work. For example, the Self-Determination Theory offers considerable experimental support for the relationship between authenticity and self-esteem. In general, much work of this type focuses on the most basic aspects of authenticity, namely, awareness and action, which are also visible in most self-esteem moments (Pyszczynski et al., 2004a). Kernis made the link quite explicit when he said,

> Depending on how these challenges are resolved, individuals may proceed further down the path toward either optimal or fragile (or low) self-esteem. No matter whether these "moments" are challenges or affirmations, they provide significant opportunities for growth and self-understanding. . . . To the extent that individuals consult their feelings and motives when deciding how to respond, they are tapping into the potential to develop more optimal self-esteem. Ultimately, their responses may follow social dictates, but if they are freely chosen and fully informed by their true self, they reflect authenticity. Authenticity, in turn, is a vital ingredient in promoting optimal self-esteem. (Kernis, 2003b, p. 89)

The connection between authenticity, self-esteem, and self-esteem moments in adult life is easiest to see in terms of moral challenges because this area is one in which the crucial aspects of authenticity, awareness, and decision making are most visible and clearly tied to a source of self-esteem. However, authenticity is also a part of many other situations that do not involve moral dilemmas, such as success or failure in making meaningful vocational choices, and acceptance or rejection by social groups that are important for an individual and that are based on positive values.

Of course, there is good and bad developmental news in that such self-esteem moments are a part of adulthood. The bad news is that most of us have to deal with these types of problematic self-esteem challenges repeatedly in life: We cannot escape the psychological vulnerability they create because it comes from who each of us is as an individual. Indeed, most of us have several such problematic self-esteem themes. For those of us with particularly poor self-esteem developmental histories, the cross of self-esteem is quite a burden. That there is no guarantee that we will resolve our self-esteem issues in a positive way is another piece of bad news. Sometimes an individual's life is severely affected by this harsh existential fact, especially insofar as low self-esteem is related to various conditions mentioned in the DSM system.

But the good news is just as potent. For one thing, this aspect of being human is like psychological karma. We do indeed reap what we sow in terms of competence and worthiness. Self-esteem, then, helps us to be psychologically and existentially honest: We cannot get away with bad choices forever. In addition, positive or authentic self-esteem provides a sense of direction in life, mainly because of the connection between self-esteem and worthiness. In this way, self-esteem is understood as a type of internal compass that is helpful in telling us where to go in difficult times. Thus, it would be genuinely terrible if we did not have a way of knowing the importance of developing and maintaining positive self-esteem in adulthood. In addition, that the fundamental structure of self-esteem is such that it "fates" us to face our particular problematic themes again and again is something to appreciate. This condition means that there is hope for the possibility of changing self-esteem in the future. In short, these self-esteem moments give us a second chance and more for development during adulthood. This existential fact also has exciting therapeutic implications that we discuss in the next chapter.

In the final analysis, then, self-esteem is likened to a bucket of water carried on a desert journey. The water, of course, represents self-esteem because it is vital for survival. Each time we encounter a potential source of self-esteem and take advantage of it, self-esteem is "added" to the bucket. The more often we are valued by significant others, act with virtue, use influence in a positive way, or reach a personal goal, the farther we walk a higher road without becoming distracted by lesser concerns. Although positive experiences with all four sources of self-esteem is probably optimal, it is important to at least find a source of competence as well as one of worthiness. Such a balance is necessary to create self-esteem and to stabilize the vessel in which it is carried. In addition, the metaphor of carrying a bucket through the desert is apt in another way: Its water can be lost, which also has existential consequences that affect our lives. One way to lose one's self-esteem is akin to the kind of evaporation that comes with neglecting to respect the importance of being diligent about our values or behaviors in minor ways. Another is to stumble hard enough in life to spill the vital contents, which is to say by acting in ways that undermine one's authenticity and self-esteem by harming others, acting without virtue, and so forth. Truly, then, it is up to us to manage self-esteem once we become adults, and there are no guarantees about what final type or level any given person may reach.

REEXAMINING THE LINK BETWEEN SELF-ESTEEM AND BEHAVIOR (CO-CONSTITUTION)

The last area to tackle in developing a comprehensive phenomenological meaning-based theory of self-esteem is to articulate the link between self-esteem and behavior from this perspective. Looking back, it appears that there are three basic approaches to understanding the connection between self-esteem and behavior. The first one, of course, is to minimize it altogether due to what appears to be a weak statistical relationship (Baumeister, Smart & Boden, 1996; Baumeister, Campbell, Krueger & Vohs, 2003; Damon, 1995; Emler, 2001; Seligman, 1990). However, we saw that there are several problems with this conclusion, especially the possibility that much of the statistical weakness might arise from defining self-esteem in a lopsided fashion, or from the difficulties associated with measuring meaning. Second, it is also possible to see self-esteem as a special type of self-fulfilling process. It is one that is based on self-esteem acting as feedback for a self-system that seeks to maintain a high degree of stability while attempting to maximize its potentials (Bednar, Derezotes, Kim & Specht, 1989; Coopersmith, 1967; Epstein, 1980, 1985).

As tempting as it might be to embrace the second possibility, there is a fundamental problem with the approach, namely, that information-processing views are highly reductionistic (Costall & Still, 1987; Dreyfus & Dreyfus, 1986). That is, likening a human being to a computer, even a sophisticated computer, reduces the fullness of the person and the richness of the human experience by making lived processes merely mechanical ones. For example, making a choice implies a certain degree of free will. However, a person is seen as making a "decision" from a cognitive point of view and even computers can do that on the basis of logic trees, parallel processing strategies, and so forth. Although such an approach is more "scientific" in the natural science sense, it fails at the descriptive level because it does not have any way to talk about explicitly human factors such as meaning.

In other words, the cognitive perspective is fine for describing such things as computational processes and perhaps even modeling how basic organisms work, but to claim that human beings function in the same way is quite a leap. In this case, the fundamental structure of self-esteem shows us that the cognitive version of the self-fulfilling prophecy does not describe how competence and worthiness are actually lived. For instance, the self-esteem matrix does not merely "process" information; it makes information *meaningful* and meaning is beyond computation. There are other, more esoteric problems with the cognitive approach to consider as well. For example, it involves what has been referred to as the "ideology of control" or a fascination with manipulating things (Dreyfus & Dreyfus, 1986), whereas a human science approach tends to appreciate that life is always richer than our ability to understand it.

Co-Constitution: A Phenomenological Alternative

Among the major ways of understanding the link between self-esteem and behavior in the traditional literature, then, we are left with Harter's (1999) description of self-esteem and directionality. There is an interesting phenomenological counterpart to this type of understanding that helps us to understand how self-esteem is linked to behavior a bit more completely. It is found in the phenomenological notion of the process of constitution (Husserl, 1970b), which is better discussed with the more contemporary term of *co-constitution*. The process of co-constitution consists of three elements: the person, the situation in which he or she currently finds himself or herself, and the relationship between the two. The term "self-world relationship" is used to refer to these three fundamental aspects of behavior.

On the "self" side of the existential picture, each person faces the world and its situations, which includes others, as well as objects, on the basis of the meanings that the individual brings to them. These meaning-making factors include a tendency to perceive events in ways that are compatible with one's cultural heritage, social background, personal identity, individual preferences (including one's genetic predispositions), current degree of self-awareness, sense of agency (purpose, motivation, and free will) and, in situations that involve competence and worthiness, one's self-esteem. The "world" side concerns what a particular situation brings to a person in terms of objects, people, possibilities, and limitations. Of course, free will is always limited by reality, which is why some of us prefer the term "situated free will" to a more open-ended understanding. Behavior is represented by the hyphen in the self-world relationship because it expresses the interaction between the two co-constitutive dynamics and the outcome of such an exchange.

Phenomenologists fully appreciate that neither side is more important or more real than the other. This is why we cannot be phenomenalists who tend to emphasize the role of the subject in behavior too much to be faithful to reality. Nor can it be said that any situation announces endless possibilities: We are limited by the structure of our bodies, brains, and so forth. Consequently, it is also not possible to say that interpretation is everything as many post-modernists tend to do. Rather, both sides of the interface between person and world interact to organize, form, create, or cooperatively constitute (hence, co-constitute) human realities. This dynamic exchange between the self and the world (including the social world) is more like a dialectic or conversation than a feedback loop in that both sides allow certain possibilities to occur and both forces shape them over time until they have either played themselves out or flowed into new scenarios.

On one hand, then, the self-esteem meaning matrix formed by our inevitable developmental concerns with competence and worthiness orients us toward the world so that we are ready to perceive, react, and respond to it in these ways. On the other hand, the world and those within it address us on a number of levels, some of which mobilize these structures of meaning and experience in minor and major ways. When that happens in a way that "captures" us in terms of our self-esteem, we are mobilized and must respond in terms of worthiness and competence. The motivation to preserve a stable sense of meaning (consistency theory) and to maximize our potentials (enhancement theory) is what connects self-esteem to behavior in terms of needs and calls, which is to say motivation in general. Because the dynamics of the situation are co-constituted by individuals and the situation in which they find themselves, cause and effect inevitably flow in both directions. It is difficult to measure such "directionality" statistically because, in addition to being based on meaning, it is also fluid. Yet, as Harter (1999) pointed out, there can be little doubt that self-esteem is *at least* phenomenologically important to the experiencing person who is trying to manage the realities of life at the lived level. It is possible to illustrate the relationship between facing challenges of living authentically and self-esteem, or the link between self-esteem and behavior, as seen in Figure 5.5.

Although this interaction may at first look like a feedback system that perpetuates itself in the form of a self-fulfilling prophecy, information should never be confused with meaning. The diagram moves from left to right and is organized in terms of time (past, present, and future); let us examine the relationship between self-esteem and behavior as it is lived chronologically. Along with many other things, part of an individual's past includes his or her history of competence and of worthiness as related, but separate, developmental themes. Slowly, these two developmental processes become increasingly tied to one another so that they become intertwined dynamically in a relationship characterized by the set

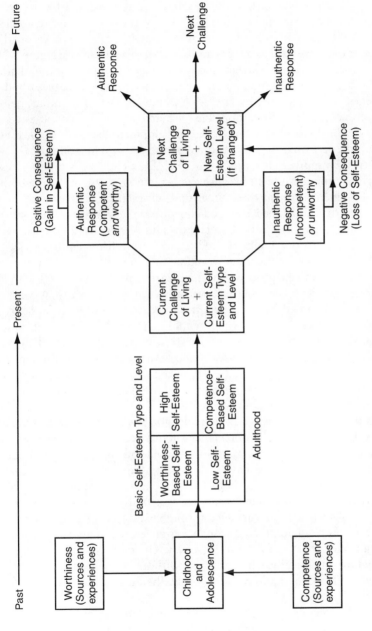

Figure 5.5   Self-Esteem and Behavior as a Co-Constitutive Process.

of checks and balances described earlier and represented by the Self-Esteem Meaning Matrix in Figure 5.1. As life is explored during adolescence, self-esteem matures to the point that it begins to take on the character of one of the basic types and levels of self-esteem (see Figure 5.2). From that point on, self-esteem emerges as a distinct phenomenon that is tied to identity. As the individual becomes increasingly capable of independent decision making by late adolescence or early adulthood, he or she becomes increasingly responsible for managing their own self-esteem, which can be done well or poorly. This development brings us to the present and the section of Figure 5.5 that represents the here and now.

Once an individual reaches this level, life's challenges take on new importance for self-esteem because they create opportunities called self-esteem moments. It is at these times that self-esteem becomes extremely active as a "variable" because it co-constitutes the structure of the situation, which means that it both influences and is influenced by what ever happens there. If one really wanted to measure self-esteem to assess its significance as a variable, these would be the times to do it! At any rate, through the complex process described earlier in this chapter, the individual resolves the situation authentically or inauthentically. When the challenge is handled in a competent and worthy fashion, it leads to a higher or positive meaning, which would be located in the upper, right-hand quadrant of the matrix. If self-esteem is already secure, then it is maintained at that level because the level was reaffirmed. If the type or level was not especially secure, then an increase in self-esteem actually occurs because it moves the matrix in a more balanced, which is to say secure, positive, healthy direction.

Unfortunately, however, things do not always go as well. On the downside of the ledger, if competence should occur without worthiness, then the outcome has little importance for self-esteem: Each of us is competent at many things that have little bearing on our self-esteem because they are not important to us in this way. If the action or failure to act is unworthy of a person, then self-esteem is actually lowered. Similarly, if worthiness is felt without earning it through exhibiting appropriate forms of competent behavior, then dissonance is generated in another way, one that can only affect self-esteem negatively. Of course, if the challenge is handled inauthentically, which is to say without competence and worthiness when they are required and possible, the outcome is certain to be a loss of self-esteem.

Finally, the last part of Figure 5.5 as we move from left to right is labeled "Future," because whatever effect the outcome of a current challenge of living has on self-esteem is meaningfully added to the matrix, which is carried into the future as a co-constitutive process along with many other psychosocial dynamics. That life never stops bringing with it new challenges of living means that self-esteem will always be a variable in our lives, sometimes weakly so, but sometimes strongly.

Co-Constitution and Stability versus Change

The last issue we need to address before moving on to showing how a phenomenological meaning-based theory can be applied at the practical level concerns understanding how self-esteem can be both relatively stable and yet open to change. We know that research concerning the development, assessment, and modification of self-esteem indicates that, once established, it becomes fairly consistent: Even unstable self-esteem constitutes a pattern of behavior that the person actually works hard to maintain, though not terribly consciously. At the same time, we also saw that self-esteem changes fairly dramatically under certain circumstances, such as when large-scale change occurs in a person's life or with regard to certain kinds of crucial challenges. By this point, it should be clear that a two-factor definition of self-esteem captures both possibilities, but now we know why. In addition, careful consideration of the matrix and the research findings in the field concerning changing self-esteem suggest that it can be altered in two ways: slow growth and sudden development.

On one hand, then, we strive to co-constitute the world so that it makes sense to us in ways that are consistent with our particular historical and social circumstances. On the other hand, the world can make maintaining stability difficult at times: It brings to us new people, different opportunities, or unexpected situations, all of which can disturb existing understandings. Some situations speak to us in terms of our competence and worthiness in ways that place additional demands on the forces that maintain stability. Challenges that are not too threatening and that are relatively easy to deal with are not terribly unpleasant because they do not require a large degree of change. This combination is one reason why the research on changing low self-esteem suggests small incremental increases may be better than larger or sudden ones (Bednar, Derezotes, Kim & Specht, 1989) for many clients, especially for people with negativistic levels of low self-esteem. At the same time, some situations unfold in ways that force us to confront our own problematic self-esteem themes more directly, meaning that they also present an opportunity for major growth or setbacks, especially with regard to authenticity or inauthenticity. The language of feedback and regulatory processes probably can be massaged into describing this existential fact, but that does not change its lived character at all. The one thing that determines whether self-esteem will change at these times is *meaning*, and there is no need to reduce that phenomenon any further.

In concluding this chapter, it is important to note that a two-factor, meaning-based approach seems to meet the requirements for a legitimate theory: It is based on a standard definition, is grounded in a tradition of work, and accounts for a great deal of research on self-esteem, some of which other theories cannot. Indeed, this approach describes how self-esteem is lived (in terms of competence and worthiness), shows how it works (on the basis of meaning), and describes the link between self-esteem and behavior (a co-constitutive process) in a way that even addresses the lack of traditional statistical support. Now let us turn to the task of moving from theory through research and to practice in order to determine whether we can use this approach to enhance self-esteem in a consistent and empirically verifiable fashion.

CHAPTER 6

A Two-Factor Self-Esteem Enhancement Program

In Chapter 4 we saw that self-esteem enhancement programs follow something of a general pattern or loose general structure. One logical way to develop a phenomenologically oriented, meaning-based enhancement program, then, is to use those same general design principles but in a way that is consistent with the fundamental structure of self-esteem. As such, this approach includes working with competence and worthiness, focusing directly on increasing self-esteem as the explicit and main focus of the work, assessing each participant in order to individualize the program, enhancing self-esteem through the use of established techniques, proceeding in a systematic fashion, and helping the participant to maintain self-esteem gains after the program ends.

There are many good clinical and research reasons for building a program on these foundations. For instance, a theoretically consistent, well-structured approach gives the client and facilitator common ground for their work together. Such a format protects the consumer because it requires the therapist to offer a specific set of guidelines and procedures instead of offering a loose collection of techniques and calling them "self-esteem enhancing." In addition, unlike more open-ended or general therapies, the steady focus provided by a structured program helps us to avoid becoming bogged down in various clinical or developmental issues that could take us far afield in the practical setting. Hence, although a good program is flexible enough to allow us to deal with issues like depression or defensiveness along the way, it is sequenced clearly enough to keep the sessions moving in a specific direction from beginning to end.

One advantage of such consistency is that it allows us to observe how people move through the process and its procedures time after time. This feature of the program means that one develops a sense of what to expect as a therapist, when to expect it, and sometimes even a sense of from whom it may come. Such information can be useful in making groups run that much more smoothly in the future. Occasionally, for example, there is a certain type of person, interpersonal response style, learning style, or personality characteristic that can interfere with the group process (Burns, 1993b; Vinogradov & Yalom, 1989). In such cases it is advantageous to anticipate when that interference is likely to happen or to plan for what might work best in a particular kind of situation based on past experience with the program. Similarly, running a reasonably well-structured program has teaching value. A structured approach allows us to identify common stumbling blocks to learning in advance of when they are likely to occur, allowing us to offer suggestions to practitioners for dealing with them from the outset. In addition, the consistency of a well-structured program has research value: It allows others to use, test, and evaluate the program in a relatively reliable, consistent fashion, which we talk more about at the end of the chapter.

Finally, if structured activities are a clear path for the facilitator, providing a look at them in advance is like also having a map for the participants. Thus, I give people an outline for the program at its beginning. This "cognitive map," which takes the form of a handout, lets them know where they are going and what self-esteem challenges they will face along the way. This simple courtesy seems to help the therapist or facilitator and participant begin to see each other as partners interested in the same quest, even though they play different roles in it. In the following pages, then, we walk through each part of the program as it is sequenced from beginning to end. The corresponding handouts for the steps that facilitate this way of searching for self-esteem are found in the appendix. It might be a good idea to turn to that section now and become familiar with the materials before moving any further.

ENHANCING SELF-ESTEEM IN THE GROUP SETTING

Although I discuss enhancing self-esteem in an individual setting later, the group version of the program is the major format for this enhancement system. This form of the program can be offered as a psychoeducational group for non-clinical populations or as a therapeutic group for clinical ones. I point out distinctions between the two when necessary and suggest guidelines to help structure them appropriately for each population. Both forms of the group are designed for about 6–12 people, plus a leader or two co-therapists. It is a good idea to keep a group designed to enhance self-esteem for clinical populations near the middle of this range, as other treatment issues are likely to crop up more frequently with this population. Combining non-clinical and clinical populations into one group is not recommended, because the latter population often moves at a much slower pace than the former. In either case, I have had the most success with groups by having a male and female working as co-therapists, but this practice is not necessary in order for the program to work. My co-therapists have been social workers, counselors, and substance abuse specialists, so the program is designed for interdisciplinary use.

The other general parameters of the program are as follows: First, its basic structure consists of a series of at least five meetings, each of which is about 2 hours long. This length of time for sessions is within recommended limits for group psychotherapy (Vinogradov & Yalom, 1989). Such a period is long enough to allow people to warm up to the session comfortably, engage in some real encounter or dialogue, and also allows some "working through" to occur. Each session is divided into approximately two 1-hour blocks with a short break between them, if necessary. I have neither run the group with people under 16-years-old, nor have I run it with clients who have less than average intelligence. It may be that such populations would do better with shorter and more frequent sessions, as Pope, McHale, and Craighead (1988) and Shrik and Harter (1999) found with their programs for children and adolescents. Second, the standard number of 2-hour sessions is five. They should be spread evenly over time, such as by meeting once per week.

How long a program should be is always an important question. The 5-week period seems to be optimal in terms of making a compromise between having enough time to work on self-esteem in a way that allows for some change to occur and for maximizing attendance in an outpatient or educational setting. On one hand, we know that changing self-esteem takes consistent time and effort. On the other hand, the simple fact is that most adults have busy lives and going beyond a limited number of sessions is likely to create problems with attendance, which would impede the group processes and diminish results. I present the program as a 5-week approach but often offer the possibility of a sixth session as a follow-up meeting. It is important to realize that although the program seems short in terms of time or length, its 10-hour treatment requirement is well within the short-term therapy format. More importantly, although the program has been shown to result in measurable change during this time period, the real aim is to teach people a set of skills that allows them to work on self-esteem well after the program stops, perhaps for a lifetime. However, people can go through the program more than once if they have such a need or interest. Thus, the criticism that the approach is "too short to help" reflects a basic misunderstanding of the program and needs to be reconsidered in this light.

For most populations, it is more realistic to create a self-esteem program that is relatively brief and well structured instead of long and open-ended. This framework also means that we are best served by using a few solid therapeutic activities rather than a large range of them, especially because there simply are not many proven self-esteem enhancement activities to consider in the first place. It takes time to learn anything well, so marathon or weekend workshops are not recommended unless one is dealing with a motivated, high-functioning audience. Also, I have found that care should be taken to do some pre-screening, even if it is only a referrals-only approach. Self-esteem is a popular topic and programs on it draw people with much more serious issues than may meet the eye. Such individuals slow down or disrupt a general population group, so it is more appropriate to refer them to a clinical or individual offering of the program. Finally, clinical groups, which often move at a slower pace and go on for a longer time, can be modified somewhat by adding a few extra sessions to make sure that everyone gets a chance to process the activities and experiences.

With these general comments out of the way, we can now go through each of the five 2-hour sessions individually. For each one, I present the basic *goal* for a given week, identify what *materials* are to be used during that period, and then present a step-by-step *procedure* to use as a method of reaching those goals. The handouts and materials are presented in the appendix instead of being included in the text so as to make them easier to use. The one thing that I cannot provide is the Multidimensional Self-Esteem Inventory (MSEI), which must be ordered separately. At the time of this writing, the address is Psychological Assessment Resources Inc., 16204 North Florida Ave., Lutz, FL 33549, Tel.: 800-331-8378. In theory, the program could be run with a simpler instrument, such as Coopersmith's Self-Esteem Inventory (1981), because its questions can be divided into those that concern competence and those that concern worthiness. Also, there is some justification for considering the use of Harter's scales if one is interested in a particular age range not covered by the MSEI (Messer & Harter, 1986). However, neither alternative includes a defensiveness scale, which is a crucial one. Of course, using other instruments would certainly require modifying some of the handouts in the program in ways that I have not tested, so I would consider using alternatives only if necessary.

Week 1: Focusing Phase

Goal

The first week is the most important for two reasons; namely, because people usually make the decision about whether to come back at this point and because it sets the general tone for the entire program.

Therefore, we have two objectives here. One is building the foundation for a focused and supportive group. This aim involves facilitating a sense of interest, comfort, and purpose so that individuals feel *safe but ready to work*. This goal represents quite a clinical challenge because it requires the facilitators to have the skills necessary to achieve rapport quickly. The other goal is to raise consciousness of self-esteem and its role in our lives because the research shows us that this should be the first task in any good, systematic self-esteem enhancement program. Ideally, the result of this initial meeting is to come to a common ground in terms of what definitions are being used in the program and what kinds of work the group will be doing together. The aim is to help each member leave the session feeling excited about coming back and stimulated to learn more about self-esteem at the next meeting.

Materials

Taken together, all of the handouts in the appendix form the basis for a self-esteem workbook. The materials that are offered in the appendix are presented here in the order in which they are used week-by-week, so that the clinician knows what to prepare before each session and how to use the corresponding materials.

1. Week 1—Handout 1: Self-Esteem Enhancement: Program Announcement. This statement simply makes it known that the program is available. It is circulated among colleagues, to potential patient populations, or to the general population, depending on the setting in which one is going to be working. The announcement also makes it clear that the group is working on self-esteem and not on other issues. The information may be written on professional stationery and modified as needed.
2. Week 1—Handout 2: Activity Schedule. This handout is the basic road map of the program, allowing people to see where they are going if they participate in the program.
3. Week 1—Handout 3: Group Guidelines and Expectations. This handout consists of the rules governing the group and the interaction between its members. The guidelines are intended to help establish a supportive, respectful code of conduct. They can also be helpful in confronting and limiting destructive or inappropriate behavior. The information is intended to facilitate the group process, encourage pro-self-esteem behavior, and address some possible ethical issues in advance.
4. Week 1—Handout 4: Defining Self-Esteem. The first stage of a standard enhancement program concerns increasing one's

awareness of self-esteem. This exercise does that by helping us to think about what self-esteem is and by taking some time to focus on competence and worthiness as we actually live them in daily life.

5. Week 1—Self-Esteem Journal. The facilitator either hands out notebooks or asks participants to buy one to use exclusively for this purpose. I recommend providing a notebook to the clients, as that tends to make the program seem more professional and actually helps motivate people to keep such a journal.

6. Week 1—Multidimensional Self-Esteem Inventory (MSEI). As mentioned in Chapter 6, this instrument is currently available through Psychological Assessment Resources Inc. This test, or something like it, is essential to the program. The leader should order this instrument well in advance. The cost for the test is relatively low and its format can easily be worked into a group setting. The fact that it is not a self-help instrument makes the program a bit more demanding on the clinician, but it also helps to distinguish it as being more empirically based.

Procedure

This session is a busy one because it serves several important functions, such as organizing the group, taking care of various administrative tasks, and beginning the program. I usually find it helpful to develop a brief program announcement such as the Self-Esteem Enhancement: Program Announcement (Week 1—Handout 1). This simple device is a convenient way of letting an agency or other therapists know that I am starting a new group and when it will be running, so that they can refer appropriate patients to it. The handout can also serve as a recruitment instrument in the private practice setting.

After the group has been announced and is gathered together for the first time, I ask everyone to sit in a semicircle so that we all can see each other. The materials are then distributed to each person. The room is always equipped with an overhead projector, chalkboard, or flip chart with plenty of blank pages, as some sort of a public workspace is needed to demonstrate some of the activities and exercises. I typically introduce myself first and offer participants a warm welcome to the "exciting search for self-esteem that we will embark upon together over the next 5 important weeks." This introduction includes letting them know a little about my credentials, background, and preference for a scientific approach to enhancing self-esteem. I usually close with some information about my own self-esteem issues and the work I am doing on them so they can know that I struggle with self-esteem, too. The use of humor whenever possible and appropriate is beneficial and I often use cartoons to illustrate points about self-esteem and its importance. However, humor must be used tastefully, especially with respect to issues concerning age, gender, and cultural diversity.

Step 1: Introducing the Program. We begin by sitting in the semicircle and looking at the Activity Schedule (Week 1—Handout 2). This outline is used to preview the program, a practice that is beneficial in several ways. In addition to providing a sense of the lay of the land, so to speak, it can put people at ease. Many individuals are a little apprehensive, even anxious, about being in the group. Sometimes they have peculiar ideas of what to expect from a psychotherapeutic or psychoeducational group. Conversely, more experienced participants can expect too much from a group. Another important point is that many people who attend such groups usually have self-esteem problems. They may feel unworthy of group attention or may feel that their social skills are limited, so it often helps them to know in advance what to expect and what is expected of them.

Part A is a general introduction to the psychology of self-esteem. I usually begin by sharing some of the more important research findings concerning self-esteem and enhancing it. The aim is to dispel some of the myths that are a by-product of the popularization of self-esteem and to give the participants a few key findings that they may trust. Although any facilitator is free to select the findings he or she feels are most important, it is often useful to talk about the "self-esteem fallacy" so that participants do not develop false expectations about rapid transformations in their self-esteem or behavior. The fallacy is, of course, that often people treat self-esteem as though it were a magic bullet for creating mental health and superior performance and that, although commonly held, this way of viewing self-esteem is incorrect. First, I point out the bad news: The research findings showing that self-esteem is only one factor affecting any given situation or behavior and often not even a statistically strong one at that. This comment tends to capture the group's attention because self-esteem has become another buzzword and I appear to contradict my own purpose. Then, I quickly follow up with the good news: Although small in effect, self-esteem is a constant force, which means that although increasing it may not make a great difference right now, even a small gain can have tremendous power over the course of time, especially a lifetime. The participants usually get this point without too much difficulty and have already begun thinking about self-esteem more realistically.

It is not a good idea to spend a long time going over the research information on self-esteem. Although tempting, to do so takes too long and the exercise is too academic: a few solid findings are easier to remember than a long list of weaker ones. Focusing on the finding that shows that the better self-esteem programs are systematic is a nice lead in to the next part of the outline, part B. This section of the material allows me to emphasize that it is possible to divide a good self-esteem enhancement program into several distinct parts and to identify them on the handout. I also quickly point out the major activities that we will be doing for each stage, which are included on the handout. This procedure helps participants to understand the specific steps that they make from week to week and that the steps are linked together to produce a cumulative effect.

This approach also helps people begin to understand that enhancing self-esteem is seen as a process rather than as an event. In addition, seeing that no threatening activities are involved in the program and assuring them that they do not have to do anything that makes them feel uncomfortable, seems to help calm those who have performance or social anxiety, a phenomenon that is to be expected in a group that consists of people who have difficulties with self-esteem. I always end this step by pointing out that we are already in the focusing phase because we are working on our awareness of self-esteem *right now*.

The next part of the introduction focuses on Group Guidelines and Expectations (Week 1—Handout 3). This material lays the foundation for how we treat one another in the group. I always try to read the guidelines and expectations aloud to stress the seriousness of the enterprise on which we are about to embark. This practice also ensures that everyone is familiar with the basic rules that govern the group and even reinforces them to some degree. The voluntary nature of the program and a statement concerning confidentially are mentioned in the introductory paragraph. Remember, the therapist, not necessarily the client, is obligated to maintain confidentiality. Therefore, it is important to make group members aware that although you are obligated to maintain their confidentiality, other group members are not. Similarly, respecting limits and differences is absolutely essential to our work, because recognizing the rights and dignity of each human being is already self-esteem enhancing. The same applies to the issue of gender, age, and cultural differences.

The comments concerning attendance are important because the program is designed in a stepwise fashion and it is difficult, though not impossible, to recover from missing even 1 week. In fact, if people anticipate missing even 2 weeks I suggest that they have to wait until another time to take the program. I encourage people to participate actively in these groups as learning and growing usually occur as a function of how much effort one puts into the process. However, it is important to remind participants that they are not required to do anything that feels uncomfortable to them and that they should let the facilitator know when they feel that way so alternatives can be offered.

By now, the participants are likely wondering if they are just going to be lectured to for 5 weeks, so at this point it is useful to engage in some basic ice-breaker activity to help them feel more comfortable and to help them see themselves as a group instead of as a collection of individuals. I typically ask participants to introduce themselves to the other members of the group by stating their first names and their interests in enhancing self-esteem. There are other standard getting-to-know-you activities that can be used here, but simple ones seem to be the least threatening. After all, it is important to remember that some people are likely to be there because they have difficulties feeling comfortable in social situations. The step takes about 30–40 minutes. It is possible to take a short break here if desired, but taking too much time tends to break the group gestalt.

Step 2: Becoming Aware of Self-Esteem. We found that a good enhancement program begins by increasing awareness of the importance of self-esteem in our lives. An excellent way to begin focusing attention on self-esteem, and to achieve a common ground from which the group can work, is by defining it. The first experiential activity of the program is guided by the material found on the handout Defining Self-Esteem (Week 1—Handout 4). It is designed to help the group do its own mini-phenomenology of self-esteem. (I seldom use that term because it is too technical for lay audiences.) I begin by presenting and explaining a simple definition of self-esteem based on competence and worthiness, which is at the top of the handout. In part I-A of the activity, participants are asked to examine their own biographies, both recent and past, for experiences in which they found themselves being competent and to describe one of them briefly on the handout. Then, they are invited to examine this experience and ask themselves what it shows about the relationship between self-esteem and competence.

A key to the exercise is taking the time to ask the group members to share these experiences and to ask what can be learned about self-esteem from them. I usually start by sharing an example of my own recent experience and then ask for volunteers to do the same. This activity helps people to see the connection between competence and self-esteem. In addition, the experiences are by and large positive, and sharing them is usually enjoyable. This work tends to help participants relax some and brings the self-esteem enhancing principle of positive feedback into play. The same procedure is repeated for worthiness in part I-B of the exercise. This one can be more difficult because worthiness is more abstract, which is why we begin with the competence dimension. Usually someone gives an example, such as an experience of helping someone, and the ball starts rolling.

Often, the effect of this activity is surprisingly strong. First, tying a definition to experience makes it more meaningful. Second, having participants share some of what they experienced or discovered helps those who might be having a hard time with this exercise, or with understanding self-esteem in terms of competence and worthiness instead of either one alone. Third, this activity makes people think about self-esteem and self-esteem moments in their own lives. Finally, this process of identifying, describing, and thinking about self-esteem is important because it prepares the group to write a self-esteem journal. As a matter of academic honesty, I also let them know that there are other ways of defining self-esteem.

Now we have shown participants that they can identify, describe, and learn from experiences of competence and worthiness in their own lives. We have also helped them to see that these experiences are connected to self-esteem and to various challenges of living. The group is now ready for its first homework assignment, which is starting the self-esteem journal as mentioned in part II of the handout. There is usually some resistance to this activity at first, probably because it requires work and people do not often write regularly. Once again, I find it helpful to give the group members a blank notebook or at least an attractively bound packet of papers for the journal. This courtesy facilitates taking the journal seriously and adds a professional touch to the program. I also point out that the group has just shown they can do this kind of work because they have already described two relevant experiences. They are told that the journal is to be written in the same way and that they should write about any positive experiences with competence and worthiness they have during the next week. It is more helpful to focus on positive experiences than on negative ones because positive reinforcement is usually more effective and because people with self-esteem problems often don't receive much of it. However, the rule is not hard and fast because "forbidding" people to write or talk about certain experiences is probably not a good idea. The importance of the journal is emphasized by adding that although they are keeping one for all the sessions, it is not graded or collected, so it can be done informally. In total, this step usually takes about 40 minutes.

Step 3: Administering the MSEI. Now we are at the end of our first meeting. Sometimes, depending on how large the group is and who is in it, participants either want to continue discussing their experiences or end the session, feeling that they have worked hard enough for the first meeting. Either way, I tell them about the research findings concerning the need to assess self-esteem. At this point, O'Brien's and Epstein's MSEI (1983, 1988) is administered *but not scored.* The form can be filled out in about 20 minutes, but some people take longer, which is why it is good to give the test at the end of the session when such differences do not require group members to wait for others to finish.

As an aside, I have found that it helps to make sure that the room being used is reserved about at least 2.5 hours to avoid any time crunches, especially for those who read or take tests slowly. Allowing people to take a little longer to fill out the form prevents them from feeling rushed: If someone else is trying to access the room, the situation may become awkward. It is important to have the testing done the first week because it stimulates participants' curiosity about themselves and encourages them to come back, if only to find out their results! We do a lot of work in this session, but people also tend to be highly motivated at this point and usually manage to complete the meeting without difficulty.

Week 2: Awareness Phase (Appreciating Self-Esteem)

Goal

The second week continues the process of increasing awareness as a first step toward enhancing self-esteem. The goal is to raise consciousness concerning the nature of self-esteem, its value, and the sources of this vital psychosocial resource. Our objectives in this work include becoming aware of the basic types and levels of self-esteem, appreciating their related problems, and identifying individual self-esteem strengths and weaknesses.

Materials

1. Week 2—Handout 1: Self-Esteem Types, Levels, and Problems. This handout is used as a general introduction to the self-esteem meaning matrix (or cross of self-esteem, depending on which metaphor is more suitable for a particular group). It is designed to introduce how problems with competence and worthiness affect self-esteem.
2. Week 2—Handout 2: Applying the Multidimensional Self-Esteem Inventory Scales. This handout is designed to help participants make sense of their scores on the MSEI, especially as the scores apply to the program.
3. Week 2—Handout 3: Finding Sources of Self-Esteem. This worksheet is based on the research findings concerning the four major sources of self-esteem. It is set up to help people get in touch with how the sources are potentially available to them.

Procedure

Step 1: Review. I usually begin this session by creating an opportunity for group members to share experiences and reflections from their self-esteem journal of the past week. Someone always seems to get the ball rolling, but sometimes it is helpful to model (which, it will be recalled, is an established self-esteem enhancement principle) by sharing my own experience. Reviewing in this way reinforces the importance of focusing on competence and worthiness as components of self-esteem, and it allows the group to see that these themes really are alive for themselves and others. In fact, all sessions begin with a review of the previous session because it facilitates the development of a cohesive group and offers an opportunity to clarify previous material.

Step 2: Determining Self-Esteem Problems. Becoming genuinely aware of the importance of self-esteem in human behavior also means knowing that there are problems associated with the lack of it. Although it is not necessary to go into great detail about the non-clinical and clinical problems, it does help the group members to become aware of how the lack or loss of competence and worthiness can lessen or impair self-esteem. The self-esteem matrix is used to do such work, which is why it is included in the handout Self-Esteem Types and Problems (Week 2—Handout 1, part I). In working with non-clinical or psychoeducational groups, it is important to stress authentic self-esteem as well as success-based, approval-based, negativistic, and, especially, medium levels of self-esteem. Although classically low, narcissistic, and anti-social levels of self-esteem are mentioned to complete the diagram; it is usually not necessary to dwell on these types. However, in working with some clinical groups, such as those who abuse substances, the more extreme areas should also receive considerable attention.

In either case, it is extremely important to emphasize that medium self-esteem is preferable to all types and levels except authentic high self-esteem. This practice is important for non-clinical or psychoeducational groups because it allows them to think about the process of moving toward the highest goals. For many clinical groups, the information lets them know that medium self-esteem is a step along the way and a worthy goal, too. Moreover, oftentimes aiming too high is an invitation to failure; for some, reaching the level of medium self-esteem is a significant achievement in itself.

The aim is to show how competence and worthiness are related to self-esteem and its problems and to address the learning styles of visually oriented participants. Sometimes there is value in asking people if they can recognize these kinds of self-esteem problems in themselves or others and to list the more common ones, as indicated in part II of the handout. Although it is necessary to talk about self-esteem problems, I try to keep the group focused on enhancing self-esteem, not on the lack of it. Group members usually are already quite good at focusing on negative phenomena, and

I do not want to reinforce that behavior. It is important to try to limit parts I and II to the first half of the session, so the best guideline to remember is to keep one's explanations clear, short, and to the point.

Step 3: Interpreting the MSEI. We know that a good self-esteem enhancement program involves assessing self-esteem and that this process can be complex. Fortunately, the MSEI is easy to administer and interpret in a group setting, providing one has the proper credentials and is familiar with the manual. However, scoring the results and writing profiles does take time and should be done by the clinician between the first and second sessions. The MSEI provides percentage and t-scores on the 11 scales for each gender, and the test manual shows how to interpret them. Remember, the normative samples are limited, and age and various cultural factors might affect scores (Sue & Sue, 1990), so I recommend a simple scoring and interpretive procedure when working in the group formation. The handout that I have designed for this purpose is labeled Week 2—Handout 2: Applying the Multidimensional Self-Esteem Inventory Scales. The handout is constructed so that it presents the 11 scales at the top of the page and then presents only 4 for a given individual: the two highest scores and the two lowest scores. This streamlined presentation of results allows me to individualize the scores in a way that is meaningful for the participant, without having to either explain t-score conversions or go over the complete profile for each person, either of which would be unwieldy in a group setting.

To save time, I begin the interpretive process by going over the 11 scales and by grouping them into three clusters: general self-esteem indices, those that are related to competence, and those that are connected to worthiness. One may even develop a brief handout that explains all the scales if that seems desirable for a particular group. Then, I ask participants to look at their two highest and their two lowest scores and to make sure they understand what those scores mean. I answer questions to make sure that everyone has the opportunity to clarify what the results are suggesting for them and then ask if they can identify with the findings. Usually most people say "Yes," which makes the test seem more credible to the group. The individual practitioner is free to present the results in other ways or to use other forms, but I caution against becoming overly technical with the reports and against getting bogged down with too many details.

The MSEI provides several kinds of information about an individual's self-esteem that can be useful in the program. The Global Self-Esteem scale, for instance, is a composite figure that tells us something about the individual's general level of self-esteem. Another general scale, the Identity Integration score, is less useful because identity is such a complex, abstract topic. However, it can give some indication about the likelihood of other psychological issues that may have to be dealt with before self-esteem can really become a project, such as finding out about one's own values (which can be done through values clarification work). I have found the Identity Integration Scale to be helpful when the individual does not find that any of the other scales speak to their experience of themselves. In this situation, for example, a person might report that they are going through a major crisis or life transition and simply do not know who they currently are. Showing them that such a phenomenon can be helped by the program gives them more confidence in the program itself; if it does not, a referral may be made to a more appropriate treatment program.

Perhaps the most useful and fascinating scale is the one for defensiveness. It is crucial to remember that scores on this scale are arranged in a way that is opposite of the others. Whereas high scores on the other scales are generally positive, high scores on the defensiveness scale usually indicate that there is likely to be a problem with self-esteem. Such scores suggest that the individual is anxious about his or her self-esteem, often in ways that are difficult to detect upon first glance, as in the case of the successful overachiever. This scale is also useful in detecting various forms of unstable or fragile self-esteem, such as being too moralistic, rigid, or self-deceptive. Occasionally, people present themselves this way and have enough insight to know about such things, but often they do not. Therefore, it is important to treat interpreting this scale, as well as those who score high on it, with as much sensitivity as possible. At first, such a person might be difficult to reach, but sometimes asking if they tend to have trouble admitting to mistakes, or if they are easily hurt by criticism even though they may not show it, allows them to get past the point of resistance. Sometimes, such individuals even become the most appreciative participants as the group moves on because they begin to make insights that bring them a sense of relief. If the person does not respond favorably, at least the scale alerts us to the need to be cautious when interacting with him or her.

The heart of the test consists of eight subscales that assess various domains of self-esteem. These basic self-esteem scales can be grouped together as reflecting either competence or worthiness. On the one hand, what the test calls Competence, Personal Power (or influence), Self-Control, and Body Functioning are behaviorally based or action-oriented qualities. Each one concerns an individual's ability to perform certain identifiable skills that can be evaluated to yield some measure of competence (or the lack of it). On the other hand, the qualities of Lovability, Likability, Moral Self-Approval, and Body Appearance are more value oriented, and they range in importance in terms of being worthy (or not).

I always close this part of the session by offering participants the opportunity to ask questions about their results.

Requiring people to consider both the areas in which they are strong as well as the areas in which they are weak is useful because there is a tendency for participants to pay too much attention to the negative aspects of their self-esteem assessment. Indeed, allowing such a negative drift to occur too often or too long in the group can actually reinforce self-esteem problems. Also, we saw that increasing success is a valid route to self-esteem and it is sometimes better to encourage this possibility by working with a client's strengths rather than with their weaknesses. Some people suffer such serious self-esteem problems that they can only afford to work on increasing what little strength they have before they can address more difficult challenges. Participants are then instructed to start tracking these positive and negative self-esteem themes in their journals, which should help them to increase their awareness of self-esteem as they live it.

Step 4: Finding Sources of Self-Esteem. Now that we have assessed self-esteem, it is important to be aware of its potential sources, especially those that are most readily available within the context of our own lives. The handout for this activity, Finding Sources of Self-Esteem (Week 2—Handout 3), lists each major source of self-esteem we found in the research, namely, personally significant achievements or successes, evidence of influence or power, acceptance or being valued by others, and virtue or acting on beliefs. It is helpful to point out that these four sources of self-esteem are based on competence (achievements and influence) and worthiness (acceptance and virtue). After I describe the characteristics of each source, I include an example of a recent experience I have had in each area. Then, the participants are asked to try and identify one or two recent experiences of their own in each of the four areas.

Some people complete this activity quite easily, but others have a hard time with it because they tend to look for only major achievements, influence, actions, or acceptance. Occasionally, people worry that they do not seem to have much material to put into one or more of the categories, so there is some value in having members share their work. Sooner or later, a person says something like, "It makes me feel good about myself when I find my child waiting for me at the door when I come home from work," or "Someone was having a problem doing something at work today and I was able to show him how to do it: that made me feel that I have something to offer." Usually, others in the group then begin to look for small, but readily available, potential sources of self-esteem in their own lives.

Another factor to be aware of when working with the group is that self-esteem environments vary considerably. For instance, some life situations make one source of self-esteem more or less accessible than others and not everyone is going to be able to readily find all four sources. The point is to let people know that these four basic sources of self-esteem really do exist and that they need to be aware of which ones are most likely to be available *in their own set of circumstances*. It is good practice to take some time to make sure that each member of the group becomes aware of at least one realistic source of self-esteem that can function as a viable option for him or her, because having access to one of them is necessary for the program to work. In some cases, presenting the self-esteem bucket metaphor through words or a diagram is helpful. The point to stress is that all that the bucket needs to be "good enough" is for "water" to be put into it from at least one source of competence and one source of worthiness with some degree of regularity. Finally, we turn to the journal and ask participants to track the ways in which these potential sources of self-esteem manifest themselves during the next week. This information is used again at the end of the program.

Week 3: Enhancing Phase (Increasing Worthiness)

Goal

The third week marks the beginning of the enhancement phase, which actually constitutes two sessions, or weeks, of the program. As before, the session begins with a review of the previous week's homework to reinforce the material that was learned and the need to be aware of the importance of self-esteem. Once again, participants are asked to share their experiences in the form of an open review. By now, they are usually comfortable enough with each other and with the group as a whole for me to begin encouraging individuals who seem to need a little help participating more actively. The group typically starts to come together as a therapeutic enterprise at this point, just as it becomes time for them to start taking some small risks by participating in activities designed to increase worthiness and competence, and therefore self-esteem.

Materials

Note that all three materials for this stage of the program come from our findings concerning the most valid self-esteem enhancement techniques.

1. Week 3—Handout 1: Enhancing Worthiness through Positive Feedback.
2. Week 3—Handout 2: Increasing Worthiness through Cognitive Restructuring.
3. Week 3—Handout 3: Pattern-Breaking Outline.

Procedure

The major activity this week is to work on what I euphemistically call self-esteem "gumption traps" (Pirsig, 1974), which is a phrase describing how we often create and fall into self-esteem problems that are particularly vexing because they lessen our sense of worthiness. If the phrase "gumption trap" seems awkward, then "self-esteem trap" may be used. These self-esteem traps are powerful, co-constitutive processes. For example, they help us to experience ourselves as being less worthy than we are and to move through the situations of life as though we are genuinely unworthy, thereby keeping us locked into our own negative self-esteem themes. These are not the times in life when we face a challenge, try our best, and still fail. Those events do lower self-esteem and challenge our competence, but having tried our best, we maintain our worthiness. Instead, we are asking people to identify the *habitual and unnecessary* ways that they work to maintain low, unstable, or fragile self-esteem. We use two exercises to facilitate this transformation. The first one is more humanistic and involves actually experiencing that about ourselves that is already worthy, even though we may tend to hide it from awareness. The second, which is based on the principles of cognitive therapy, involves identifying and disrupting the habits of mind often called "thinking patterns" that lead to a lower than appropriate sense of worthiness.

Step 1: Enhancing Worthiness. This exercise is usually a rather pleasant, highly meaningful activity that is designed to help participants get in touch with their positive (worthy) qualities and to do so in a supportive environment where others are genuinely accepting of them. The exercise involves asking participants to fill out the Enhancing Worthiness through Positive Feedback sheet (Week 3—Handout 1, part A), which involves writing down 10 positive qualities or attributes about oneself. The list is also shared with the group in part B.

Occasionally, a person is unable to complete the list. There are two reasons this situation occurs. First, people tend to look for unusually significant achievements or outstanding qualities. Many of us would have a hard time coming up with 10 of those, so it is important to tell participants that things we easily overlook are also indications of worthiness, such as being a good parent, being faithful to one's word or spouse, and so on. Second, low or competence-based self-esteem can interfere with a person's ability to perceive or identify worthy things about himself or herself. Sometimes the individual feels so unworthy that he or she thinks there is *nothing* good to say about himself or herself. Indeed, I still remember one woman who dropped out of a group because she felt unworthy of feeling worthy about herself! Fortunately, she went back to individual therapy. However, this experience taught me that worthiness is more of an issue than sometimes meets the eye, especially when working with someone who led a lifestyle that incurred considerable social disapproval, such as addiction, prostitution, and so forth. Offering the group a small number of realistic examples and giving participants time to reflect on their positive qualities seems to help them complete the activity, although, occasionally, some still do not fill in all the blanks. When this happens, it can be helpful to ask if they heard anything on someone else's list that applies to them and, if so, to add it to their own list.

Reading the lists aloud should be done with considerable sensitivity because some people learn that saying positive things about themselves is "wrong" (a sign of a being a braggart or a violation of the principle of humility), or they are only accustomed to vocalizing their negative qualities. I usually begin by reading my own list to show participants that it is all right to say positive things about oneself and to get the ball rolling. Then I ask for volunteers and try to make sure everyone has an opportunity to participate. It is easy to dismiss this exercise as a popular psychology gimmick, such as reading the list every morning while standing before a mirror. There is little evidence that such methods work and it is important to make sure people know that doing such a thing is *not* the point. Instead, the exercise is designed to be done once, as part of the group, and that it is done for two good reasons.

First, some people feel so unworthy about themselves or come from environments that affirm so little about who they are, that they may even weep when they realize that they actually have a number of real, identifiable, positive qualities. At such times, the rest of the group sees how special the moment is and respond with comments of affirmation and appreciation; these words are often more healing than those any therapist can offer. For example, sometimes group members spontaneously give a soft round of applause or begin to share their own difficulties in thinking or speaking well of themselves. These self-esteem moments can be moving and certainly are self-esteem enhancing. Second, although this activity has less empirical support for its effectiveness than others, it is actually a variation of established self-esteem enhancement techniques we discuss in Chapter 3: increasing self-esteem through acceptance and by using positive feedback. This activity helps us make the transition from mere learning to learning in an atmosphere that involves sharing, camaraderie, and above all, acceptance, which are necessary for a self-esteem group to be effective.

Step 2: Introducing the Concept of Cognitive Restructuring. The first part of the session usually takes about a half hour. Then, we turn to the handout Week 3—Handout 2: Increasing Worthiness Through

Cognitive Restructuring. Most mental health professionals are familiar with this practice and we have already found that it is used in self-esteem work. Because the concept is discussed earlier, it is not to be detailed again here. However, it is important to remember that this information is often new to clients. Therefore, it is best to present the information clearly and walk them through it step-by-step. First, it is helpful to explain the basic idea behind this cognitive intervention, which is part A of the handout. This procedure usually involves a discussion about self-talk, the self-fulfilling prophecy, and self-defeating behavior. I tend to use those terms instead of meaning, directionality, or co-constitution because people are more familiar with them, and because the terms are often used in the cognitive literature with which more therapists (and clients) are familiar. The important things to emphasize are (1) the idea that distorted, irrational, illogical, or unwarranted thinking (whichever term one prefers) leads to unwarranted perceptions, negative feelings, and dysfunctional behavior; and (2) if we correct such cognitive mistakes, then our perceptions, feelings, and behaviors are likely to change as well.

Next, we turn to parts B and C and combine them by giving people an example of making such errors from one's own life and what it means to do so. For instance, I might begin by telling them about a time when a relationship I was involved in was ended by the other person and how my "self-talk" (meaning making) at the time helped create (co-constitute) a higher degree of pain for me than was actually necessary. "There I sat in my lonely apartment," I might say, "convinced that no one would ever love me again because I was such a loser." Then, I ask participants to identify which "traps" I had fallen into as they look over the list of common mistakes presented in the handout. Usually, there are several possibilities to consider.

In this example, labeling often comes to mind fairly quickly, which suggests that the group is learning to use the terms in an appropriate way. I take some time to point out that it is usually necessary and appropriate for a person to be sad over a loss; otherwise, participants may develop exaggerated expectations about the value or effectiveness of this technique. Then, I emphasize that the point is that one does not have to suffer *unduly* over a negative event, such as by becoming depressed. This activity may be done with good humor, as well as instruction. Indeed, sometimes the session becomes quite lively as we all learn to laugh at ourselves a bit more easily. Be careful about what is disclosed, however, because it may be similar to what someone in the group is currently working on, which means that you may fall prey to a transference situation. One time, for instance, I used this example and a person in the group who had just left someone reacted poorly to the anecdote, and it was necessary to work through that before moving on in the session.

The idea is to help individuals become aware of the negative patterns or "worthiness traps" they happen to use most often. In earlier editions, I limited myself to 10 "standard" terms associated with well-known approaches to show that the technique is supported by clinical literature. Since then, this practice has become so well accepted that it is not necessary to proceed in that way. In fact, when I compared several of the major lists available (Burns, 1980; Leahy, 2003; McKay & Fanning, 2000) I found that there are over 20 terms that are used to describe cognitive errors, flaws, or distortions that get in the way of realistic perception and experience. Although it might be helpful to list all the terms, the same item is often defined in different ways by different authors and keeping all of them in mind would be quite a task. A more useful approach is to look for those that run across the major lists.

The result of such an examination is as follows: With minimal modification, five basic terms were used in all three approaches: Labeling, Filtering, Overgeneralizing (which also showed up in the research on self-esteem in Chapter 3), Personalizing, and Emotional Reasoning. Some version of several more terms also showed up on at least two lists: Mind Reading, Fortune Telling, Catastrophizing, Dichotomous Thinking, and Should Statements. In other words, there are a number of good, standard terms from which to choose. The list I offer in the handout consists of the first set of five because they are the most universal terms. It also turns out that the most frequently discussed errors are negative in a way that tends to undermine a sense of worthiness more than competence, which is, of course, what makes them most appropriate to this part of the program. However, a number of lines are left blank in the handout so that a clinician can add ones that he or she is comfortable with too. For example, I usually include catastrophizing because it is a common cognitive distortion and people seem to relate to it well, including the author. Of course, it is helpful to go over each term, give examples of each one, and allow the group members to ask questions to ensure that everyone understands what is meant.

Step 3: Using Cognitive Restructuring. Now comes the time to show the group how to use the technique to alter patterns that help to co-constitute a life of fragile, unstable, or low self-esteem. Once again, there are several systems from which to choose (Freeman, Pretzer, Fleming & Simon, 1990) such as those I mentioned earlier. The main difference between them is that the number of steps they use to reduce the negative effects of such habits of thought varies. In any case, the general idea is straightforward. First, it involves teaching people how to examine situations that bring them pain and to note the thoughts they have during those times. Then, the individual examines the cognitions for ones that fit a given list of common errors. Each mistake is identified, named, and corrected. At the end of the process, the individual re-evaluates his or her feelings to determine whether he or she has changed in appropriate ways. The process is then repeated until the person's reactions correspond to the events as realistically as possible. The aim is threefold: to help the group understand how people trap themselves in ways that generate excessive pain, to learn how to identify that process when it is actually happening, and to become able to control thinking and feeling in a way that increases a sense of worthiness rather than suffering the usual decrease that otherwise occurs.

Whatever version of this approach is selected by the therapist, it is *essential* to walk people through the process step-by-step and to do so several times. I happen to use a seven-step method when starting out because it is usually the most detailed approach and reveals the entire process most clearly to beginners. We turn to the material labeled Week 3—Handout 3: Pattern-Breaking Outline when moving into this stage of the work. After identifying the seven steps presented in the handout in part A, I usually show how they are to be used by working one of my own recent problems in front of the group. That procedure is represented as part B of the handout.

Typically, I begin by drawing a long horizontal line across the board, flip chart, or screen in front of the group and number sections of it 1 through 7. Then, I describe a situation that is troubling me and identify it under as step 1 on the line. Next, I name my strongest feelings and rate their intensity to complete the second step. In step 3, I reflect on what was going through my mind at the time (without embarrassing myself too much) and try to simply state my own thoughts as they actually occurred. Step 4 involves asking the group to help me identify the illogical, "irrational" (Ellis & Harper, 1977), "distorted" (Burns, 1980), or generally dysfunctional part of my thinking, according to the list of errors or distortions presented in the previous handout. Now that the group is involved, I ask them to offer a rational alternative for my distorted thinking to complete step 5. Then, we proceed to step 6 and reevaluate my own feelings in front of the group, showing that there is a real gain involved in doing this kind of work. I always point out that even a "measurable" reduction in intensity is better than what I was experiencing before we went through the exercise. Finally, we move to step 7 and begin with the next strongest feeling I had, repeating the process until I feel a significant reduction in distress.

I emphasize that it is important to outline every step by writing them down, because we can fall into these worthiness eroding self-esteem traps easily or fool ourselves by thinking it is sufficient to do the steps mentally. It is helpful to point out that, like any bad habit, these cognitive patterns have been learned over the course of a lifetime and that it is difficult to unlearn them quickly. The authors of these techniques have had their work confirmed by independent research, and each of them stresses the importance of the work of writing things down and going through *all* the steps on paper. These habits of meaning making are so well practiced and ingrained that it takes something like writing to slow down cognitive and perceptual patterns enough to identify, let alone disrupt, them. Changing such habits of mind requires even more work, which is why the process has to be repeated many times before progress occurs. Being methodical also helps reinforce the importance of thinking more realistically.

To be sure the participants get the point and to ensure that they know how to use the program, I turn to part C. Here, I ask a participant to allow me to help him or her work through the system in front of the group using a recent experience that affected self-esteem. This part of the session is always done after obtaining permission from an individual. All the work is shown on the board, in front of the group, and in an accepting fashion. After one or two times, the group typically becomes relaxed. People begin to volunteer to have their experience processed and eventually I have the group tell me what to put on the board as we go through each of the steps. This part of the process is crucial to the program's success and can be fun. Finally, the last step of the activity involves a homework assignment, which is to continue to practice the technique and record results in the journal. Of course, it is possible for a clinician to use a similar cognitive restructuring technique, providing it can be worked into the same time frame.

Week 4: Enhancing Phase (Increasing Competence)

Goal

The fourth week continues the enhancement phase of the program, but the focus shifts from working on worthiness to developing competence. This phase may be lengthened to include more activities than I have included here. If, for instance, we were working in a long-term group situation, then we could focus on learning to stand up for ourselves through assertiveness training. However, learning such sophisticated skills usually takes several weeks (Rakos, 1990). Therefore, the fourth session aims to round out the enhancement phase by increasing competence in other ways.

Materials

These materials are designed to aid the group's work on skills and abilities and not just making group members feel good about themselves; the latter is the major criticism of the anti–self-esteem movement mentioned in Chapters 1 and 3. The group can help accomplish this task by remembering that the fundamental structure of self-esteem shows us how competence balances worthiness and vice versa. Thus, the next set of activities focuses on the behavioral dimensions of self-esteem, or how we *earn* it.

1. Self-esteem journal data.
2. Week 4—Handout 1: Enhancing Competence: Problem-Solving Method.
3. Week 4—Handout 2: Enhancing Competence: Problem-Solving Worksheet.

Procedure

Step 1: Review. The session begins with a review of the cognitive restructuring technique. I start by asking the group to share examples from their journals, but this time I also ask permission to diagram one situation on the board and have the group work through it with me from beginning to end. I repeat this procedure until I am sure everybody knows how to use the technique. There are several reasons for beginning this way. One is that we are trying to help people acquire a new skill that must become a habit to work effectively. Such learning takes time and people often make mistakes in the early stages, just as any novice might. Also, the old habits are so powerful and so automatic that people are likely to be trapped by them again and again, despite attempts by others to intervene. Repeating the process reinforces new ways of dealing with these old self-esteem traps. Finally, by going over them publicly participants get to see that someone else in the group actually found relief using this method. Often, hearing others talk about how they broke out of a trap, even if momentarily, lends credibility to the technique, gives hope for the future, and underscores the program's value.

It should be noted that some of the cognitive (co-constitutive) distortions we commit are trickier to deal with than others. Working through participants' problems on the board allows us to use our professional expertise to help with some of the more subtle self-esteem traps. For instance, I find that one of the most difficult distortions with which to deal is that of a person who co-constitutes a situation through what Burns (1980) called "emotional reasoning." I like to call this particular distortion "Yeah, but," which is a phrase a student of mine coined when she noticed that those seem to be the words people use most often when they are engaged in emotional reasoning. Let me illustrate this phenomenon because it can be disruptive to the group process if it is not dealt with successfully.

Typically, those who reason emotionally begin by presenting a situation that is genuinely unpleasant. They work what happened through the steps but see only a slight reduction in feeling intensity. Rather than just accept the fact that the situation is simply an uncomfortable one, or instead of being satisfied with a realistic reduction in negative affect, they start up all over again. Usually, such individuals offer superficial agreement by saying something like "Yes, I see what you mean, but . . .," then slip right back into reasoning illogically through the overuse of emotion. Although it may take several repetitions of going through the steps, having the individual work on each "Yeah, but" often helps them to understand how they are distorting the situation to keep it more painful than it needs to be. For example, someone might keep going back to being betrayed in a relationship again and again and again because the feeling of anger allows him or her to avoid facing the loss that comes with endings. "If only this . . . or if only that. . ." is another variation on this theme that can be used to achieve the same distorted end. When a participant manages to realize the nature of this particular trap in the session, the event can be a powerful lesson for the individual, as well as for the group, because it shows that even the most stubborn distortions can be broken.

Step 2: Enhancing Competence through Problem Solving. The second activity of the session, which usually comes after the break, continues to follow the two-factor, meaning-based theory of self-esteem by building on the connection between self-esteem and competence. The goal is to help participants learn a skill that increases their ability to better deal with the challenges of life. The single most powerful tool for this purpose is learning to solve problems effectively. After all, increasing this ability should increase an individual's chance of success in a variety of situations, which, in turn, could lead to a greater demonstration of competence over time.

D'Zurilla and Goldfried (1971) pioneered work in this area and D'Zurilla and Nezu (2001) refined it later. Pope, McHale, and Craighead (1988) applied this technique to helping children enhance self-esteem. Like correcting mental errors, problem solving therapy has evolved into several different types of formats. However, the ideas and practices remain fairly stable: Learning how to better solve problems of living involves understanding that something is a problem, developing a plan of action, and then implementing it. This technique is chosen here because it is theoretically sound, nicely compatible with a theory of self-esteem based on competence and worthiness, reasonably well researched, and relatively easy to both demonstrate and use.

We begin by turning to the first handout for this session, Enhancing Competence: Problem-Solving Method (Week 4—Handout 1). Although the temptation is to go directly to the problem-solving steps listed in part B, it is important to spend some time on the theory behind good problem solving in part A. This practice helps participants appreciate that feeling, thinking, and behaving are distinct parts of the process, which is important because sometimes they have trouble distinguishing between one or more areas. For instance, I still find that men tend to have more difficulty than women with recognizing feelings, which often means that men have more trouble detecting early signs of a developing problem. All too often this tendency means that things have to get worse before they can get better. Thus, taking the time to explain the value of being able to identify and listen to feelings is helpful for many clients who have not been socialized in this way. Then, I present and describe the 8 steps identified in part B.

The next part of the session consists of walking the participants through the steps of the problem-solving process format presented in the handout for this part of the session, Week 4—Handout 2: Enhancing Competence: Problem-Solving Worksheet, much in the way that we did with cognitive self-esteem traps. I usually begin by listing in order all the steps and procedures from part A on the board, which may be done in a vertical or horizontal fashion, although I find the latter more useful. Next, I take a problem I am facing in my own life that is not too personal or overly complex and work it through the process step-by-step. In other words, I first identify a problem and list it. Then, as step 2 indicates, I stop and think about the difficulty and try to articulate what is really bothering me about this problem so that we are able to take the third step and decide what a *realistic* goal would be in dealing with this particular issue.

Next, we think about potential solutions to this particular problem and do some group brainstorming to generate a number of possibilities. This fourth step of identifying possible solutions may be a little tricky because people tend to want to evaluate the relative merits of each possible solution as it is offered. Someone, for instance, often says, "Well, that sure won't work," and I have to remind the group that we are not yet evaluating solutions, just trying to list as many possibilities as we can. After writing all the possible solutions on the board, we move to the fifth step, where we evaluate the alternatives individually. The typical approach is to think about the likely consequences for each one. Putting them in some kind of order in terms of what a solution "gets me" versus what it will "cost me" is helpful. Next, in the sixth step, I select the best alternative listed earlier. Note that what makes this step "best" is that it is the one that offers something of a real solution but at a cost an individual is willing to pay. In other words, the most effective solution is sometimes not chosen because it requires more work than the individual is willing to do. Then, of course, it is important to take the time to make a realistic plan of how to implement the decision I made. Paying close attention to detail is important because people usually make plans that are doomed to fail. Therefore, in this seventh step I ask the group to help me identify each specific activity that must be completed to implement the solution and to assist me in placing them in the order that is necessary for them to take me to the goal. Finally, I add another step that is not on most of the other versions of the technique, which is the need to practice problem solving before deciding on whether or not it works. Many people try the method, find that it did not make the problem go away, and give up on the technique. Reminding them of this aspect of the learning process helps reduce frustration and helps participants increase their problem-solving skills.

After going through this practice run, we make the exercise more realistic by asking people to volunteer problems for part B. Of course, we work each one out on the board by asking the group to process the problem each step of the way. As the facilitator, I clarify their responses and write them on the board for all to see. The same procedure is repeated until we run out of time, and then the whole group is instructed to practice using this technique for the next week and to record their experiences in their self-esteem journals. Participants often seem pleased to be receiving training in problem solving, and even the most skeptical group members tend to see it as a tangible benefit of the program that is readily transferable to real life. Usually, someone agrees to think about what has been done here, use the technique on a particular problem, and report back to us on his or her experience of the problem at the next meeting.

There are some points to remember in working both the cognitive restructuring and the problem-solving activities. For one thing, it is helpful to model them for the group, which in this case, is done both by the facilitator's working through a problem and by working through problems from the group. Modeling not only shows each step of the process more clearly but, as we have already seen, is itself a valid self-esteem enhancement technique that is tied to competence. Trying things out also allows us to help dispel certain kinds of difficulties, such as the mistaken belief that these techniques make one feel great or work overnight. For example, participants might say that even though their pain or uncomfortable feelings have been reduced by this or that technique, they still feel bad. At this point it is necessary to emphasize that the goal is to be realistic, which means understanding that sometimes circumstances are simply uncomfortable. In these situations, even a reduction in pain or anxiety is a net gain, which fully justifies using the technique. This happens with problem solving in that some participants say something like "OK, I've done what you want, but I still have a problem" or "None of the alternatives are good ones." It is often necessary to remind people that these techniques are not magical, just rational, and that they at least help us find the best ways to deal with problems or challenges of living.

Finally, we must consider the fact that the principle of practice is more important at this point in the program than ever before. By this time, people tend to groan about the journal writing (and sometimes that does fall off). However, by now they also see the importance of doing the actual work, so I often try to reinforce the value of practicing by using the following analogy. The idea is to compare learning how to restructure one's thinking and response patterns with other forms of learning that participants can relate to more easily, like weight lifting or joining an exercise class: One starts out slowly and the first few attempts are crude and uncomfortable, but gains come if one sticks to the activity for a reasonable length of time. In other words, increasing self-esteem is just like any other complex learning activity: It takes time and work. I conclude by asking once again, "Why should you expect anything else when so many years have gone into learning to develop a self-esteem problem?"

Week 5: Management Phase (Maintaining Self-Esteem)

Goal

The fifth week deals with two related issues. First, the group meetings are coming to an end. Any experienced clinician knows about the importance of dealing with issues such as termination, separation anxiety, and the sadness of losing something. Second, and more important, ending the group means that its members no longer are able to count on the discipline or structure offered by weekly meetings to help them focus their awareness or to reinforce the gains that have been made during the program. The group members might need to be reminded that complex learning takes time and that they have invested only a few weeks. Thus, the finding we uncovered—that good programs must deal with the problem of maintaining self-esteem—turns out to be an important one indeed, and this concern becomes the focus of the last regular meeting. Note that I use the term *managing* instead of maintaining self-esteem because management is much more active, dynamic, and future oriented than is maintenance, which implies holding ground more than making advances.

Materials

The fundamental structure of self-esteem was found to consist of competence, worthiness, and the relationship between them. Consequently, the following materials are designed to bring together the work that we have done on both components in a balanced fashion so that they work together to create more self-esteem.

1. Self-esteem journal data.
2. Week 5—Handout 1: Building a Self-Esteem Enhancement Project.
3. Week 5—Program Evaluation Sheet (clinician's design).

Procedure

Step 1: Review. As usual, the session begins with a review of what the members of the group did with the problem-solving homework from the last session. Usually, one person presents a positive experience and another presents an example in which the technique failed. Both experiences are good grist for the therapeutic mill: the former reinforces, as any testimonial tends to do, and the latter gives us an opportunity to practice once again. At this point, I have the group tell me what steps should be used as we walk through the particular problem. Such an active review reminds participants to use the method correctly and practicing it serves as an opportunity to reinforce the learning process. This step should take no more than 45 minutes.

Step 2: Introducing the Concept of Managing Self-Esteem. Remember, self-esteem involves facing the challenges of living in a worthy way over time. The key to the program, then, is to help people find ways to build on the work done to date and take it into the future with them. The critical aspects of this endeavor include offering a way of continuing to be aware of self-esteem as a vital psychosocial resource in everyday life; finding individualized ways of becoming more worthy as a person and more competent at living; and remembering how important it is to manage self-esteem effectively so that, throughout life, self-esteem is earned more often than it is lost. One way to help participants that also fulfills these requirements is to show them how to make self-esteem an ongoing personal project, something that is done by developing a "self-esteem action plan."

The activity for this week, which is presented in Building a Self-Esteem Enhancement Project (Week 5—Handout 1), is divided into two parts. Part I is a visual representation of the idea of a self-esteem action cycle. I organize this information as a cycle to show people how maintaining or increasing self-esteem works conceptually. Also, the diagram is helpful in explaining the process before we go through its steps. Thus as the chart indicates, participants are told that the current (or lived) status of their self-esteem is where we must start, no matter where it is. Moving clockwise, the next step is to identify one self-esteem issue to work on that is especially important or appropriate *right now* in one's life. Once such a goal is identified, we can use the information acquired from other parts of the program to build an individualized self-esteem project. This means targeting a source of self-esteem that is capable of increasing worthiness or competence, or both, and setting up a plan to get there by using our problem-solving skills. We work on reaching the goal through practice, which eventually results in new learning and in an increase of competence, worthiness, or both. Because acquiring more competence and more worthiness is additive (Harter, 1999), completing the cycle in this way shifts our position on the self-esteem matrix in a positive direction. Sometimes it is helpful to make a copy of Figure 5.5, which shows how self-esteem is lived in adulthood, so that participants understand why they are being asked to construct such a plan and how it will help them in the future. I also point out that one may always repeat the process and that always keeping a self-esteem project "going" at least maintains our awareness of self-esteem over time.

Step 3: Building a Self-Esteem Action Plan. Now we move to part II of the handout and walk participants through the steps one at a time in a way that requires them to build a plan. There are two reasons for doing so. First, this practice allows us to check the work to see if participants really understand the cycle. Second, the exercise is designed to move into that future with them: if done correctly, the plan that is developed here also becomes the first self-esteem project that they work on once the group is over. Once again, the worksheet for this step is set up to be done in a stepwise fashion under the direction of the facilitator who acts as teacher, coach, and troubleshooter for this process.

First, in part II-A, group members are asked to identify a self-esteem area that they wish to improve. Our work with the MSEI on identifying self-esteem strengths and weaknesses becomes important once again. A person whose self-esteem is relatively healthy is best served by building a project around a content area that scored low on the test. Such an individual is likely to be able to tolerate looking at shortcomings without becoming defensive or discouraged, which helps them to take a "fast track" toward increasing self-esteem. However, a person with a more serious self-esteem problem already focuses on his or her vulnerabilities, so that individual is better served by taking another slower and more gentle approach. In this case, working to improve functioning in an area where one is already doing at least moderately well is more effective. This type of plan leads to an increase in the self-confidence that success brings with it, which could help the person gain enough confidence to move on to more complex tasks. I usually leave the choice up to the members, but I do suggest these basic guidelines to them as they are selecting an area for improvement.

Next, members are instructed to match the nature of their self-esteem theme with an appropriate source of self-esteem by using the four basic sources they worked with in Week 2—Handout 3. This information is to be written in part II-B on the worksheet for the current step to help focus awareness. The activity also helps participants build an efficient program because they can begin to look for the kinds of self-esteem opportunities they need to make a given project successful. Individuals who suffer from difficulties with competence, for instance, might think about increasing various skills that could help them to have more achievements or influence. Some relevant possibilities in this regard include learning how to speak more effectively and taking a leadership-training course. Those who score lower on worthiness scales might seek out interpersonal opportunities that could lead to being accepted or valued more, such as doing volunteer work. Or they could look for ways to act more virtuously, even if it is just to work on eliminating a bad habit. Indeed, it is important to note that it is useful to deal with a negative behavioral pattern that undermines self-esteem in a given individual's life. Behaviors that end up making a person experience a loss of worthiness because they feel "wrong" to begin with, such as giving in to a negative temptation, are especially detrimental to self-esteem.

Notice that although either competence or worthiness is emphasized in any given project, the other component is active as well. When encouraging the individual to increase competence, we also want them to do that to reach worthy goals, not unworthy ones. When helping someone to increase their sense of worthiness, we want them to do so by being virtuous or by behaving in ways that facilitate being valued for positive qualities that they actually demonstrate, not through mere passive acceptance or blanket approval. Self-esteem always involves both competence and worthiness because it takes one to balance the other in theory and in practice.

The next part, labeled II-C on the activity sheet, brings the problem solving skills work done during the last session into play. Here, we ask individuals to examine their self-esteem needs, to consider the ways in which the source of self-esteem they are focusing on manifests itself concretely in their own lives, and to generate some goals that are realistic in terms of their own situation and abilities. Once again, the tendency is for people to set their sights a little too high, so I help by asking them to decide on one or two goals that are meaningful and realistic. Sometimes it is helpful to go around the room asking participants what they are targeting as a goal so that others get some ideas. It is also possible to ask participants to work in pairs to help in this fashion.

The final part, II-D, is the most difficult and important. Again, it relies on the problem-solving skills learned in the last session. The task is to help members create a practical program; one that involves clear, realistic steps that result in reaching a reasonable self-esteem–enhancing goal.

A good self-esteem project is therefore highly individualized. It must accommodate a personal range of possibilities, take into account various individual qualities, and fit with the current environment or unique circumstances. For instance, a self-esteem enhancement project aimed at increasing competence for an individual who is challenged mentally would look different from one for a person who was doing reasonably well in life but who wishes to do better. In the first case, the goal of learning how to find the right bus home from work might be a major achievement. In the second, aiming for an award or promotion might be a fitting goal. Sometimes people doom themselves to failure by picking goals that are too high for them right now or by selecting ones that cannot be supported by their current environments, which is why we must often help them to make realistic adjustments in their plan. In all cases, developing a self-esteem project is like preparing for a trip in that the more planning one does, the more likely one is to reach the destination.

Now, we ask people to write down each and every step they must take to reach the goal they have identified. If the aim, for instance, is to work on bodily functioning (which includes physical functioning, as well as body image issues) by developing an exercise program, then the individual is asked to be specific about how this will happen. It might mean trying out several sports. If so, then the individual must indicate the initial steps needed to experiment in this way such as calling the YMCA/YWCA, joining a club, or finding a friend involved in a relevant activity. If the individual decides to join the "Y", then he or she must find out how much the program costs, set aside a day to go to the gym, talk with a trainer, try a certain number of activities, and so on. If someone makes becoming more likable the goal, then he or she needs to consider such things as becoming involved in a community activity or learning better interpersonal communication skills. Depending on which activity is selected, there is often a need to develop a list of organizations, contact friends, make phone calls, meet with a few groups, and try out the activity until something suitable is found. Similarly, assertiveness training is a popular project and a well-established self-esteem enhancement activity. But it also means finding a qualified trainer nearby, seeing how much it costs, finding low-cost alternatives if necessary, and making schedules compatible.

Focusing on these mundane details is positive for a number of reasons, ranging from such platitudes as "A journey of a thousand miles begins with a single step," or "Inch by inch, it's a cinch," to the simple fact that small successes can lead to larger ones. At this point, I present my own self-esteem enhancement goals and ask members to help me develop the specific action steps necessary to improve in this area so that they can see how it is done through modeling. Then, I encourage volunteers to present their plans to the group. As before, I put the steps on the board and walk the group through a volunteer's plan so that we help improve it and so that I can reinforce the need for the plans to be detailed. This process is repeated until about the last 10 or 15 minutes of the session.

Finally, the end of the session nears and I use the remaining time as an opportunity for members to share their experience about the five weeks, mention their plans for the future (sometimes they have already acquired the phone numbers of people they have linked up with for further support), and assess the value of the group. The last activity gives me feedback concerning what participants found to be useful or not and what they would like to have done more or less of in the program. Not surprisingly, I want to remind them of the crucial roles that hard work and time play in increasing self-esteem. Therefore, the last step in the activity is to point out to participants that the journal is a way of keeping these important ingredients in mind. The program ends by asking them to complete whatever evaluation tool the facilitator wishes to use to obtain feedback about their experience.

Week 6 (Optional): Follow-Up Session

One last possibility needs to be mentioned. There is real value in adding a sixth session after the group has ended as a kind of follow-up or "booster" meeting. We know that increasing self-esteem requires hard work and that it can take a long time. But sometimes people start out well intentioned and then become discouraged or bogged down for one reason or another. A follow-up meeting may help participants to strengthen their resolve or to see the progress they have made, both of which can be powerful reinforcers. There are several things we do during this meeting to reinforce managing self-esteem effectively. For instance, we ask participants to share their experiences about how they were successful and where they had difficulty, so that everyone can see how hard people have to work at managing self-esteem. Material from any of the sessions may be reviewed on request. Special group attention might be given to an individual self-esteem project or need. The follow-up session could also be used to remind people about the learning curve, how long they have had a problem with self-esteem, and the need to continue to practice. Finally, for those leaders who are research oriented, the follow-up session may involve using the MSEI as a post-test to track significant differences.

Although most of my groups do not include this extra session, there is good reason to invest in this additional time upon occasion. This meeting may be included in the program from the beginning by making it a 6-week program instead of 5. The advantage here is that attendance is likely to be good. However, the disadvantage of having only a week lapse before the "boost" is that it might feel just like a regular meeting and the potency of the technique is diminished. However, it is also possible to schedule a 1-month follow-up after the five sessions end. In fact, this arrangement is mentioned in the short-term psychotherapy literature and is purported to have an enhancing effect (Wells, 1982). The risk of going this route is that attendance is likely to be lower than the usual group meetings because of such things as time limitations; schedule conflicts; and the resurgence of old, poor self-esteem habits. Nevertheless, in general I have found that clients often seem pleased with the progress they have made and wish to share their success with others.

ENHANCING SELF-ESTEEM
IN THE INDIVIDUAL SETTING

We saw earlier that self-esteem enhancement programs may also be designed for the individual setting (Bednar, Wells & Peterson, 1989; Pope, McHale & Craighead 1988; and Shirk & Harter, 1996). It is also possible to organize the program offered here in a way that is compatible with individual work. This version is based on a planned short-term treatment model (Wells, 1982) that continues to gain in popularity for at least two reasons: it reduces costs (which seems to please managed care programs) and the literature on the subject tells us that it is reasonably effective. Of course, there are several general characteristics of this approach that distinguish it from longer-term models, the most important of which is that it is a time-limited arrangement. However, another crucial distinction is that rather than being open-ended and general, short-term work is usually structured and focused. Typically, the client and therapist identify a particular problem or issue that is to be the center of their work and relationship. Long-term problems involving such goals as general personality reorganization or extremely psychotic conditions are not well suited to short-term work (Mann, 1973), which means that careful screening and diagnosis are a part of the process. Finally, there are psychodynamic, behavioral, cognitive, and even humanistic approaches to short-term work, which allows it to be used by clinicians from a number of persuasions.

The general approach is to simply adapt the enhancement program to fit the short-term framework without changing the essential character of either one. That is, we would begin a standard intake evaluation to make sure that this type of work is appropriate for the client and then use the same steps found in the group format to organize the treatment. Because most clinicians tend to work with individual clients in 1-hour appointments, the program could be broken up into 10 steps instead of 5 without much logistical difficulty. For example, the steps are 2 hours long and already have a break or transition built into them, which could be used to mark the point where they would be divided into two 1-hour sessions. In short, one way of adapting the program to individual work is by making its steps the basis of a short-term therapeutic contract, the primary focus of which is to work on enhancing self-esteem. Indeed, I have been investigating this approach and offer the format that is used for such work in the part of the Appendix labeled "Supplement I" for examination. It is possible to expand the number of sessions in various phases such as increasing worthiness or increasing competence. However, doing so turns the program into longer-term work, which is beyond the research scope of the individual program as it has been developed so far. Of course, it is important to note that no supporting evidence is being offered here for or against the individual format at this time.

Just as there are some advantages to working in the group format, the individual setting offers its own unique opportunities. For one thing, it allows us to focus more directly on the client as a unique and special person, which, among other things, allows us to take better advantage of assessment. For example, in this setting we are free to use the MSEI to explore all the domains of self-esteem it evaluates, rather than just identifying the areas with the highest and lowest scores. Such work is likely to increase awareness of self-esteem in general, but it also allows us to develop a much better understanding of how the components and dimensions of self-esteem are alive in a particular person's life. Thus, in addition to exploring each domain, this approach also allows us to look for, and to identify, self-esteem themes that are especially important for the person in his or her life.

Also, individual work is better positioned to use naturally occurring self-esteem moments, especially those involving problematic self-esteem themes. After all, the longer a client is in treatment, the more such opportunities are likely to arise. This aspect of individual work can be beneficial for two reasons. First, we know that the positive resolution of such self-esteem challenges can genuinely modify underlying problematic self-esteem themes in a positive direction. Indeed, we saw work that supports the idea that this format could be a more direct route to enhancing self-esteem in Chapters 3 and 5. Second, as Bednar and colleagues (1989, 1995) pointed out, individual therapy adds new elements to the situation that make a meaningful difference in their outcomes. For example, the client does not have to face the challenges of living alone in this therapeutic arrangement. Here, the therapist helps to increase the client's awareness of what is really at stake: dealing with a challenge that involves significant biographic themes and the potential to be a self-esteem turning point. Indeed, the clinician even helps the person to navigate these situations in a pro-self-esteem fashion. In other words, the presence of a knowledgeable, skilled, supportive ally during such periods could tip being at stake in these crucial ways toward a positive outcome. For as we saw in Chapters 1 and 5, such an event can be a powerful positive moment in the development of self-esteem. Even if a client fails, we help the individual to understand how that happened and think about ways to improve his or her chances the next time such a challenge occurs.

However, a word of caution is in order, even if just researching such individual work. The relationship between the client and therapist is more important in this format than in the group setting because there is no one else to bring into the picture. Given the nature of the relationship between self-esteem and authenticity, this work is much more existential than pedagogical which, among other things, means that both client and therapist are more actively engaged with each other here. Therefore, it is important to realize that there are two limits to considering this approach. First, the therapist should be well acquainted with the program before beginning to use it in the individual setting. Second, clinicians should pay close attention to the usual possibilities that occur in more intensive therapeutic relationships such as transference, countertransference, acting out, and so forth, and be prepared to handle them according to the standards of practice.

One last word about formats and the program in general is in order. It should be clear that group and individual approaches have their respective strengths and weaknesses. For instance, the former has rich dynamics of the group process to rely upon such as multiple perspectives, spontaneous opportunities, group affirmation, and reduced cost, whereas the latter offers more personal and individualized attention. However, the step-by-step character of either one may seem somewhat rigid to those who are more comfortable with a traditional humanistic or psychodynamic approach. If so, then it is important to realize that, although structured, the program cannot be successfully run in a mechanical fashion. Indeed, much of the program's effectiveness is predicated on the research that identified the interpersonal attitudes of acceptance, care, and respect for others, or the so-called "common factors" of therapy, as one of the primary agents for changing self-esteem (Arkowitz, 1997; Seligman, 1995a). If the quality of interpersonal contact is poor, then the effectiveness of the program is likely to suffer, perhaps even fail. Thus, the therapist is not just a good technician or a skilled teacher: he or she also becomes an important source of worthiness through acceptance, and of competence through modeling. In other words, it is important that the therapist "connect" with the individuals in the group (Mruk & Hartzell, 2003). Although the program's steps show people where to go, it is the therapist's unique and authentic presence that takes them there.

VALIDITY REVISITED

We are at the end of our phenomenological search for self-esteem, which means that I address one last issue. From the beginning, I have stressed the importance of basing the program on good research as well as on solid theory. For example, I attempted to show how the program meets the criteria for construct validity in two ways. First, we found that a valid approach to understanding self-esteem must be able to accommodate important insights and findings made by other researchers, theoreticians, and clinicians. The idea was that validity increases in relation to the descriptive power of the approach, in this case the ability of a phenomenological framework to integrate the major research findings on self-esteem. The approach actually seemed to do quite well in this regard in that the work on the definitions of self-esteem, the self-esteem paradoxes, and the research findings on self-esteem were all shown to be compatible with the fundamental structure of self-esteem and the meaning matrix. Second, it was said earlier that a valid approach would be one that is theoretically consistent. And we just saw how the phenomenological approach uses the definitions of competence and worthiness to move from research to theory and end with practice in an extremely consistent fashion.

Ideally, I would like to demonstrate the validity of both the theory and its application with convincing empirical aplomb because that is what our society respects the most about the scientific method. If one accepts the data of human experience as empirical enough to be subject to qualitative analysis, then it is likely that we have already demonstrated the validity of our fundamental finding, which is that self-esteem consists of both competence and worthiness. But the practical aspect of the program means that we are also interested in applying psychological knowledge to human life, which makes validity a practical, as well as a scientific, issue. Therefore, as a clinician I must insist on more traditional forms of empirical validation concerning program effectiveness as well. Of course, we can never expect the social sciences to reach the same levels of "uncertainty reduction" (Tryon, 1991) seen in the natural sciences: scientific expectations must always be tempered by the fact that things are more complicated at the lived level than they are in the lab. Nevertheless, there have been considerable advances in studying the effectiveness of psychotherapy over the past 2 decades and some work has been done on using this self-esteem enhancement program in the clinical setting.

Traditional forms of empirical evidence that lend credibility to a program consist of reliability and validity. As noted earlier, the reliability of a program, or the degree to which it can be implemented in a consistent way by others over time, is important for two reasons. First, it provides consistency to the use of the process, which is important clinically. Second, reliability is the key to consistent data-generating activities, especially if the information is going to come from a number of settings, through a range of practitioners, or over any period of time, all of which apply to clinical practices.

There is good reason to believe that this meaning-based two-factor program is reliable for working on self-esteem in adulthood. For instance, the group version of the program is highly structured in that it involves clear steps that are to be followed in a sequential fashion. The handouts, the testing instrument, and the materials for the activities are all reasonably standardized as well. Next, the same basic program has been used successfully by other therapists. In addition to training mental health therapists to use the approach in a community mental health system with which I am associated, for example, I have also offered it to traditional and non-traditional college populations and to general audiences. In addition, the program has been used by others who followed the book and then wrote or talked to me about their experiences afterward. These individuals work in diverse settings, ranging from inner city environments to college counseling centers. In addition, the program has been taught to graduate students at several institutions and has been presented at major professional conferences. In short, the theoretical consistency and step-by-step nature of the program does seem to give it a fairly high degree of reliability in both the research and clinical settings.

There is still the question of measured or quantifiable validity, which is most important if we are to apply the program to real lives with any degree of confidence. Some degree of empirical validity is seen in the fact that it was one of the things we looked for when researching the self-esteem enhancement techniques to be used in the program. Although the degree of such support for any particular technique varies, all of them have been tested by other authors and have stood the tests of persistence and significance. Indeed, some of the techniques, such as cognitive restructuring and problem solving, have done quite well in the empirically oriented literature on therapeutic efficacy. Even the MSEI has more research accompanying it than most self-esteem tests. Yet, there is no substitute for measurement. Fortunately, though small in number, the program has also been subjected to more rigorous examination, which includes the use of comparison groups, statistical analysis of effectiveness, and publication in peer-reviewed journals, all of which should be expected if one is thinking of using it in clinical or educational work.

One such endeavor was conducted by Hakim-Larson and Mruk (1997). I collected the data and she analyzed it to minimize my obvious bias. Some 32 subjects came from a large midwestern, hospital-based, multi-county, comprehensive, community mental services program. The participants ranged in age from late teens to mid-60s and were over-represented in terms of women and underrepresented in terms of minorities, although some of the participants were men and others were individuals from minority populations. These parameters are fairly typical of the community mental health environment. The subjects were divided into six medium-sized groups. I led each group with a co-therapist who differed from group to group. Two of the groups were composed of individuals from the general population who were not in treatment at the mental health facility. Two of the groups consisted of people with non-psychotic mental health diagnoses who were in treatment at the center. The remaining two groups were from the chemical dependency population: One consisted of people with a diagnosis who were in treatment at the facility; the other involved "co-dependent" family members, most of whom were not related to people in the other treatment groups. All of the participants were given the MSEI at the beginning of the treatment, and all of those who completed the program were tested once again at the end. They were also asked to fill out a qualitative questionnaire concerning their experience of the program and changes in themselves related to competence and worthiness.

The research design was not perfect in that we did not have the luxury of using a control group. Like most "real world" environments, the community mental health system is funded by state and local tax dollars, and forcing people to wait for service is ethically questionable. However, the conditions in this study were the ones most therapists are likely to encounter in practice. And there is considerable literature on the importance of doing research under these conditions using methods similar to our own (Kazdin, 1992; Seligman, 1995a). In addition, the study did include a comparison group of participants who were not diagnosed as having a mental health problem at the time. Also, the results of the research were surprisingly robust. Finally, there were no significant pretest differences between those participants who dropped out and those who stayed, suggesting that the results were not being influenced by this kind of selection factor.

Most important, every MSEI scale for self-esteem showed statistically significant positive changes between pre- and post-testing, which is exactly what we would expect if the program worked. Moreover, the qualitative data corroborated these statistical findings in that the subjects reported a high degree of satisfaction with the program and with positive changes in their self-esteem as it is defined by the program. We also did a follow-up session 6 months later, which is a long time in the community mental health situation. Subjects who attended the meeting reported continuing change and satisfaction with the program. These findings and issues concerning doing research in real-life settings are discussed in more detail in the article and the reader is referred to it if he or she is interested in such matters. More and better work is, of course, necessary and welcome.

Additional work of this type appears to be taking place. For example, Edward O'Brien, the primary author of the MSEI, and Mia Bartoletti have researched the effectiveness of the program with various populations (Bartoletti & O'Brien, 2003). Although done with small numbers of subjects, this work also involved pre- and post-testing using the MSEI and compared levels of self-esteem with relation to immunocompetence. The results showed that participating in the self-esteem program correlated positively with increases in immunocompetence as well as self-esteem. In other words, although there is always room for improvement, there does appear to be good reason to take the position that a two-factor, meaning-based approach to the research, theory, and practice of self-esteem stands up to several qualitative and quantitative indices of validity. In addition, this orientation surely meets or exceeds the standards of practice for enhancing self-esteem as they exist today. Perhaps the future will present the opportunity to revisit the efficacy of the program through additional research once again. If so, my questions would simply be, "What have we found out about self-esteem since the last time we looked at the field and what has been learned about this particular approach to researching and enhancing it?"

CHAPTER 7

Self-Esteem and Positive Psychology

Although most of the chapters in this book have been heavily revised to remain current, this chapter is a completely new addition because there was no need for it until now. For more than a century, self-esteem has held a significant place in psychology and related disciplines that few other concepts or phenomena have found: It figures prominently in personality, clinical, and social psychology, whether viewed from the psychodynamic, social learning, cognitive, evolutionary, or humanistic perspectives. However, two recent developments challenge the stature of self-esteem in social science today. One is that the limits of defining self-esteem in terms of competence or worthiness alone finally have been reached. This development challenges the value of the concept in various ways. For example, there are those such as Baumeister, Smart, and Boden (1996); Baumeister, Campbell, Krueger, and Vohs (2003); Emler (2001); Damon (1995); and Seligman (1995b) who criticize the importance of self-esteem when it is defined primarily in terms of worth or worthiness which, we have seen, it most often is. Similarly, there are those who take issue with the phenomenon when it is defined in a way that makes self-esteem contingent on any external standard of competence or success (Crocker & Nuer, 2003, 2004; Crocker & Park, 2003, 2004). Questioning any self-esteem study that is based on a lopsided or incomplete definition is certainly welcome in a two-factor approach. However, the criticism has become so great that we may have reached the point where the entire concept of self-esteem is in danger of being discarded.

If that situation does not represent a significant challenge to the field, then another one certainly does. This issue concerns the question of what kind of intellectual and clinical space self-esteem occupies in the positive psychology of human behavior that is becoming popular today (Seligman, 2002; Seligman & Csikszentmihalyi, 2000; Snyder & Lopez, 2002). This field of psychology is defined in several ways but Martin Seligman, perhaps its leading proponent, stated that it has several major identifying characteristics. Above all, positive psychology is *"A science of positive subjective experience, positive individual traits, and positive institutions [that] promises to improve quality of life and prevent the pathologies that arise when life is barren and meaningless"* (Seligman & Csikszentmihalyi, 2000, p. 5). At first glance, such qualities and objectives lead one to expect that self-esteem occupies a respected, if not prominent, place in this new field. After all, as we understand it, self-esteem is based on positive subjective experience; competence and worthiness are certainly positive individual traits, especially when combined; and institutions that foster this combination are surely positive in terms of helping to offer meaning and to prevent pathology. Unfortunately, however, this newly emerging psychology may not be particularly welcoming of, or interested in, self-esteem work.

The effect of these two developments creates a situation that threatens to relegate self-esteem to a far corner of the modern psychological stage. Indeed, we have already seen that some of the criticisms against self-esteem work have been harsh. Similarly, a review of several major handbooks in this new positive psychology is quite sobering in this regard. For example, self-esteem rarely occurs as a chapter, prominent theme, or even a key issue in such texts. In fact, self-esteem did not even make the "first cut" of basic individual strengths in this new positive psychology's classification of human strengths and virtues (Peterson & Seligman, 2004). However, there are two good reasons to object to such views: One is to understand how self-esteem has always been a part of positive psychology and the other is to realize that when defined in terms of competence and worthiness, self-esteem continues to warrant an important place in positive psychology today, no matter what form it takes. In other words, "Perhaps it is appropriate in this time of positive psychology to reclaim the positive in self-esteem" (Heatherton & Wyland, 2003, p. 39). Our final task is to demonstrate the merit of this position.

In order to understand the relationship between self-esteem and positive psychology, it is necessary to clarify what is meant by the latter. Although the phrase "positive psychology" may be traced to at least 1882 (Taylor, 2001), today the concept is primarily used in two ways. For example, we just saw that it is possible to understand positive psychology as a particular field of study within psychology. However, for a long time now the phrase has also been used to describe an entire approach to psychology, namely, humanistic psychology. Of course, we will see that there are several key distinctions between them. For instance, it will become clear that the type of positive psychology that Seligman and colleagues present is more empirical in the traditional sense and is based on logical positivism as the foundation of science. This form of positive psychology is also just emerging. Hence, it may be referred to as the "new" or "positivistic" positive psychology. The other type of positive psychology is much older and is connected to the humanistic tradition, which takes issue with logical positivism and its approach to science. Therefore, we may refer to this form of positive psychology as the "original" or "humanistic" positive psychology. As we shall see, both psychologies share a concern with understanding positive human phenomena and using that knowledge to help people, but they go about those activities very differently. This paradigmatic possibility was discussed in Chapter 2, so it should not be a surprise to find ourselves talking about self-esteem in relation to both approaches to positive psychology, which we shall do throughout this chapter.

SELF-ESTEEM AND THE ORIGINAL, HUMANISTIC POSITIVE PSYCHOLOGY

More than half a century ago, psychiatrists realized that the social sciences were failing to live up to an important aspect of their commitment to study human behavior, particularly its richer and higher dimensions. Initially, several individuals were concerned with the failure of the sciences of human behavior to study such things as positive subjective experience, human strengths and virtues, and positive social institutions that would foster such experiences and characteristics, all of which we have just seen to be the earmarks of positivistic positive psychology. Occasionally, individuals such as Adler (1927) or Horney (1937) struggled with this issue independently. Later, several psychologists, such as Gordon Allport and Gardner Murphy, addressed similar themes (Taylor, 2001). However, the first organized positive response was offered by humanistic psychology.

Like most movements, humanistic psychology began as a core of ideas around which an identity forms. The most central idea for humanistic psychology was general disagreement with the reductionistic philosophical foundations of the psychological perspectives that were dominant at the time, especially the psychodynamic and behavioral points of view. Both of these mainstream positions were based on the logical positivism of psychology practiced as a natural science, which was seen as too limiting to understand the full richness of human experience, especially its higher or more positive possibilities. Thus, humanistic psychology began as a protest, one that was "directed against the entire orientation of psychology since Hobbes and Locke, against its Newtonian and Darwinian models of man and against its mechanistic, deterministic, and reductionist character" (Misiak & Sexton, 1973, p. 115). Taking issue with this approach at the deepest level, the editors of the *Journal of Humanistic Psychology* defined humanistic psychology as the following:

> Primarily an orientation toward the whole of psychology rather than a distinct area or school. It stands for respect for the worth of persons, respect for differences of approach, open-mindedness as to acceptable methods, and interest in exploration of new aspects of human behavior. As a "third force" in contemporary psychology it is concerned with topics having little place in existing theories and systems; e.g., love, creativity, self, growth, organism, basic need-gratification, self-actualization, higher values, being, becoming, spontaneity, play, humor, affection, naturalness, warmth, ego-transcendence, objectivity, autonomy, responsibility, meaning, fairplay, transcendental experience, peak experience, courage, and related concepts. (Maslow, 1964, pp. 70–71)

Instead of a rigid insistence on the strict use of naturalistic methods, the humanistic approach welcomed a diversity of methods by including more qualitative ones such as those discussed in Chapter 2.

Humanistic psychology continues its original mission but has matured to the point that it is also characterized by a general set of positive psychological themes, issues, and concerns that carve out a reasonably clear, though not dominant, place in psychology. Tageson (1982) identified them as including a holistic approach to understanding the person (instead of a reductionistic approach), a concern with self-actualization (human development and the good life), self-determination (intrinsic motivation and autonomy), authenticity (healthy psychological functioning), self-transcendence (especially in relationships with others), and person-centeredness (appreciation of our essential humanity).

Contemporary humanistic psychology also includes a focus on developing more sophisticated methods for researching human experience and behavior (Greenberg, Koole & Pyszczynski, 2004); several refereed scientific publications such as the *Journal of Humanistic Psychology* and the *Humanistic Psychologist*; and various professional organizations that support its efforts, including a division in the American Psychological Association's (APA) Division of Humanistic Psychology. In short, the humanistic approach is well established as the first organized form of positive psychology.

There can be little doubt that self-esteem occupies a secure place in the humanistic tradition and its view of positive psychology. For example, Maslow (1968) identified self-esteem as one of the basic developmental issues that all human beings face. Indeed, so fundamental is this need that it is often characterized as a "D" or deficiency need, meaning that it is a part of the natural cycle of human development, something we all need and must contend with in one way or another. Although one may criticize such a characterization as being largely theoretical, we have seen research that identifies self-esteem as one of the three most important types of need-based human experiences (Sheldon, Elliot, Kim & Kasser, 2001). We have also found that understanding self-esteem as a fundamental aspect of human development gives self-esteem tremendous psychological significance in at least two ways. One, it means that self-esteem has motivational power: It drives behavior in a way that forces us to master life's challenges so that we may feel valued and respected by ourselves and by others. Failing to fulfill this need means that behavior is driven in another direction, one that is not healthy. In this case the individual attempts to compensate for a lack of self-esteem which, depending on how great the deficiency is, may manifest itself through all types of negative behaviors ranging from ordinary neurosis to a host of pathological conditions both within the DSM structure and beyond it.

Two, self-esteem is also directly tied to one of the most important and distinguishing aspects of humanistic psychology: growth and self-actualization. Rogers (1951, 1961), for instance, felt that self-esteem is necessary for people to become "fully functioning," which is one of the reasons he stressed the need for "unconditional positive regard" in childhood and in the therapeutic relationship. Of course, when discussing this aspect of humanistic psychology, it is important to remember that unconditional positive regard is a concept that often has been misused and mistakenly criticized. Such a stance toward others does not mean welcoming or even accepting everything a child or client does. Rather, unconditional positive regard involves respecting the intrinsic worth and value of the other person as a unique human being at all times, even though it is necessary to disapprove of certain forms of unworthy, incompetent, or unhealthy behavior when they are inappropriate. The point is that self-esteem is important in this positive psychology because it is tied to human development in general. For example, if one does not value one's worth as a person in an authentic fashion, then it is difficult to know what to actualize in the first place.

Similarly, even if one understands what merits actualization, it does not happen without a sufficient degree of competence. Finally, if one suffers from low self-esteem, then one may also risk being thrown off one's intrinsic developmental track in ways that matter. For instance, such a developmental derailment increases the risk of developing one of the many mental disorders we saw connected to self-esteem earlier or, perhaps even worse, living an inauthentic life. In short, the place of self-esteem is well established and secure in the original vision of positive psychology.

THE NEW POSITIVISTIC POSITIVE PSYCHOLOGY

The origins of the new form of positive psychology cannot be too closely tied to those of the older or original one because instead of taking issue with the reductionism of the positivistic paradigm, the emerging field fully embraces that approach. Instead, Seligman and Csikszentmihalyi (2000) see the development of positivistic positive psychology in relation to certain events associated with the aftermath of World War II. In particular, the negative effects of the war on various soldier and civilian populations coupled with a huge influx of federal and academic money toward treatment shifted the very foundations of American psychology: It moved from a traditional academic footing to a more applied one, especially one that focuses on dealing with psychopathology and mental problems. One result of this development is that most of modern clinical psychology focused on negative rather than positive behavior. The new positive psychology is offered as an antidote to this condition. In short, positivistic positive psychology gaining momentum today is preceded by an older, original, humanistic positive psychology that shared the same concerns except for one: the question of paradigms, which were encountered in Chapter 2.

Basic Ideas

To examine the place of self-esteem in positivistic positive psychology, we must first understand what it is. The general intent of this approach is clearly defined by its adherents in almost all of their basic writings on the topic: This positive psychology aims to correct an important deficiency that characterizes much of traditional psychology.

> The message of the positive psychology movement is to remind our field that it has been deformed. Psychology is not just the study of disease, weakness, and damage; it also is the study of strength and virtue. Treatment is not just fixing what is wrong; it is also building what is right. Psychology is not just about illness or health; it is also about work, education, insight, love, growth, and play. And in this quest for what is best, positive psychology does not rely on wishful thinking, self-deception, or hand waving; instead, it tries to adapt what is best in the scientific method to the unique problems that human behavior presents in all its complexity. (Seligman, 2002, p. 4)

Thus, positivistic positive psychology aims to offer a corrective balance to traditional psychology. This effort starts at the theoretical level by reminding psychology that although it should be concerned with studying negative human behavior to help ease humanity's suffering, it may be more important to keep the other, more positive, end of the continuum of human behavior in mind as a goal. The new positive psychology then takes this message to the level of research by encouraging psychologists and others to study the positive or healthy aspects of human behavior more seriously than has been done in the past. In this case, phenomena such as love, growth, and play are seen as being just as important to study as problems and pathologies, because the former are more promising than the latter in terms of understanding and actualizing human potential. Finally, positivistic positive psychology extends theory and research to the practical level, which completes a circle by reminding social scientists that their efforts may benefit society in myriad ways. In addition to spending resources on healing, for example, we might also focus on increasing our knowledge and skills of nurturing. In the long run, fostering healthier people should reduce suffering and help people to live the "good life."

Core Themes

In addition to an overarching framework that spans theory, research, and practice, positivistic positive psychology is concerned with three basic themes, levels, or dimensions (Compton, 2005). First, the focus is on positive or healthy human experience such as "well-being, contentment, and satisfaction (in the past); hope and optimism (for the future); and flow and happiness (in the present)" (Seligman & Csikszentmihalyi, 2000, p. 5). Thus, the general tone of this positive psychology is true to its stated intent: to balance what is considered psychology's emphasis on illness and problems by concentrating on understanding positive human phenomena that are healthy and that reflect the joy of living a full, good life. Second, this approach focuses on positive human qualities and characteristics including "the capacity for love and vocation, courage, interpersonal skill, aesthetic sensibility, perseverance, forgiveness, originality, future mindedness, spirituality, high talent, and wisdom" (Seligman & Csikszentmihalyi, 2000, p. 5). In just a few years the new field has already produced several impressive works on these topics (Aspinwall & Staudinger, 2003). The third focus is on understanding the relationship between group or social behavior and basic human values, especially "the civic virtues and the institutions that move individuals toward better citizenship: responsibility, nurturance, altruism, civility, moderation, tolerance, and work ethic" (Seligman & Csikszentmihalyi, 2000, p. 5). This dimension expands the scope of new positive psychology beyond traditional psychology: To achieve healthy human functioning, people are best served by a society that is actively concerned with fostering optimal growth and development. In this sense, positivistic positive psychology is also a social, as well as psychological, project.

Applied Focus

Finally, its focus on treatment and prevention make it clear that positivistic positive psychology is not envisioned as just another academic enterprise. Positive treatment involves concentrating on strengths, as well as dealing with weaknesses. This applied goal may be reached by incorporating traditional therapeutic techniques into a positive format. However, positivistic positive therapies also aim at developing and applying new approaches such as the "well-being" therapy that is being developed by Fava (1999) and others. In addition, new positive psychology emphasizes the importance of prevention. Like most attempts at prevention, the new positive psychology is concerned with helping to prevent problems at the individual level through such things as parenting programs, school-based programs for children, and so forth. However, positivistic positive psychology sees long-term prevention as being just as important, if not more so, given its ultimate goal of creating healthy societies. This view of prevention involves reshaping entire institutions along positive lines. The hope is that by doing so, we create a virtuous cycle of subjective, individual, and social well-being. Hence, positivistic positive psychology is also a political, as well as a social and psychological, project.

SIMILARITIES AND DIFFERENCES
BETWEEN THE TWO POSITIVE PSYCHOLOGIES

At this point, it should be easy to identify the similarities between the two positive psychologies. For example, both the new and the original positive psychologies set their point of origin in the context of a mainstream psychology that is characterized by an excessive focus on negative human behavior. In this case, the criticism of the disease model by positivistic positive psychology is roughly equivalent to what Maslow and others in an earlier day said about the psychodynamic preoccupation with neurosis. Similarly, both approaches are concerned with the same three dimensions in their views of positive psychology. For instance, what is meant by psychological well-being in the positivistic positive approach is similar to various aspects of the self-actualizing individual or fully functioning person of the humanistic approach, especially in terms of being open to experience, living the good life, and so forth. Similarly, both psychologies talk about the importance of researching and fostering positive individual characteristics and their development. In fact, when we examine the quotations of what each version of positive psychology wishes to focus upon that were cited earlier in the chapter, we find that they even mention some of the same positive qualities, namely, love, hope, and play.

In addition, both views of positive psychology go well beyond a focus on the individual. Each of them points out a need to change group behavior; alter institutional values; and, in general, shift society in ways that help people to move toward the "farther reaches of human nature," to paraphrase the point with the title of one of Maslow's (1971) more famous works. Finally, both approaches understand human beings as, in essence, "good" rather than "evil," and adaptive rather than fixed. Each psychology sees human problems as stemming from the imposition of environmental or developmental factors that stunt a natural desire to function in a healthy way, not as a result of a lack of desire or ability. Accordingly, each vision of positive psychology aims at creating a nurturing environment that fosters development, in addition to helping those who already suffer from the lack of it. In some crucial ways, then, the new positive psychology is not at all new.

Indeed, positivistic positive psychology does make it clear that it is "not a new idea" and that it "has many distinguished ancestors" (Seligman & Csikszentmihalyi, 2000, p. 13), most of whom were associated with humanistic or third force psychology and psychiatry. However, the new positive psychology goes to great lengths to emphasize that there are fundamental differences that clearly separate it from its predecessor, especially embracing the vision of psychology practiced within the traditional naturalistic paradigm and the superiority of its quantitative methods.

> Unfortunately, humanistic psychology did not attract much of a cumulative empirical base, and it spawned myriad therapeutic self-help movements. In some of its incarnations, it emphasized the self and encouraged a self-centeredness that played down concerns for collective well-being. Further debate will determine whether this came about because Maslow and Rogers were ahead of the times, because these flaws were inherent in their original vision, or because of overly enthusiastic followers. However one legacy of the humanism of the 1960s is prominently displayed in any large bookstore: The "psychology" section contains at least 10 shelves on crystal healing, aromatherapy, and reaching the inner child for every shelf of books that tries to uphold some scholarly standard. (Seligman & Csikszentmihalyi, 2000, p. 7)

Of course, the crucial word to keep in mind is "empirical," because positivistic positive psychology claims to differentiate itself from the original positive psychology by a commitment to traditional quantitative research.

Humanistic positive psychology, by contrast, is characterized as being far too open methodologically, particularly in terms of emphasizing qualitative work. Thus, positivistic positive psychology maintains that it is important to stay with the naturalistic paradigm and its focus on observation, measurement, experimentation, and so forth. The hope is that this approach enables the new positive psychology to do the one thing that humanistic positive psychology failed at: generating a large body of scientifically acceptable studies that are presented in rigorous scientific journals with enough frequency to reach the critical mass of general acceptance. If this effort is successful, then it is thought that positivistic positive psychology will wield enough academic and scientific clout to be recognized in mainstream social science, perhaps even enough to turn it in a positive direction.

If one reviews the literature generated by this emerging field today, it is clear that this strategy helps positivistic positive psychology progress toward its goals. For example, in just a few short years the field has gone from an APA presidential address to several large, empirically oriented, edited handbooks on the major dimensions of positive psychology mentioned earlier. The nearly 800-page *Handbook of Positive Psychology* (Snyder & Lopez, 2002) consists of 55 chapters covering the entire field that positivistic positive psychology addresses; *A Psychology of Human Strengths: Fundamental Questions and Future Directions for a Positive Psychology* (Aspinwall and Staudinger, 2003) focuses on this important dimension of the field, which was identified as its second level; and *Positive Psychology in Practice* (Linley & Joseph, 2004) takes the new approach to the applied area where change and prevention are of concern. In addition, the movement now includes special issues in the *American Psychologist,* several large-scale research projects and dedicated journals, and an ever growing Web presence. In short, positivistic positive psychology is making a concerted effort to do just what it said it would do: use traditional methods to make acceptable contributions to mainstream psychology in a way that gives the new positive psychology the credibility that the original one never achieved. The fact that so much work has occurred in such a short time is genuinely impressive no matter what side one supports.

Several powerful forces fuel the movement of positivistic positive psychology toward this three-pronged goal of research, accumulation, and influence or power. First, this vision of positive psychology is well positioned in regard to major professional organizations, such as the APA. Such an affinity ensures the legitimacy of this approach in terms of disseminating information through conference presentations, publications in important professional journals, and contracts with major book presses. This factor alone may stimulate many academic psychologists to look in this direction because it opens up a new, major publishing track that presents important opportunities for those who are seeking tenure or a reputation in the field.

Second, positivistic positive psychology appeals to significant sources of private funding, such as major philanthropic foundations, at a time when research money is becoming increasingly unavailable. Such support is helpful because a body of published material influences a field over time. In addition to attracting mature researchers, teachers, and practitioners, funding may also target projects that encourage younger professionals. The long-term effect of this development may be a cadre of bright, interested minds for the future. Many may teach or assume leadership positions, both of which may help to extend positivistic positive psychology from one generation to the next in a way that achieves the goals of critical mass and influence.

It is important to realize, of course, that pointing out these academic and economic processes is not meant as a criticism: It is simply the way of science. In its day, humanistic psychology also enjoyed similar benefits. For example, Maslow and Rogers were both presidents of the APA, supportive professional organizations and journals were created, and funding for behavioral research was more readily available than it is now. The important difference is this: Positivistic positive psychology has one more leg on which to stand. Where humanistic psychology takes issue with psychology based on the paradigm of natural science, the new positive psychology embraces this positivistic approach. In supporting logical positivism as its scientific foundation, the emerging positive psychology is less likely to encounter resistance that humanistic psychology endured and continues to suffer from today.

HUMANISTIC RESPONSE

Although still alive, the humanistic approach to a positive study of human behavior has not had the effect on psychology that its supporters had hoped to achieve in the early days of its conception. However, those who are within this perspective speak about the reasons for this situation in a different way. For example, positivistic positive psychology often contends that humanistic psychology stumbled because it "somehow failed to attract a cumulative and empirical body of research to ground their ideas" (Seligman, 2002, p. 7). But Tom Greening, editor of the *Journal of Humanistic Psychology*, took issue with such thinking in a special edition dedicated to a humanistic response to positivistic positive psychology.

> When I first read Martin Seligman's articles in the *APA Monitor* announcing his advocacy of the study of positive human qualities and actions such as self-actualization, I was pleased to see the long-standing agenda of humanistic psychology getting mainstream APA attention. However, it soon became apparent the he was making no connections with and giving no credit to humanistic psychology. It was as if the field did not exist, in spite of a four-decade history, countless publications, and a Division of Humanistic Psychology within APA itself. (Greening, 2001, p. 4)

Others use even stronger language to show how this type of criticism ignores a large body of high quality, publishable and published literature on humanistic positive psychology and positive topics.

For instance, Eugene Taylor, who specializes in the history and philosophy of psychology, pointed out in the same issue of the journal that there is a long line of work by Henry Murray, Gardner Murphy, Gordon Allport and others that called for more positive work. He said that subsequent humanistic psychology introduced by Maslow, Rogers, and others has, in fact, generated a substantial body of research and findings. Taylor supported his argument by first pointing out that considerable laboratory-based work on meditation has been performed from a humanistic perspective. He then noted that key humanistic concepts, ones that are also central to the new positive psychology, have been researched empirically and published significantly by humanistic psychologists since 1960.

> A simple search of PsychInfo shows that the construct of self-actualization has appeared in psychological literature in more than 2,700 articles since the 1960s. Moreover, most of these studies refer to the measurement of self-actualization as a personality construct using Shostrom's Personal Orientation Inventory, obviously now a well-established research tool in psychology. (Taylor, 2001, p. 21)

Meditation and self-actualization are only two examples of humanistic literature about positive psychological phenomena and there are many more. Therefore, it is unlikely that the humanistic approach to positive psychological studies has been limited by its ability to stimulate a significant body of publishable or published results. In other words, something else prevented the kind of recognition that is usually awarded such a body of work. The only other reasonable explanation concerns paradigmatic conflicts and the scientific, as well as economic, politics that surround them.

In discussing the history of humanistic psychology, Taylor (2001) noted that it began as an academic movement that emerged from an interface among three disciplines: personality theory, educational counseling, and motivational psychology. From the beginning, humanistic psychology was concerned with positive growth and development across the board in personal, academic, educational, organizational, social, and applied settings. However, he also pointed out that the combination of disciplines, tolerance of multiple methodologies, and an active interest in generating change quickly spiraled out of the academic setting into a myriad of disciplines and therapies. Both forms of positive psychology generally agreed that one result of this openness was that the humanistic version of positive psychology was diluted and popularized. Even though as an academic discipline humanistic psychology is more rigorous than may meet the eye, the fact that it is often embraced by popular and self-help psychology makes humanistic positive psychology guilty by association. Perhaps positivistic positive psychologists drew a line between themselves and this body of work to avoid a similar fate. Although understandable, limiting access to material in this way is both regrettable and, as we shall see momentarily, unnecessary.

The other factor that limits humanistic psychology's influence in positive psychology is specifically paradigmatic, although methodological openness is a case in point. We saw this deeper, more structural issue in Chapter 2 when we compared the scientific paradigms used to research self-esteem. For one thing, mainstream psychology is founded on the logical positivism of psychology practiced as a natural science, which is to say that it is objective and factual but reductionistic and deterministic. Thus, when positivistic positive psychology calls for empirical research, it means quantified studies; those based on the right side of the methodological continuum and that support a clear hierarchy of value in terms of what is acceptable.

Humanistic psychology is not as uniform in its approach because it realizes the need for multiple methods, both quantitative and qualitative. This aspect of the human science paradigm is seen as a strength because it allows researchers to access phenomena as they are actually lived. However, methodological diversity also generates a less uniform body of work. Thus, whenever humanistic psychology attempts to bring its material to the psychological table, such as the one for positive psychology, it must jump two hurdles right from the beginning: skepticism toward its work *in principle* and a range of findings that are too diverse to be placed under a single roof. Consequently, it is easy to see how the naturalistic form of positive psychology dismisses as irrelevant, non-scientific, and so forth, humanistic work on positive topics. In this light, it also is not difficult to comprehend why the human science approach fires back with ugly charges of hegemony, intellectual imperialism, and the like.

Fortunately, however, things are not as clear-cut as they seem. For example, the following quotation appears in a special issue of the *American Psychologist* only 1 year after the first article on this topic in that prestigious and important journal.

> Positive psychology is thus an attempt to urge psychologists to adopt a more open and appreciative perspective regarding human potentials, motives, and capacities. Such an endeavor is surprisingly difficult within psychology's reductionist epistemological traditions, which train one to view positivity with suspicion, as a product of wishful thinking, denials, or hucksterism. It is probably appropriate that psychologists receive such training because all people are prone to be taken

in, at least at times, by their own delusions and wishes. However, we suggest that such skepticism, taken too far, may itself constitute a negativity bias that prevents a clear understanding of reality. (Sheldon & King, 2001, p. 216)

Instead of focusing on differences, perhaps both approaches should look at points of convergence, complementarity, and integration. After all, we saw that it is possible to bring both paradigms and their methods together on one positive topic, self-esteem. Perhaps other, more integrated understandings occur elsewhere. In other words, instead of standing at odds, the two approaches could work together for the betterment of positive psychology.

Fortunately, such integration is happening in what might be called the "second generation" of new positive psychology, particularly among clinicians. For example, P. Alex Linley and Steven Joseph, who focus on the clinical application of positivistic positive psychology, suggested that the distinction between the two approaches blurs significantly at the level of real life.

We are aware that the relationship between positive psychology and humanistic psychology has been a subject of debate. To be sure, there are differences between positive psychology and humanistic psychology, but we believe that these differences are far outweighed by their similarities. Hence, we have worked hard in this volume to speak to readers from the traditions of both positive psychology and humanistic psychology. Our knowledge will advance all the more quickly if we are able to acknowledge similarities, constructively explore our differences, and work together in the joint pursuit of our common goals. (2004, pp. xv–xvi)

In other words, although the relationship between the two positive psychologies has often been characterized by dismissal if not antagonism, there is hope. In addition to arguing that the study of self-esteem has an important and rightful place in positivistic positive psychology, this topic may also be particularly well suited to the kind of cooperation that Linley and Joseph suggest. Giving voice to this possibility is the last, but certainly not the least, aim of this book.

SELF-ESTEEM AND POSITIVE PSYCHOLOGY

We saw that self-esteem holds a significant and secure place in the humanistic vision of positive psychology. Although its position in traditional social science is not as secure as it was, self-esteem is still an important theme. For example, the fact that high-level professional journals such as *Psychological Inquiry* continue to devote entire issues to it is a testament to the importance of self-esteem. Similarly, that the rate of publishing articles on the topic remains extremely high compared with other subjects also indicates that self-esteem is alive and well in psychology today. Yet, the status of self-esteem in the new positive psychology is far less clear. Often, for instance, when a positivistic positive psychologist discusses Maslow's famous hierarchy in the context of understanding self-actualization or when identifying fundamental human values, the concept of self-esteem is omitted. Instead, the phrase "cognitive needs" is used. Although technically correct, this terminology stands in contrast to the more commonly used name for the fourth stage, which is self-esteem.

Taken collectively, the three major handbooks on positive psychology mentioned earlier in this chapter present 110 chapters on topics deemed important to positivistic positive psychology such as well-being, positive affect, emotional intelligence, problem solving, adjustment, authenticity, moral virtue, and so on. However, only one chapter focuses on self-esteem. Even that section is primarily concerned with "deconstructing" self-esteem as a "new emotion" that arises in response to social forces characteristic of modern Western societies (Hewitt, 2002, p. 144). Such an approach certainly reveals how culture affects whether competence or worthiness is emphasized, and it is important to know how different societies affect the ways in which members obtain competence or worthiness. However, this view is at serious odds with the body of work presented earlier that sees self-esteem as a basic human concern. For example, such a culturally relativistic perspective does not address the cross-cultural research on the importance of self-esteem discussed in Chapter 3. Similarly, reducing self-esteem to a mere cultural artifact fails to address the basic evolutionary significance of this phenomenon that many other theories endorse as seen in Chapter 4.

It is unclear whether positivistic positive psychology is simply missing the work on self-esteem, examining but dismissing it as insignificant, or systematically attempting to relegate self-esteem to that distant corner of psychology mentioned at the beginning of this chapter. Perhaps one reason that self-esteem is in this situation stems from the quantitative focus toward which positivistic positive psychology aspires. If self-esteem is understood in terms of worthiness, for instance, then interest in the phenomenon may lessen because much of that type of work on self-esteem involves weak statistical evidence for its vitality as a concept. Similarly, a worthiness-based definition of self-esteem is often associated with the "feel good" approach of the self-esteem movement, which the new psychology clearly wishes to differentiate itself from by emphasizing its positivistic character.

However, we already saw that such criticisms do not apply to self-esteem work based on defining it in terms of competence and worthiness. In addition, such two-factor research is investigating some of the same themes that concern the emerging positive psychology and often by using the same methods. For example, competence involves acquiring problem-solving skills, dealing with the challenges of living effectively, having an attitude of self-efficacy, and so forth. Worthiness requires having a sense of values and making meaningful connections with others. These sets of topics are of vital interest to self-esteem work and to the work on positive psychology in general. Also, there is a considerable degree of convergence among self-esteem work, positivistic positive psychology, and humanistic positive psychology in certain areas such as an interest in effective action, subjective and psychological well-being, and living the good life. Finally, both forms of positive psychology involve a number of topics in which we saw the role of self-esteem to be quite prominent such as in work on authenticity (Kernis, 2003a, b; Koole & Kuhl, 2003), positive affect and emotional stability (Greenberg, Pyszczynski & Solomon, 1995; Pyszczynski, Greenberg & Goldberg, 2003), and healthy self-regulation (Leary, 2004a, b; Leary & Downs, 1995; Leary & McDonald, 2003; Leary & Tangney, 2003), to mention a few. Yet, the self-esteem aspect of such work, which is central to it, is hardly mentioned by positivistic positive psychology literature on those topics, even when it refers to the same research or material.

Over all, then, it is really quite surprising to find so little reference to self-esteem in the new field. One result of this situation is that instead of reviewing the place of self-esteem in positivistic positive psychology, it is more appropriate to end this book on a different, but perhaps more important, note: establishing a place for self-esteem in the new positive psychology. This work aims to show that by defining self-esteem in terms of competence and worthiness, it is not necessary to discard the concept with the water that has been muddied by the lopsided definitions of the past. Discussing all of the possibilities that characterize the full extent of the existing and potential interface between the psychology of self-esteem and positivistic positive psychology requires another book. However, we have been dealing with two points of convergence in these pages, so it is possible to use them as examples of the interface between the fields of self-esteem and the new positive psychology.

One of them concerns researching topics such as authenticity and their implications for well-being or for living the good life. The other takes on a more practical character and is found in work that concerns dealing with the problems of living and fostering the development of positive qualities through what is called "applied positive psychology" (Linley & Joseph, 2004). Let us briefly examine the connections between self-esteem work and positivistic positive psychology in these two areas as a way of making the point that there is a legitimate and important place for self-esteem in this new field. Using examples from both academic and applied areas such as these also illustrate the fact that self-esteem work is important for at least two levels or dimensions of positivistic positive psychology.

Self-Esteem, Authenticity, and Positive Psychology

When examining research findings in Chapter 3, we found that the field of self-esteem has been interested in the phenomenon of authenticity for quite some time. Positivistic positive psychology also identifies authenticity as a primary human strength and supports work in this area (Peterson & Seligman, 2004, p. 249). Much of the existing work on authenticity involves self-esteem, but that fact is not given much attention when the new positive psychology makes use of this literature. In theory, perhaps the problem with including self-esteem in positivistic positive psychology is the idea that humanistic work on the topic does not meet the standards of the naturalistic paradigm. For example, perhaps a true, inner, or "intrinsic" self, which is essential to the notion of authenticity, is far too "qualitative" of a concept to meet the traditional empirical standards of the new positive psychology.

However, the fact is that contemporary work on self-esteem goes well beyond such a limitation. A case in point is Self-Determination Theory (SDT), which operates from an explicitly existential and "organismic," which is to say humanistic, point of view. SDT holds that there are three most basic human needs: autonomy, competence, and relatedness. To paraphrase Ryan and Brown (2003, p. 73) this view understands autonomy as a combination of "volition and ownership, and initiative," competence as the "ability to respond to challenges effectively," and relatedness as "feelings of belonging and connectedness," which I characterize in terms of providing a sense of acceptance or worth.

Although SDT does not see self-esteem as one of the most basic human needs, self-esteem is still regarded as an important phenomenon because it affects such things as self-regulation and authenticity, both of which are vital to SDT. For example, if a person suffers from low, fragile, contingent, paradoxical, or unstable self-esteem, then much of self-regulation will be defensive. Understanding oneself as having a poor degree of competence impairs autonomous functioning, because such a perceived deficiency makes it difficult to take the risks associated with acting on one's own. Similarly, basing one's sense of worth on external rather than internal standards creates a condition of dependence on others that constrains one's ability to function on the basis of intrinsic motivation.

Thus, the lack of competence, autonomy, and worth are conditions that decrease one's ability to function authentically and increase the likelihood of living life inauthentically.

In contrast, having a good sense of oneself as being fairly competent, autonomous, and connected results in what SDT called "true self-esteem" (Deci & Ryan, 1995). In this case, defensiveness is minimal, which allows the individual to get in touch with intrinsic values more easily. This awareness helps the person to know what to actualize and to take appropriate risks in that direction. In other words, self-esteem is important because depending on whether it is positive or negative, it helps create a virtuous cycle of authenticity or a vicious cycle of inauthenticity.

In addition to offering important insights into the nature of self-esteem, one of the most important things about SDT is that it is an existentially oriented approach to understanding human behavior *that is supported by just the type of empirical studies and methods that appeal to positivistic positive psychology*. For example, some experimental and longitudinal work has been done showing that people work longer, harder, and with more enjoyment when pursuing intrinsic goals rather than extrinsic ones (Sheldon & Kasser, 2001). Indeed, most major principles of SDT are supported by such research, which has now reached the point where its accumulated volume is substantial enough to be recognized by mainstream psychology. For example, the *Handbook of Experimental Existential Psychology* (Greenberg, Koole & Pyszczynski, 2004) contains many examples of traditionally based research on humanistically oriented topics such as terror of death, the importance of meaning, making choices, motivation, authenticity, and so forth, several of which are important to the new positive psychology as well.

Notice that I am *not* saying that SDT work on self-esteem necessarily supports the view of it being presented in this book. For instance, I argue that self-esteem is a basic human need when it is defined in terms of competence and worthiness. SDT does not, even though self-esteem shows up among the top three basic human needs in a study performed by Sheldon, Elliot, Kim & Kasser (2001) that both positions use to bolster their points. Similarly, competence, which SDT does make prominent use of, was actually fourth on that list of needs and is included in the definition of self-esteem being used here. Nevertheless, the real point is that work on authenticity is directly tied to self-esteem and vice versa and yet, we do not see the new positive psychology exploring this dimension of authenticity with much vigor at this time.

Michael Kernis may be making even more headway into the interface between self-esteem and authenticity while using more traditionally empirical methods. He began by identifying four basic components of authenticity. They are *awareness,* especially of feelings, thoughts, values, hunches, and the ability to trust them; *unbiased processing,* which involves a certain degree of openness to internal and external realities; *action,* or the ability to function in ways that are consistent with one's authentic self; and *relatedness,* which includes awareness of the importance of others. When added together, "Authenticity can be characterized as reflecting the unobstructed operation of one's true, or core, self in one's daily enterprise" (Kernis, 2003a, p. 13). Koole and Kuhl (2003) noted that Kernis was able to "operationalize" high, secure self-esteem based on this approach and did so in ways that resulted in traditionally empirical support for his work on self-esteem and authenticity.

Kernis' work also illustrates another potential link between self-esteem and positivistic positive psychology, one that is surely important for reaching what is called "psychological well-being" as it is presented there. In this case, the connection occurs in terms of what he called "optimal self-esteem."

> I believe that optimal self-esteem involves favorable feelings of self-worth that arise naturally from successfully dealing with life challenges; the operation of one's core, true, authentic self as a source of input to behavioral choices; and relationships in which one is valued for who one is and not for what one achieves. . . . Moreover, it is characterized by favorable implicit feelings of self-worth that stem from positive experiences involving one's actions, contextual factors, and interpersonal relationships. (Kernis, 2003a, p. 13)

Dealing with life's challenges, operating from one's authentic self, and affirming relationships make this approach to self-esteem much different than one that is based on worthiness or competence alone. Researching self-esteem moments that involve facing major challenges of living certainly ought to be of interest to positivistic positive psychology, too. For example, we saw that acting with virtue is an important source of self-esteem. It is one that is usually connected with handling some sort of moral dilemma competently, which is to say that it brings the individual a sense of dignity or worth as a person. Other self-esteem moments include acting with courage in the face of overwhelming odds, overcoming temptation to make more worthy choices, placing higher values such as justice or care for others over personal needs, and so on. All of these positive human experiences and characteristics, as well as the work that accompanies it, should be of interest to the new positive psychology given its stated priorities and goals.

Although certainly not contingent in the fashion that Crocker and Park (2003, 2004) suggested, there is a way in which self-esteem depends on meeting certain standards: Having authentic self-esteem means that one has fared reasonably well while facing the "big choices" in life. Existentially, self-esteem is always at risk because it may be challenged by various situations of life at any time. If we handle them competently, then all is well and good: We *earn* a feeling of worth that reflects our basic humanity and connectedness to others. If we do not, then our humanity is diminished in a significant way and we are usually aware of that, too. As mentioned in Chapter 5, one of the most appealing things about self-esteem when it is seen structurally is that it acts like a behavioral compass. Those who find the value of facing challenges of living in a worthy fashion are more likely to strive to act in ways that maintain such an existential, behavioral, positive "true north" in the future. It would be difficult to understand how a psychology that attempts to focus on positive human behavior and positive human potential is not interested in self-esteem when it is seen in this way.

In sum, researching self-esteem moments can make a significant contribution to both forms of positive psychology. Such situations and the experiences that they bring can be identified, described, analyzed, and even cataloged. Not only can such self-esteem knowledge increase our ability to understand important existential situations and how decisions are made in them, but also it can lead to practical applications. For instance, in addition to allowing people to think about such possibilities in advance, knowledge about the types of situations that can affect self-esteem can be useful in helping parents create environments that foster its development, in assisting organizations that are concerned with promoting virtue, and so forth. Such activities are priorities of positivistic positive psychology, which implies that self-esteem should have an important place in this approach to healthy living and optimal functioning, just as it has in the original positive psychology.

Self-Esteem and Applied Positive Psychology

The other natural tie-in between the established field of self-esteem and the emerging field of positivistic positive psychology is more concrete and practical. Since its inception, the new positive psychology has expressed an interest in applying its principles to everyday life (Seligman & Csikszentmihalyi, 2000). Two general strategies are mentioned in this regard. One involves helping people to deal with existing problems and issues in a positive way, which is sometimes called "positive clinical psychology" (Peterson & Seligman, 2004). The other focus is on prevention, particularly through enhancing the development of various positive human qualities, such as courage, wisdom, resilience, and so forth, as well as facilitating the kinds of social processes and institutions that foster them (Seligman & Csikszentmihalyi, 2000).

In both cases, positivistic positive psychology aims at fostering the development of psychological well-being, which is defined as reflecting "engagement with and full participation in the challenges and opportunities of life" (Linley & Joseph, 2004, p. 5). Although subjective well-being, or what is usually known as "happiness," is a part of psychological well-being, the latter goes far beyond hedonistically positive affective feelings and states. The ultimate goal of this psychology is to facilitate the living of the "good life," which is largely seen in an Aristotelian sense: one that involves striving to live a rich and full, but dignified and balanced, life. Recently, finding ways of dealing with problems and living life in such a positive way have come together in what is called applied positive psychology. The branch of the emerging field that is defined as "the application of positive psychology research to the facilitation of optimal functioning" (Linley & Joseph, 2004, p. 4). To this end, the new positive psychology has developed the beginnings of a classification system of positive characteristics (Peterson & Seligman, 2004) and urges further work on identifying and understanding them in the hope of helping people move toward psychological well-being and the good life. Let us conclude our work by considering how the psychology of self-esteem fits in with this practical aspect of positivistic positive psychology.

One dimension of this area of convergence between the two fields is more clinically oriented. For example, we have seen that there is considerable evidence in work on self-esteem to show that it plays an important role in helping people deal with stress. In this sense, self-esteem acts as a buffer (Pyszczynski et al., 2004a) and serves as a "stock of positive feelings that can be a valuable resource under some conditions" (Baumeister, Campbell, Krueger & Vohs, 2003, p. 37). In addition, it was already shown that self-esteem may be seen as a pivotal variable (Rosenberg, 1965), particularly when people face and deal with various problems and challenges of living (Epstein, 1979; Jackson, 1984; Kernis, 2003a; Mruk, 1983). Finally, evidence indicates that self-esteem is related to healthy human functioning. For example, self-esteem is hedonically positive in that it is characterized by positive affect and "feels good" (Baumeister, Campbell, Krueger & Vohs, 2003). However, self-esteem is positive in terms of eudaimonia as well because it is connected to optimal functioning and the good life by virtue of the relationship between authenticity and self-esteem (Kernis, 2003a, b). All things considered, it stands to reason that work on increasing self-esteem should be of considerable interest to any form of positive psychology in terms of treatment and prevention.

Self-Esteem and Positive Therapy

In discussing positive therapy, Linley and Joseph start out with a position that may seem surprisingly friendly to humanistic psychology given the history of controversy between these two approaches that we reviewed earlier in this chapter.

> It is not our intention to advocate new ways of working therapeutically, but rather to ask what it is to work therapeutically within a positive psychology framework. Can some therapies be considered positive therapies? Our answer to this is yes. In particular, those therapies based on the theoretical premise of an organismic valuing process and an actualizing tendency appear to be most consistent with what the positive psychology research is now telling us. (2004, p. 354)

On deeper reflection, however, there are several good reasons that this position is found in the more clinical literature of the new positive psychology. Where researchers, theoreticians, and academicians are relatively free to debate subtle distinctions concerning such things as the origins and relative superiority of various concepts, theories, or positions, clinicians are not: They must be more concerned with what helps, regardless of such nuances. Thus, programs that reduce human suffering and increase the ability to handle life's challenges by helping people through self-awareness and authentic action are welcomed additions to the therapeutic arsenal by practitioners, no matter what their particular theoretical foundations may be. When seen in this light, it is possible to argue that the self-esteem program offered in Chapter 6 may also stand as a "positive therapy," thereby showing an applied connection between self-esteem and positivistic positive psychology.

One way to evaluate the compatibility of this program with the new positive psychology is to compare it with existing positive therapies. Fava's "well-being therapy" (WBT) has been cited as a primary example of positive therapy in two of the major source books on positive psychology (Linley & Joseph, 2004; Snyder & Lopez, 2002), so it may be used to offer some guidelines as to what constitutes such an approach. This form of therapy was originally designed to deal with the problem of relapse that is a major issue in the treatment of affective disorders (Fava, 1999). The approach is based on the finding that "psychological well-being could not be equated with the absence of symptomology, nor with personality traits" (Ruini & Fava, 2004, p. 371). Instead, psychological well-being is associated with the development of human potential, which both humanistic and positivistic psychologists would call self-actualization, even if one only has brief episodes of it. Historically, of course, well-being has not been the focus of treatment, particularly in modern psychiatry because it is largely oriented toward symptoms and diseases. Yet, Fava and other researchers have found that when this aspect of life is supported by therapeutic interventions, people who live various forms of affective disorders suffer fewer relapses and report greater satisfaction with life than those who are left untreated in this way.

WBT is a short-term approach that is based on the idea that people who suffer negative affective conditions tend to ignore positive ones, *even when they do occur.* Chronically low levels of satisfying experience increase the likelihood of negative responses to life which, in turn, facilitates the occurrence of relapse. If so, breaking this cycle of negative affect and experience with positive ones may prevent relapse, if not assist in recovery. Ruini and Fava (2004) specify that the treatment consists of eight 30- to 50-minute sessions that are offered either once a week or once every other week. The sessions are roughly grouped into three sets or phases. The initial meetings focus on helping patients to identify episodes of well-being that they do experience, describe the circumstances that surrounded them when they occurred, record the situations and experiences in a diary that is kept for this purpose, and then rate the degree of well-being they experienced on a scale of 0–100, with the latter being the highest. Of course, even realizing that one has moments of well-being in the midst of severe illness may be helpful in itself.

The middle or intermediate sessions aim at identifying the ways in which people either short circuit or prematurely end such experiences. This phase also involves teaching them how to avoid doing that, often through cognitive restructuring work. The last cluster of sessions focus on helping the therapist and client identify specific problem areas that impair their ability to experience well-being so that special efforts can be made to address them. This aspect of the program's work involves more detailed assessment using the Well-Being Scales (WBS) (Ryff & Singer, 2002). Then, certain areas of positive functioning related to psychological well-being are given special consideration. They are environmental mastery, personal growth, purpose in life, autonomy, self-acceptance, and positive relations with others. So far, research on well-being therapy for this population generates considerable support as indicated by pre- and post-testing using the scale (Ruini & Fava, 2004; Ryff & Singer, 2002).

Although designed at different times and for different purposes, it should be apparent that there are several significant similarities among the goals and structure of well-being therapy and the self-esteem enhancement program offered in Chapter 6. The most obvious similarities are quite easy to see. For example, each approach is time limited (8 vs. 10 hours of work, respectively) and the sessions are divided into a number of sequential phases (3 vs. 4). Both systems aim to increase self-awareness concerning positive life experience (moments of well-being vs.

self-esteem moments) and both use similar methods to do that (a diary or a journal). Each approach uses a standard assessment instrument as a way to develop treatment that fits the individual rather than a simple manualized program (the WBS and the MSEI). In addition, both programs turn to standard therapeutic techniques to remove obstacles that hinder living more effectively (e.g., cognitive restructuring). Finally, each approach has generated some empirically based work that supports its efficacy based on pre- and post-testing.

In addition, however, the two programs are also similar on another more important level, one that involves what positivistic positive psychology calls "deep strategies" (Peterson & Seligman, 2004; Seligman, 2002). Deep strategies are thought to be especially important therapeutically because they occur as common factors across all major forms of therapy when it is done effectively. Whether moments of well-being or powerful self-esteem moments, one way that both programs work at this deeper level is to take advantage of positive experiences that occur naturally by building them into the therapeutic process right from the beginning. As such, they both work from a strengths perspective, not from a weakness or disease model. WBT focuses on six dimensions of well-being: environmental mastery, personal growth, purpose in life, autonomy, self-acceptance, and positive relations with others. In one way or another, we saw that most of them are also a part of the self-esteem program.

For example, where WBT focuses on environmental mastery, the self-esteem program fosters the development of competence, which is involved in mastery. Personal growth, which is characterized by helping clients feel a sense of ongoing development as an individual human being, is an important goal in either system. Purpose in life, which involves the client having goals and a sense of direction, is central to WBT. Developing a self-esteem project also involves setting goals that are personally meaningful and working toward them provides a sense of direction. Autonomy depends on independence, self-determination, and evaluating oneself by one's own standards: So does self-esteem when it is defined in terms of competence and worthiness. Self-acceptance is an important dimension of psychological well-being that is important to WBT, and we also saw that it is at the heart of worthiness in the self-esteem program. Naturally, there are differences between the two programs in design and in these six areas: after all, the two therapies have their respective goals and concerns. However, by now it should be clear that the similarities are substantial, indeed.

Finally, it is important to point out that the three criteria positivistic positive psychology uses to characterize its positive therapy may also be used to applied self-esteem work, at least when it is done on the basis of competence and worthiness. First, positive psychology aims to facilitate the development of positive aspects of human behavior. What could be more positive than fostering competence when it is balanced by worthiness? Second, we have seen that positive therapy aims at helping people to reach psychological well-being, as well as subjective well being; so does helping them deal with life's challenges in a competent and worthy way over time. Finally, we saw that Linley and Joseph stated that positive therapy also is concerned with "organismic values" and self-actualization. They, too, have been shown to be a part of self-esteem and enhancing it, especially in terms of intrinsic values and authenticity. In sum, enhancing self-esteem is clearly a form of positive therapy and should be seen that way, regardless of whether positive is defined in newer or older ways.

Self-Esteem and Prevention: Working with a Human Strength

Another dimension of the practical connection between self-esteem work and new positive psychology occurs in relation to prevention, which is among its chief characteristics. As Seligman and Csikszentmihalyi said early on in the movement,

> Prevention researchers have discovered that there are human strengths that act as buffers against mental illness: courage, future mindedness, optimism, interpersonal skill, faith, work ethic, hope, honesty, perseverance, and the capacity for flow and insight, to name several. Much of the task of prevention in this new century will be to create a science of human strength whose mission will be to understand and learn how to foster these virtues in young people. (2000, p. 7)

Although important at the individual level, fostering strengths or virtues also has larger, more social, and longer lasting implications. For example, healthy people are more likely to demand healthy institutions, work for their creation, remove obstacles that threaten them, and care for them because of the intrinsic value of the project. In this way, the strengths perspective may set up a virtuous cycle that could expand over time to include more and more people. At the Utopian level, perhaps this positive dynamic could even include the entire world. Of course, anyone who is familiar with Maslow's work knows that humanistic positive psychology proposed such a long range and encompassing vision as well.

At this point it should be clear that there is a place for self-esteem in positivistic positive psychology. If not, then it is important to ask the question of what would it take for the new positive psychology to pay attention to self-esteem in this way? Some positive psychologists have identified 10 criteria by which human characteristics and qualities may be identified or understood as constituting a positive strength or virtue

(Peterson & Seligman, 2004). Although it is not clear how much ambiguity any particular criterion tolerates, it is stated that a given human quality or characteristic must meet "most" (p. 16) of them to qualify in this regard, though it is not certain whether that means six or more. Perhaps briefly taking self-esteem through this "test" will help us determine whether it is possible to argue that this human characteristic merits such consideration when defined as a relationship between competence and worthiness.

The first criterion concerns fulfillment: whether a quality fulfills an individual in a way that is consistent with an Aristotelian view of the "good life." This indicator is also known as the "deathbed test" (p. 17). The test is that if a person was dying, would the individual be likely to wish, in the face of death, that he or she would have spent more time living in a particular way (or exhibiting a particular characteristic), if he or she had not done enough of it already in life? It seems to me that many self-esteem moments suggest that facing challenges of living in a worthy way over time certainly would be something that one would hope to say they had done enough of at the end of a life. If not, it seems just as likely that they would wish they had, either of which meets this test. The second criterion focuses on whether a particular strength or quality is morally valued in its own right. The type of self-esteem that comes with acting in a virtuous way and from being worthy in general certainly seems relevant in this regard. The third criterion is the stipulation that a true human strength does not diminish other people in any way. Of course, it is possible to argue authentic self-esteem qualifies at this level, because self-esteem only fails such a test when it is defined in terms of competence or worthiness alone.

The fourth criterion is more difficult to consider because it may be less clear or straightforward than the others. It concerns the degree to which "Being able to phrase the 'opposite' of a putative strength in a felicitous way counts against regarding it as a character strength" (p. 22). This criterion may mean that the opposite of authentic self-esteem needs to be examined for certain types of contradiction. Low self-esteem does not have many characteristics that are desirable, at least according to the self-esteem matrix and the DSM IV-TR, so perhaps self-esteem is acceptable in this regard. However, Peterson and Seligman also noted that this particular criterion may not be applicable to "bipolar" characteristics and self-esteem could be seen as one of them because it ranges in positive and negative ways. Thus, it is not clear whether self-esteem is to be assessed in this way. The fifth criterion is that the characteristic or quality must occur in a range of situations or behaviors, much as a trait would. Self-esteem certainly meets this criterion: We saw in Chapters 3 and 5 that self-esteem may be stable, low, unstable, fragile, secure, and so forth but tends to be reasonably consistent, much like a personality trait, and can even be measured like one.

The sixth criterion is that a positive strength must be "distinct from other positive traits in the classification and cannot be decomposed into them" (p. 24). If self-esteem is "decomposed" into its components of competence and worthiness, we lose something important, namely how they balance each other to create something greater than either one alone. As Tafarodi and Vu (1997) pointed out, four lines do not create much of anything unless they stand in relation to each other to make a shape. If balance is added as a requirement, then only one figure, that of a square, will do, which means that self-esteem seems to pass this test too. The seventh criterion is that a character strength is "embodied in consensual paragons (p. 24)" such as stories, fables, and so forth. One would be hard pressed to talk about self-esteem "fables." However, it is possible to point to any number of stories about individuals who struggled to do the right thing in trying circumstances and we know that such behavior is tied to self-esteem. The eighth criterion does not to apply to all strengths, but some of them involve young people who demonstrate extraordinarily high degrees of a particular characteristic. Of course, we do not speak of self-esteem prodigies and ask them to perform for us. Yet, most parents, teachers, coaches, counselors, and ministers have noted with approval that this or that child seems to have unusually high or solid self-esteem. Thus, this criterion could be counted from a particular point of view as well.

The ninth criterion defines a positive characteristic by noting how negative behavior is when the quality is absent. It is difficult to imagine anyone praising the virtues of having classical low self-esteem as defined here, so it certainly passes muster in this regard. The tenth criterion concerns whether social institutions foster the development of the positive characteristic. In this case, I would point out that parents certainly work hard to let their children know that they are accepted and loved as worthy individuals. Teachers struggle daily to help their students gain competence in ways that will serve them well. After that, of course, we are on our own. However, adults admire people who display a balance of competence and worthiness when we encounter them at the work place or in the community.

Of course, it is possible to further develop each point of the argument supporting the position that self-esteem, when defined as a balance of competence and worthiness, "passes the test" for inclusion into positivistic positive psychology as a positive human strength or characteristic. However, given the thrust of this book, it is also possible to claim that the results of any examination presented here could be biased. Therefore, it is up to the reader and others to accept, reject, refine, or otherwise evaluate self-esteem against the criteria for themselves. Even so, it is also possible to point out that there are other powerful reasons that self-esteem should be considered as a positive strength according to the tenants of the new positive psychology itself.

For example, the list of strengths that the positive psychology classification system has developed so far includes the quality of *integrity*. It is placed under the moral category of *courage* because it takes courage to maintain integrity, especially over time. However, integrity is a complex quality and comes in many forms. Thus, the term is bracketed to include authenticity and honesty so that the phrasing actually reads, "Integrity [Authenticity, Honesty]" (p. 29). We saw that all three of these qualities are connected to self-esteem and vice versa in the more intense types of self-esteem moments and in the research on authenticity. When self-esteem is defined as facing life's challenges in a worthy way over time, then it certainly means having "integrity." Therefore, it seems reasonable to suggest that, at least, the classification should be modified to read "Integrity [Authenticity, Honesty, Authentic Self-Esteem]."

A Final Point

One last point that goes beyond mere psychology needs to be made in closing the case for seeing self-esteem as a positive quality or human strength and for including self-esteem in positivistic positive psychology. It is important to remember that the new positive psychology bases its view of the good life in large part on Aristotelian foundations (Jorgensen & Nafstad, 2004, pp. 16–17). Students of philosophy know that this perspective, which is one of the most influential in the entire history of the world, includes a specific view of virtue and virtuous characteristics. Although it is not possible to present Aristotle's entire line of reasoning here, he does make it clear in Book II, Chapter 6 of *Nicomachean Ethics* that every virtue "both brings into good condition the thing of which it is the excellence and makes the work of that thing be done well" (McKeon, 1941, p. 957). When defined in terms of competence and worthiness, self-esteem certainly seems to demonstrate this aspect of virtue. For when someone deals with a challenge of living in a worthy fashion, they have been found to actually "bring into good condition," (make positive) their "excellence" (worth as a human being), by doing something "well" (resolving a challenge competently).

Moreover, it is necessary to appreciate that self-esteem may be a virtue in Aristotle's own classification of such characteristics. For example, when discussing virtues he pointed out that many, if not most, aspects of life may be lived in terms of excess (too much), defect (too little), or in terms of an "intermediate" (balance) between the two.

> Virtue, then, is a state of character concerned with choice, lying in a mean, i.e. the mean relative to us, this being determined by a rational principle, and by that principle by which the man of practical wisdom would determine it. Now it is a mean between two vices, that which depends on excess and that which depends on defect; and again it is a mean because the vices respectively fall short of or exceed what is right in both passions and actions, while virtue both finds and chooses that which is intermediate. (McKeon, 1941, p. 959)

The "intermediate," of course, is "that which is equidistant from each of the extremes" (p. 958) and provides the foundation for the Greek standard known as the "Golden Mean." Aristotle went on to show how this approach to defining virtue may be applied to human characteristics. For example, he reasoned, as does positive psychology, that courage is a virtue: It is the intermediate of fear and confidence. In this case, the extreme of too much fear could take the form of such deficits of character or behavior as cowardice or panic, whereas an excess of confidence may result in such dangerous extremes as rashness or foolhardiness. Courage, of course, is equidistant from both: It is a balance of the recognition of real danger and a willingness to act because it is necessary.

Similarly and most important, Aristotle noted that "With regard to honor and dishonour the mean is proper pride, the excess is known as a sort of 'empty vanity,' and the deficiency is undue humility" (p. 960). In a real sense, the modern-day language for such "proper pride" is nothing other than authentic self-esteem. For we have seen that an excess of worthiness that is not balanced by competence results in problems associated with vanity or even narcissism. Similarly, we found that an abundance of competence without the counterbalance of worthiness is characterized by a lack of honoring the value of the self, whether it be one's own or that of others. Self-esteem is the intermediate of competence and worthiness because it is the point where one balances the other. We saw this "Golden Mean" of behavior in the self-esteem matrix, in the analogy of a square, and now in Aristotle, who provides some of the more important foundations of positivistic positive psychology. Therefore, it would be difficult to understand how self-esteem, when defined as a balance of worthiness and competence, could be anything less than a positive human characteristic or virtue for the new positive psychology, just as it always has been for the original one.

So far, positivistic positive psychology has not taken up the question of self-esteem with the seriousness that it deserves. However, the situation may be changing because a new generation of positivistic positive psychologists is emerging, and they may be more open to such a dialogue.

Humanistic psychology is a broad church, and there are parts of it that we would not recognize as positive psychology; but in our view, the ideas of the main humanistic psychology writers, such as Rogers and Maslow, deserve to be set center stage within positive psychology. Theirs was an empirical stance, explicitly research-based, albeit lacking in the sophistication of current psychology research methods. We ought to respect this lineage, and we encourage those who are not familiar with this earlier work to visit it. (Linley & Joseph, 2004, p. 365)

There can be little doubt that self-esteem occupies an important place as a central idea in humanistic psychology, so it certainly deserves to be thought about as one of the ideas to which Linley and Joseph refer. In addition, self-esteem is also a part of traditional psychology and has been almost since its beginnings. Moreover, we have seen that there is an approach to defining self-esteem that deals with the limits of traditional work. Finally, it is philosophically plausible to see self-esteem as a basic human virtue or strength. Therefore, it becomes difficult to understand why positivistic positive psychology has not yet embraced the importance of self-esteem as a basic human phenomenon. Perhaps now is the time to give self-esteem its rightful place in the research, theory, and practice of the emerging field of positive psychology.

Self-Esteem Enhancement 5-Week Program

WEEK 1—HANDOUT 1: PROGRAM ANNOUNCEMENT

Self-Esteem Enhancement: Program Announcement

This 5-week program is a group experience designed to increase our understanding and awareness of self-esteem. Participants have the opportunity to assess their self-esteem, to understand its basic components, and to learn how to work on self-esteem issues. You also create your own self-esteem improvement program and use group exercises to help you work on increasing your self-esteem during the program and afterward.

The program is run by _____, who is credentialed as a _____, and who is interested in helping people to increase their self-esteem. The group sessions are based on a psychoeducational format, so learning is emphasized. The program is a focused one, meaning that we deal with one theme, self-esteem, as the main topic of all meetings and activities. Anyone currently involved in treatment for a mental health condition is advised to discuss whether to be in this program with his or her therapist.

We will meet on _____ from _____ for 5 consecutive weeks. Attendance at all meetings is strongly encouraged because the program is designed to move in a step-by-step fashion. We hope to see you there, so please be sure that you reserve a place through _____ who may be reached at _____ before _____ as there are a limited number of seats.

WEEK 1—HANDOUT 2: ACTIVITY SCHEDULE

I. Self-esteem enhancement program steps

    A. Introduction to self-esteem and basic research about it

    B. Procedure

        1. Week 1: *Focusing phase:* Defining self-esteem
          a. Discussing basic concepts
          b. Assessing individual self-esteem

        2. Week 2: *Awareness phase:* Appreciating self-esteem
          a. Understanding common self-esteem problems
          b. Understanding the sources of self-esteem

        3. Week 3: *Enhancing phase:* Increasing worthiness
          a. Understanding cognitive restructuring
          b. Removing "self-esteem traps"

        4. Week 4: *Enhancing phase:* Increasing competence
          a. Introduction to problem solving
          b. Practicing problem-solving techniques

        5. Week 5: *Management phase:* Maintaining self-esteem
          a. Planning your own self-esteem action programs
          b. Evaluating the approach: Strengths and limits

WEEK 1—HANDOUT 3: GROUP GUIDELINES AND EXPECTATIONS

Group Guidelines and Expectations

The self-esteem enhancement program is run by _____, who is credentialed as a _____. The group sessions are based on a psychoeducational format, so learning is emphasized. The program is a focused one, meaning that we will deal with one theme, self-esteem, as the main topic of all meetings and activities. Anyone currently involved in treatment for a mental health condition is advised to discuss whether to be in this program with his or her therapist.

We will meet on _____ from _____ for 5 consecutive weeks. Some basic rules will help us to create a positive, supportive group environment.

1. Confidentiality: Mutual trust among group members is important. Each of us has a right to privacy, and we all depend on each other to have it.
2. Respect: For the program to enhance your appreciation of self-esteem, it is important that all members treat each other with the respect that each unique human being deserves. Although we may have differences of opinion, it is essential that we welcome diversity.
3. Attendance: Attendance at all meetings is strongly encouraged because the program is designed to move in a step-by-step fashion. Also, group processes cannot work well if a large number of people are not present or if attendance is sporadic. Each of us depends on all the others in this regard, so do your best to be here for yourself and others.
4. Participation: The benefits of most therapeutic or psychoeducational activities are related to how much you participate in the process. However, other than following the previously listed rules, you are not required to do anything that you do not feel comfortable doing.

WEEK 1—HANDOUT 4: DEFINING SELF-ESTEEM

I. Self-esteem comes from facing life's challenges in a way that is competent and worthy and doing so over time.

    A. Experience of competence.
        1. Briefly describe such an experience.

        2. What did the experience show you about competence?

    B. Experience of worthiness.
        1. Briefly describe such an experience.

        2. What did it tell you about worthiness?

II. Keeping a self-esteem journal.

WEEK 2—HANDOUT 1: SELF-ESTEEM TYPES, LEVELS, AND PROBLEMS

I. Self-esteem matrix: basic types and levels

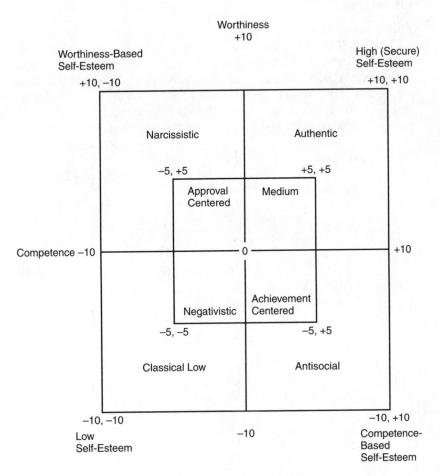

II. Common self-esteem problems (to be discussed)

WEEK 2—HANDOUT 2: APPLYING
THE MULTIDIMENSIONAL SELF-ESTEEM
INVENTORY SCALES

Self-Esteem Profile

Self-esteem profile for _____ Date _____

The MSEI has 11 scales. The scales describing general levels of self-esteem are Global Self-Esteem, Identity Integration, and Defensiveness. Competence-related scales are Competence, Personal Power, Self-Control, and Bodily Functioning. Worthiness-related scales are Lovability, Likability, Moral Self-Approval, and Bodily Appearance. The test results focus on the two highest and the two lowest areas, which for you are:

    A. Current self-esteem strengths (most positive scores)
        1. _____ The positive scale on which you scored highest.
        This scale suggests that:

        2. _____ The positive scale on which you scored second highest.
        This scale suggests that:

    B. Potential self-esteem growth areas
        1. _____ The scale on which your lowest score occurred, including defensiveness if that was high.
        This scale suggests that:

        2. _____ The scale on which your second lowest score occurred, including defensiveness if that was high.
        This scale suggests that:

WEEK 2—HANDOUT 3: FINDING SOURCES OF SELF-ESTEEM

I. Personal achievements or successes

II. Evidence of influence or power

III. Acceptance or being valued

IV. Virtue or acting on beliefs (doing the "right thing")

WEEK 3—HANDOUT 1: ENHANCING WORTHINESS THROUGH POSITIVE FEEDBACK

A. List positive features.

1. _____
2. _____
3. _____
4. _____
5. _____
6. _____
7. _____
8. _____
9. _____
10. _____

B. Group sharing (reading aloud).

WEEK 3—HANDOUT 2: INCREASING WORTHINESS THROUGH COGNITIVE RESTRUCTURING

I. Common cognitive self-esteem traps

  A. Concept: Mistakes in thinking and perceiving that keep us stuck or in pain.

  B. List of common self-esteem traps:

    1. Emotional Reasoning—Letting feelings overrule rational thoughts, such as frequently saying, "Yeah, but" or "if only."

    2. Filtering—Focusing attention on the negative aspects of a situation or event and ignoring or minimizing positive possibilities.

    3. Labeling—Using negative labels to describe self or others, such as calling yourself or others a "loser," "a wimp," or a "dummy."

    4. Overgeneralizing—Extending the negative meanings of an event beyond what is necessary so that it seems worse than it is.

    5. Personalizing—Being too sensitive about an incident or event so that it becomes more painful than realistically necessary.

    6. _____

    7. _____

    8. _____

    9. _____

    10. _____

  C. Facilitator's example of making an error

WEEK 3—HANDOUT 3: PATTERN-BREAKING OUTLINE

I. Implementation of the cognitive restructuring process

   A. Seven-step method

     1. *Describe the situation* that lessened self-esteem.

     2. *Note the strongest feelings* you had in the situation and rate them on a scale of 1–10.

     3. *Identify ALL the thoughts* you were actually having in the situation as accurately as possible.

     4. *Name ALL the errors* by examining your thoughts for those that reflect one or more of the mistakes people make in reacting to events on the list of frequent errors.

     5. *Make corrections* by substituting a realistic thought or reaction for each thinking error you made.

     6. *Reevaluate your feelings* about the situation as they are now on the same scale and compare them with the results of step 2.

     7. *Repeat* the process until errors no longer occur.

   B. Facilitator's example (Work all the steps on the board.)

     1.

     2.

     3.

     4.

     5.

     6.

     7.

   C. Participant's examples (Work problems offered by the group on the board.)

WEEK 4—HANDOUT 1: ENHANCING COMPETENCE: PROBLEM-SOLVING METHOD

A. Basic problem-solving theory
1. Feelings often let us know that a problem is developing.
2. Thinking helps us to understand the problem better.
3. Actions allow us to solve the problem.

B. Basic problem-solving steps
1. Realize that there is a problem.
2. Stop and try to understand it well.
3. Decide on a goal.
4. Identify possible solutions.
5. Think about the likely consequences of each solution.
6. Choose the best, most realistic solution.
7. Make a detailed plan for carrying out the solution.
8. Practice!

WEEK 4—HANDOUT 2: ENHANCING COMPETENCE: PROBLEM-SOLVING WORKSHEET

A. The problem-solving process.

Step	Procedure
1. Identifying a problem.	Look for emotional cues.
2. Stop and understand.	Ask, "What is the problem?"
3. Decide on a goal.	Ask, "What do I want here?"
4. Identify possible solutions.	Brainstorm possibilities.
a.	
b.	
c.	
5. Think about likely consequences.	Ask, "What will happen if this occurs?"
a.	
b.	
c.	
6. Choose the best alternative.	Ask, "Which am I willing to live with?"
7. Make a plan.	Ask, "What needs to be done, step-by-step?"
a.	
b.	
c.	
8. Learning: Practice, practice, and more practice!	

B. Select examples and work through each of the steps.

WEEK 5—HANDOUT 1: BUILDING A SELF-ESTEEM ENHANCEMENT PROJECT

I. Self-esteem action cycle

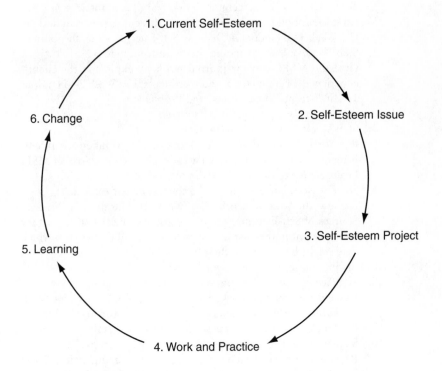

II. Self-esteem action plan: Increasing and maintaining self-esteem

A. Identify a self-esteem strength or weakness to work on.

B. Match the issue with the four sources of self-esteem.

C. Identify a realistic goal or outcome.

D. Write specific, workable action steps for the goal or outcome.
   1.

   2.

   3.

   4.

SUPPLEMENT 1: ACTIVITY SCHEDULE FOR RESEARCHING THE INDIVIDUALIZED PROGRAM

A. Focusing phase: Defining self-esteem.
    1. Step/Week 1: Introduction to the program.
      To be done after screening, intake, and diagnostic work are completed. Build rapport and go over this entire program outline. Use Week 1—Handout 4: Defining Self-Esteem. Set up the journal.
    2. Step/Week 2: Understanding the self-esteem matrix.
      Give the MSEI. Review journal work by exploring the client's experiences of competence and worthiness. Use Week 2—Handout 1: Self-Esteem Types, Levels, and Problems.
B. Awareness phase: Appreciating self-esteem.
    3. Step/Week 3: Assessing self-esteem.
      Use Week 2—Handout 2: Applying the Multidimensional Self-Esteem Inventory Scales. Review the journal work. Go over MSEI Profile, but explore all the scales instead of just two.
    4. Step/Week 4: Understanding the sources of self-esteem.
      Review the journal work. Use Week 2—Handout 3: Finding Sources of Self-Esteem. Explore the sources of self-esteem as they were present in the past for the individual and the ways in which they might be present in their lives today.
C. Enhancing phase: Increasing worthiness.
    5. Step/Week 5: Introduction to cognitive restructuring.
      Review the journal work. Explore worthiness by using Week 3—Handout 1: Enhancing Worthiness through Positive Feedback, explore areas and feelings in some detail.
    6. Step/Week 6: Removing cognitive "self-esteem traps."
      Review Journal. Teach cognitive restructuring using Week 3—Handout 2: Increasing Worthiness through Cognitive Restructuring; and Week 3—Handout 3: Pattern-Breaking Outline.
D. Enhancing phase: Increasing competence.
    7. Step/Week 7: Introduction to problem solving.
      Review journal work, use Week 4—Handout 1: Enhancing Competence: Problem-Solving Method. Use Week 4—Handout 2: Enhancing Competence: Problem-Solving Worksheet.
    8. Step/Week 8: Practicing problem-solving techniques.
      Review journal work, review previous lessons on cognitive restructuring and problem solving.
E. Management phase: Maintaining your self-esteem.
    9. Step/Week 9: Planning your own self-esteem action programs.
      Review journal work. Use Week 5—Handout 1: Building a Self-Esteem Enhancement Project.
    10. Step/Week 10: Evaluating the approach.
      Strengths and limits. Deal with termination issues.
F. Optional follow-up: Booster session or sessions.

References

Aanstoos, C. (Ed.). (1984). *Exploring the lived world: Readings in phenomenological psychology* (Vol. 23). Atlanta: West Georgia College.

Aanstoos, C. (Ed.). (1995). From the editor's bookshelf. *The Humanistic Psychologist, 23,* 121.

Adler, A. (1927). *Understanding human nature.* New York: Fawcett.

Alberti, R. E., & Emmons, R. L. (1982). *Your perfect right: A guide to rational living* (4th ed.). San Luis Obispo, CA: Impact Publishers.

American Association of University Women (1991). *Shortchanging girls, shortchanging America.* Washington, DC: Author.

American Psychiatric Association. (2000). *Diagnostic and statistical manual of mental disorders* (4th ed., text rev.). Washington, DC: Author.

Arkowitz, H. (1997). Integrative theories of therapy. In P. Wachtel & S. Messer (Eds.), *Theories of psychotherapy: Origins and evolution* (pp. 227–288). Washington, DC: American Psychological Association.

Aspinwall, L. G., & Staudinger, U. M. (Eds.). (2003). *A psychology of human strengths: Fundamental questions and future directions for a positive psychology.* Washington, DC: American Psychological Association.

Bandura, A. (1997). *Self-efficacy: The exercise of control.* New York: W. H. Freeman & Co.

Bartoletti, M., & O'Brien, E. J. (2003). *Self-esteem, coping and immunocompetence: A correlational study.* Poster session presented at the annual meeting of the American Psychological Association, Toronto, Canada.

Battle, J. (1992). *Culture-free self-esteem inventories* (2nd ed.). Austin, TX: Pro-ed.

Baumeister, R. (Ed.). (1993). *Self-esteem: The puzzle of low self-regard.* New York: Plenum.

Baumeister, R. F., Campbell, J. D., Krueger, J. I., & Vohs, K. D. (2003). Does high self-esteem cause better performance, interpersonal success, happiness, or healthier lifestyles? *Psychological Science in the Public Interest, 4,* 1–44.

Baumeister, R., Smart, L., & Boden, J. (1996). Relation of threatened egotism to violence and aggression: The dark side of self-esteem. *Psychological Review, 103,* 5–33.

Beane, J. (1991). Sorting out the self-esteem controversy. *Educational Leadership, 49,* 25–30.

Bednar, R., & Peterson, S. (1995). *Self-esteem: Paradoxes and innovations in clinical theory and practice* (2nd ed.). Washington, DC: American Psychological Association.

Bednar, R., Wells, G., & Peterson, S. (1989). *Self-esteem: Paradoxes and innovations in clinical theory and practice.* Washington, DC: American Psychological Association.

Berger, P. L. (1967). *The scared canopy.* New York: Doubleday.

Bhatti, B., Derezotes, D., Kim, S., & Specht, H. (1989). The association between child maltreatment and low self-esteem. In A. M. Mecca, N. Smelser & J. Vasconcellos (Eds.), *The social importance of self-esteem* (pp. 24–71). Berkeley: University of California Press.

Block, J., & Thomas, H. (1955). Is satisfaction with self a measure of adjustment? *Journal of Abnormal and Social Psychology, 51,* 257–261.

Bradshaw, P. (1981). *The management of self-esteem.* Englewood Cliffs, NJ: Prentice Hall.

Branden, N. (1969). *The psychology of self-esteem.* New York: Bantam.

Branden, N. (1983). *Honoring the self.* Los Angeles: Tarcher.

Branden, N. (1994). *The six pillars of self-esteem.* New York: Bantam.

Brockner, J., Wiesenfeld, B., & Raskas, D. (1993). Self-esteem and expectancy-value discrepancy: The effects of believing that you can (or can't) get what you want. In R. Baumeister (Ed.), *Self-esteem: The puzzle of low self-regard* (pp. 219–241). New York: Plenum.

Brown, J. D., Collins, R. L., & Schmidt, G. W. (1988). Self-esteem and direct versus indirect forms of self-enhancement. *Journal of Personality and Social Psychology, 55*(3), 445–453.

Burger, J. M. (1995). Need for control and self-esteem: Two routes to a high desire for control. In M. H. Kernis (Ed.), *Efficacy, agency, and self-esteem* (pp. 217–233). New York: Plenum.

Burns, D. (1980). *Feeling good: The new mood therapy.* New York: Signet.

Burns, D. (1993a). *Ten days to self-esteem.* New York: Quill.

Burns, D. (1993b). *Ten days to self-esteem: The leader's manual.* New York: Quill.

Campbell, J. D. (1999). Self-esteem and clarity of the self-concept. In R. Baumeister (Ed.), *The self in social psychology* (pp. 223–239). New York: Taylor & Francis.

Campbell, J., & Lavallee, L. (1993). Who am I? The role of self-concept and confusion in understanding the behavior of people with low self-esteem. In R. Baumeister (Ed.), *Self-esteem: The puzzle of low self-regard* (pp. 4–20). New York: Plenum.

Campbell, W. K., Rudich, E. A., & Sedikides, C. (2002). Narcissism, self-esteem, and the positivity of self-views: Two portraits of self-love. *Personality and Social Psychology, 28*(3), 358–368.

Clark, J., & Barber, B. (1994). Adolescents in post divorce and always married families: Self-esteem and perceptions of father's interest. *Journal of Marriage and Family, 56,* 608–614.

Colaizzi, P. (1973). *Reflection and research in psychology: A phenomenological study of learning.* Dubuque, IA: Kendall/Hunt.

Cole, C., Oetting E., & Hinkle, J. (1967). Non-linearity of self-concept discrepancy—the value dimension. *Psychological Reports, 21,* 56–60.

Compton, W. (2005). *An introduction to positive psychology*. Belmont, CA: Thomson.

Cooley, C. H. (1909). *Human nature and the social order*. New York: Scribner.

Coopersmith, S. (1959). A method for determining types of self-esteem. *Journal of Abnormal Social Psychology, 59,* 87–94.

Coopersmith, S. (1967). *The antecedents of self-esteem*. San Francisco: Freeman.

Coopersmith, S. (1981). *Adult form SEI Coopersmith inventory*. Palo Alto, CA: Consulting Psychologists Press.

Costall, A., & Still, A. (Eds.). (1987). *Cognitive psychology in question*. New York: St. Martin's Press.

Crocker, J., & Nuer, N. (2003). The insatiable quest for self-worth. *Psychological Inquiry, 14*(1), 31–34.

Crocker, J., & Nuer, N. (2004). Do people need self-esteem? Comment on Pyszczynski et al. *Psychological Bulletin, 130*(3), 469–472.

Crocker, J., & Park, L. E. (2003). Seeking self-esteem: Construction, mainte-nance, and protection of self-worth. In M. R. Leary & J. P. Tangney (Eds.), *Handbook of self and identity* (pp. 291–313). New York: Guilford.

Crocker, J., & Park, L. E. (2004). The costly pursuit of self-esteem. *Psychological Bulletin, 130*(3), 392–414.

Damon, W. (1995). *Great expectations: Overcoming the culture of indulgence in our homes and schools*. New York: Free Press.

Deci, E. L., & Ryan, M. R. (1995). Human autonomy: The basis for true self-esteem. In M. H. Kernis (Ed.), *Efficacy, agency, and self-esteem* (pp. 31–51). New York: Plenum.

Devos, T., & Banaji, M. R. (2003). Implicit self and identity. In M. R. Leary & J. P. Tangney (Eds.), *Handbook of self and identity* (pp. 153–175). New York: Guilford.

Diggory, J. C. (1966). *Self-evaluation: Concepts and studies*. New York: Wiley.

Dijksterhuis, A. (2004). I like myself but I don't know why: Enhancing implicit self-esteem by subliminal evaluative conditioning. *Journal of Personality and Social Psychology, 82*(2), 345–355.

Dreyfus, H. L., & Dreyfus, S. E. (1986). *Mind over machine: The power of human intuition and expertise in the era of the computer*. New York: Free Press.

DuBois, D. L., & Flay, R. R. (2004). The healthy pursuit of self-esteem: Comment on and alternative to Crocker and Park (2004) formulation. *Psychological Bulletin, 130*(3), 415–420.

D'Zurilla, T. J., & Goldfried, M. R. (1971). Problem solving and behavior mod-ification. *Journal of Abnormal Psychology, 78,* 107–126.

D'Zurilla, T. J., & Nezu, A. M. (2001). Problem solving therapies. In K. S. Dobson (Ed.), *Handbook of cognitive behavioral therapies* (2nd ed.) (pp. 211–245). New York: Guilford.

Ellis, A., & Harper, R. (1977). *A new guide to rational living*. North Hollywood, CA: Wilshire Book Company.

Emler, N. (2001) *Self-esteem: The costs and causes of low self-worth*. York, England: York Publishing Services, Joseph Rowntree Foundation.

Epstein, S. (1979). The ecological study of emotions in humans. In K. Blankstein (Ed.), *Advances in the study of communications and affect* (pp. 47–83). New York: Plenum.

Epstein, S. (1980). The self-concept: A review and the proposal of an integrated theory of personality. In E. Straub (Ed.), *Personality: Basic aspects and current research* (pp. 83–131). Englewood Cliffs, NJ: Prentice Hall.

Epstein, S. (1985). The implications of cognitive-experiential self-theory for research in social psychology and personality. *Journal for the Theory of Social Behavior, 15,* 283–309.

Epstein, S., & Morling, B. (1995). Is the self motivated to do more than enhance and/or verify itself? In M. H. Kernis (Ed.), *Efficacy, agency, and self-esteem* (pp. 9–30). New York: Plenum.

Erikson, E. (1983). *The life cycle completed.* New York: Norton.

Fava, G. A. (1999). Well-being therapy: Conceptual and technical issues. *Psychotherapy and Psychosomatics, 68,* 171–179.

Finkelhor, D., & Browne, A. (1985). The traumatic impact of child sexual abuse: A conceptualization. *American Journal of Orthopsychiatry, 55,* 530–541.

Fischer, C. (1986). *Individualizing psychological assessment.* Belmont, CA: Wadsworth.

Franks, D. D., & Marolla, J. (1976). Efficacious action and social approval as interacting dimensions of self-esteem: A tentative formulation through construct validation. *Sociometry, 39*(4), 324–341.

Freeman, A., Pretzer, J., Fleming, B., & Simon, K. (1990). *Clinical applications of cognitive therapy.* New York: Plenum.

Freud, S. (1957). *On narcissism: An introduction* (standard ed.). London: Hogarth Press. (Original work published 1914.)

Frey, D., & Carlock, C. J. (1989). *Enhancing self-esteem* (2nd ed.). Muncie, IN: Accelerated Development.

Frey, D. E., Kelbley, T. J., Thomas, J., Durham, L., & James, J. S. (1992). Enhancing self-esteem of selected male nursing home residents. *Gerontologist, 32,* 552–557.

Gecas, V. (1971). Parental behavior and dimensions of adolescent self-evaluation. *Sociometry, 34*(4), 466–482.

Gecas, V. (1982). The self-concept. *Annual Review of Sociology, 8,* 1–33.

Gecas, V., & Schwalbe, M. L. (1983). Beyond the looking-glass self: Social structure and efficacy-based self-esteem. *Social Psychology Quarterly, 46*(2), 77–88.

Gergen, K. J. (1991). *The saturated self: Dilemmas of identity in contemporary life.* New York: Basic Books.

Giorgi, A. (1970). *Psychology as a human science: A phenomenologically based approach.* New York: Harper & Row.

Giorgi, A. (1971). Phenomenology and experimental psychology: 1 & 2. In A. Giorgi, W. Fischer, & R. Von Eckartsberg (Eds.), *Duquesne studies in phenomenological psychology* (Vol. 1, pp. 6–28). Pittsburgh, PA: Duquesne University Press.

Giorgi, A. (1975). Convergence and divergence of qualitative and quantitative methods in psychology. In A. Giorgi, C. Fischer, & E. Murray (Eds.),

Duquesne studies in phenomenological psychology (Vol. 2, pp. 72–79). Pittsburgh, PA: Duquesne University Press.

Giorgi, A. (1984). Towards a new paradigm for psychology. In C. Aanstoos (Ed.), *Exploring the lived world: Readings in phenomenological psychology* (Vol. 22, pp. 9–28). Atlanta: West Georgia College.

Greenberg, J., Koole, S., & Pyszczynski, T. (Eds.). (2004). *Handbook of experimental existential psychology*. New York: Guilford.

Greenberg, J., Pyszczynski, T., & Solomon, S. (1995). Toward a dual-motive depth psychology of self and social behavior. In M. H. Kernis (Ed.), *Efficacy, agency, and self-esteem* (pp. 73–99). New York: Plenum.

Greenier, K. D., Kernis, M. H., & Waschull, S. B. (1995). Not all high (or low) self-esteem people are the same: Theory and research on stability of self-esteem. In M. H. Kernis (Ed.), *Efficacy, agency, and self-esteem* (pp. 51–71). New York: Plenum.

Greening, T. (2001). Commentary by the editor. *Journal of Humanistic Psychology, 41*(1), 4–7.

Guindon, M. H. (2002). Assessment and diagnosis: Toward accountability in the use of the self-esteem construct. *Journal of Counseling & Development, 80*(2), 204–214.

Gurwitsch, A. (1964). *The field of consciousness*. Pittsburgh, PA: Duquesne University Press.

Hakim-Larson, J., & Mruk, C. (1997). Enhancing self-esteem in a community mental health setting. *American Journal of Orthopsychiatry, 67,* 655–659.

Harter, S. (1985). *The perceived competence scale for children*. Unpublished manuscript, University of Denver, Denver, CO.

Harter, S. (1993). Causes and consequences of low self-esteem in children and adolescents. In R. Baumeister (Ed.), *Self-esteem: The puzzle of low self-regard* (pp. 87–111). New York: Plenum.

Harter, S. (1999). *The construction of the self: A developmental perspective*. New York: Guilford.

Harter, S. (2003). The development of self-representations during childhood and adolescence. In M. R. Leary & J. P. Tangney (Eds.), *Handbook of self and identity* (pp. 610–642). New York: Guilford.

Harter, S., & Whitesell, N. R. (2003). Beyond the debate: Why some adolescents report stable self-worth over time and situation, whereas others report changes in self-worth. *Journal of Personality, 71*(6), 1027–1058.

Harter, S., Whitesell, N. R., & Junkin, L. J. (1998). Similarities and differences in domain-specific and global self-evaluations of learning disabled, behaviorally disordered, and normally achieving adolescents. *American Educational Research Journal, 35*(4), 653–680.

Hathaway, S. R., & McKinley, J. C., with Dahlstrom, W. G. Graham, J. R. Tellegen, A., & Kaemmer, B. (1989). *The Minnesota multiphasic personality inventory-2*. Minneapolis: University of Minnesota Press.

Havighurst, R. J. (1972). *Developmental tasks and education* (3rd ed.). New York: McKay.

Heatherton, T. D., & Wyland, C. (2003). Why do people have self-esteem? *Psychological Inquiry, 14*(1), 38–41.

Heidegger, M. (1962). *Being and time.* New York: Harper & Row. (Original work published 1927.)

Heisenberg, W. (1950). *Physical principles of quantum theory.* New York: Dover.

Hewitt, J. P. (2002). The social construction of self-esteem. In C. R. Snyder & S. J. Lopez (Eds.), *Handbook of positive psychology* (pp.135–158). Oxford: Oxford University Press.

Horney, K. (1937). *The neurotic personality of our time.* New York: W.W. Norton & Co.

Howard, G. (1985). *Basic research methods in the social sciences.* Glenview, IL: Scott Foresman.

Husserl, E. (1970a). *The crisis of European sciences and transcendental phenomenology.* Evanston, IL: Northwestern University Press. (Original work published 1954.)

Husserl, E. (1970b). *Logical investigations II* (J. Findlay, Trans.). New York: Humanities Press.

Jackson, M. (1984). *Self-esteem and meaning: A life historical investigation.* Albany: State University of New York.

James, W. (1983). *The principles of psychology.* Cambridge, MA: Harvard University Press. (Original work published 1890.)

Johnson, K. (1998). Self-image is suffering from a lack of esteem. *New York Times,* p. F7.

Jordan, C. H., Spencer, S. J., Zanna, M. P., Hoshino-Browne, E., & Correll, J. (2003). Secure and defensive high self-esteem. *Journal of Personality and Social Psychology, 85*(5), 969–978.

Jorgensen, I. S., & Nafstad, H. E. (2004). Positive psychology: Historical, philosophical, and epistemological perspectives. In P.A. Linley, & S. Joseph. (Eds.), *Positive psychology in practice* (pp.14–34). Hoboken, NJ: John Wiley & Sons.

Kazdin, A. (1992). *Research design in clinical psychology.* Needham Heights, MA: Allyn & Bacon.

Kernis, M. H. (1995). *Efficacy, agency, and self-esteem.* New York: Plenum.

Kernis, M. H. (2003a). Toward a conceptualization of optimal self-esteem. *Psychological Inquiry, 14*(1), 1–26.

Kernis, M. H. (2003b). Optimal self-esteem and authenticity: Separating fantasy from reality. *Psychological Inquiry, 14*(1), 83–89.

Kernis, M. H. (2006). *Self-esteem: Issues and answers.* Oxford, UK: Psychology Press.

Kernis, M. H., & Goldman, B. M. (2003). Stability and variability in self-concept and self-esteem. In M. R. Leary & J. P. Tangney (Eds.), *Handbook of self and identity* (pp. 106–127). New York: Guilford.

Kitano, H. H. (1989). Alcohol and drug use and self-esteem: A sociocultural perspective. In A. M. Mecca, N. J. Smelser & J. Vasconcellos (Eds.), *The social importance of self-esteem* (pp. 294–326). Berkeley: University of California Press.

Koole, S. L., & Kuhl, J. (2003). In search of the real self: A functional perspective on optimal self-esteem and authenticity. *Psychological Inquiry, 14*(1), 43–48.

Krauthammer, C. (1990). Education: Doing bad and feeling good. *Time,* p. 78.

Kuhn, T. (1962). *The structure of scientific revolutions.* Chicago: University of Chicago Press.

Leahy, R. L. (2003). *Cognitive therapy techniques: A practitioner's guide.* New York: Guilford.

Leary, M. R. (2004a). The sociometer, self-esteem, and the regulation of interpersonal behavior. In R. F. Baumeister & K. D. Vohs (Eds.), *The handbook of self-regulation: Research, theory, and application* (pp. 373–391). New York: Guilford.

Leary, M. R. (2004b). The function of self-esteem in terror management theory and sociometer theory: Commentary on Pyszczynski (2004). *Psychological Bulletin, 130*(3), 478–482.

Leary, M. R., & Downs, D. L. (1995). Interpersonal functions of the self-esteem motive: The self-esteem system as a sociometer. In M. H. Kernis (Ed.), *Efficacy, agency, and self-esteem* (pp. 123–144). New York: Plenum.

Leary, M. R., & MacDonald, G. (2003). Individual differences in self-esteem: A review and theoretical integration. In M. R. Leary & J. P. Tangney (Eds.), *Handbook of self and identity* (pp. 401–418). New York: Guilford.

Leary, M. R., & Tangney, J. P. (Eds.). (2003). *Handbook of self and identity.* New York: Guilford.

Leary, M. R., & Tangney, J. P. (2003). The self as an organizing construct in the behavioral and social sciences. In M. R. Leary & J. P. Tangney (Eds.), *Handbook of self and identity* (pp. 3–14). New York: Guilford.

Leo, J. (1990). The trouble with self-esteem. *U.S. News and World Report,* p. 16.

Leo, J. (1998). Damn, I'm good! *U.S. News and World Report,* p. 21.

Levin, J. D. (1993). *Slings and arrows: Narcissistic injury and its treatment.* Northvale, NJ: Aronson.

Linley, P. A., & Joseph, S. (2004). *Positive psychology in practice.* Hoboken, NJ: Wiley.

Mack, F. (1987). Understanding and enhancing self-concepts in black children. *Momentum, 18,* 22–28.

Maddux, J. E., & Gosselin, J. T. (2003). Self-efficacy. In M. R. Leary & J. P. Tangney (Eds.), *Handbook of self and identity* (pp. 218–238). New York: Guilford.

Mann, J. (1973). *Time-limited psychotherapy.* Cambridge, MA: Harvard University Press.

Marcel, G. (1964). *Creative fidelity.* New York: Noonday Press.

Maslow, A. H. (1954). *Motivation and personality.* New York: Harper & Row.

Maslow, A. H. (1964). *Religions, values, and peak-experiences.* New York: Viking.

Maslow, A. H. (1968). *Toward a psychology of being.* Princeton, NJ: Van Nostrand.

Maslow, A. H. (1971). *The farthest reaches of human nature.* New York: Viking.

McKay, M., & Fanning, P. (2000). *Self-Esteem* (3rd ed.). Oakland, CA: New Harbinger.

McKeon, R. (Ed.) (1941). *The basic works of Aristotle.* New York: Random House.

McReynolds, C. J., Ward, D. M., & Singer, O. (2002). Stigma, discrimination, and invisibility: Factors affecting successful integration of individuals diagnosed with schizophrenia. *Journal of Applied Rehabilitation Counseling,* 33(4), 32–39.

Mead, G. H. (1934). *Mind, self, and society.* Chicago: University of Chicago Press.

Mecca, A. M., Smelser, N.J., & Vasconcellos, J. (Eds.). (1989). *The social importance of self-esteem.* Berkeley: University of California Press.

Merleau-Ponty, M. (1945/1962). *The phenomenology of perception.* New York: Humanities Press.

Messer, B., & Harter, S. (1986). Adult self-perception profile. Unpublished manuscript, University of Denver, Denver, CO.

Michel, W., & Morf, C. (2003). The self as a psycho-social dynamic processing system: A meta perspective on a century of the self in psychology. In M. R. Leary & J. P. Tangney (Eds.), *Handbook of self and identity* (pp. 15–43). New York: Guilford.

Miller, R. (Ed.). (1992). *The restoration of dialogue: Readings in the philosophy of clinical psychology.* Washington, DC: American Psychological Association.

Miller, T. (1984). Parental absence and its affects on adolescent self-esteem. *International Journal of Social Psychiatry,* 30(4), 293–296.

Misiak, H., & Sexton, V. S. (1973). Phenomenological, existential, and humanistic psychologies: A historical survey. New York: Grune and Stratton.

Mruk, C. (1981). *Being pleased with oneself in a biographically critical way: An existential-phenomenological investigation.* Unpublished doctoral dissertation, Duquesne University, Pittsburgh, PA.

Mruk, C. (1983). Toward a phenomenology of self-esteem. In A. Giorgi, A. Barton & C. Maes (Eds.), *Duquesne studies in phenomenological psychology* (Vol. 4, pp. 137–148). Pittsburgh, PA: Duquesne University Press.

Mruk, C. (1984). Integrated description: A phenomenological technique for researching large scale, emerging human experience and trends. *Advances in Consumer Research, 3,* 566–570.

Mruk, C. (1994). Phenomenological psychology and integrated description: Keeping the science in the human science approach. *Methods: A Journal for Human Science* (annual edition), 6–20.

Mruk, C. (1995). *Self-esteem: Research, theory, and practice.* New York: Springer.

Mruk, C. (1999). *Self-esteem: Research, theory, and practice* (2nd ed.). New York: Springer.

Mruk, C. (2006). Defining self-esteem: An often overlooked issue with crucial implications. In M. Kernis (Ed.), *Self-esteem issues and answers: A source book of current perspectives.* New York: Psychology Press.

Mruk, C., & Hartzell, J. (2003). *Zen and psychotherapy: Integrating traditional and nontraditional psychotherapies.* New York: Springer.

Neiss, M. B., Stevenson, J., & Sedikides, C. (2003). The genetic bases of optimal self-esteem. *Psychological Inquiry,* 14(1), 63–65.

Newman, B., & Newman, P. (1987). *Development through life: A psychosocial approach* (4th ed.). Chicago: Dorsey Press.

O'Brien, E. J., Bartoletti, M., & Leitzel, J. D. (2006). Self-esteem, psychopathology and psychotherapy. In M. Kernis (Ed.), *Self-esteem issues and answers: A source book of current perspectives.* New York: Psychology Press.

O'Brien, E. J., & Epstein, S. (1983, 1988). *MSEI: The multidimensional self-esteem inventory.* Odessa, FL: Psychological Assessment Resources.

O'Brien, E. J., Leitzel, J., & Mensky, L. (1996). *Gender differences in the self-esteem of adolescents: A meta-analysis.* Poster session presented at the annual meeting of the American Psychological Association, Toronto, Canada.

Pallas, A. M., Entwisle, D. R., Alexander, K. L., & Weinstein, P. (1990). Social structure and the development of self-esteem in young children. *Social Psychology Quarterly, 53,* 302–315.

Peterson, C., & Seligman, M. (2004). *Character strengths and virtues: A handbook and classification.* Oxford: Oxford University Press.

Pettijohn, T. F. (1998). *Sources: Notable selections in social psychology.* Guilford, CT: Dushkin/McGraw-Hill.

Piers, E., & Harris, D. (1969). *Piers–Harris children's self-concept scale.* Los Angeles: Western Psychological Services.

Pirsig, R. (1974). *Zen and the art of motorcycle maintenance.* New York: Morrow.

Pope, A., McHale, S., & Craighead, E. (1988). *Self-esteem enhancement with children and adolescents.* New York: Pergamon Press.

Pyszczynski, T., Greenberg, T., & Goldberg, J. L., (2003). Freedom versus fear: On the defense, growth, and expansion of self. In M. R. Leary & J. P. Tangney (Eds.), *Handbook of self and identity* (pp. 315–343). New York: Guilford.

Pyszczynski, T., Greenberg, J., Sheldon, S., Arndt, J., & Schimel, J. (2004a). Why do people need self-esteem? A theoretical and empirical review. *Psychological Bulletin, 130*(3), 435–468.

Pyszczynski, T., Greenberg, J., Sheldon, S., Arndt, J., & Schimel, J. (2004b). Converging toward an integrated theory of self-esteem: Reply to Crocker and Nuer (2004), Ryan and Deci (2004), and Leary (2004). *Psychological Bulletin, 130*(3), 483–488.

Rakos, R. F. (1990). *Assertive behavior: Theory, research, and training.* London: Routledge.

Raskin, R., Novacek, J., & Hogan, R. (1991). Narcissistic self-esteem management. *Journal of Personality and Social Psychology, 60,* 911–918.

Regier, D. A., Narrow, W. E., Rae, D. S., Manderscheid, R.W., Locke, B. Z., & Goodwin, F. K. (1993). The de facto mental and addictive disorders service system. Epidemiologic catchment area prospective 1-year prevalence rates of disorders and services. *Archives of General Psychiatry, 50*(2), 85–94.

Rodewalt, F., & Tragakis, M. W. (2003). Self-esteem and self-regulation: Toward optimal studies of self-esteem. *Psychological Inquiry, 14*(1), 66–70.

Rogers, C. (1951). *Client centered therapy.* Boston: Houghton Mifflin.

Rogers, C. (1961). *On becoming a person.* Boston: Houghton Mifflin.

Roid, G. H., & Fitts, W. (1988). *Tennessee self-concept scale.* Los Angeles: Western Psychological Services.

Rosenberg, M. (1965). *Society and the adolescent self-image.* Princeton, NJ: Princeton University Press.

Rosenberg, M. (1979). *Conceiving the self.* New York: Basic Books.

Rosenberg, M. (1986). Self-concept from middle childhood through adolescence. In J. Suls & A. G. Greenwald (Eds.), *Psychological perspectives on the self* (Vol. 3). Hillsdale, NJ: Lawrence Erlbaum.

Rosenberg, M., & Owens, T. J., (2001). Low self-esteem people. In T. J. Owens, S. Sheldon & N. Goodman (Eds.), *Extending self-esteem theory and research: Sociological and psychological currents* (pp. 400–436). New York: Cambridge.

Rosenberg, M., Schooler, C., Schoenbach, C., & Rosenberg, F. (1995). Global self-esteem and specific self-esteem: Different concepts and different outcomes. *American Sociological Review, 60,* 141–156.

Rosenberg, M., & Simmons, R. G. (1971). Black and white self-esteem: The urban school child [Monograph]. *Social Psychological Implications IX,* Rose Monograph Series. Washington, DC: American Sociological Association.

Ruini, C., & Fava, G. A. (2004). Clinical applications of well being therapy. In P. A. Linley & S. Joseph (Eds.), *Positive psychology in practice* (pp. 371–388). Hoboken, NJ: Wiley.

Ryan, R. M., & Brown, K. W. (2003). Why we don't need self-esteem: On fundamental needs, contingent love, and mindfulness. *Psychological Inquiry, 14*(1), 71–76.

Ryan, R. M., & Deci, E. L. (2003). On assimilating identities to the self: A self-determination theory perspective on internalization and integrity within cultures. In M. R. Leary & J. P. Tangney (Eds.), *Handbook of self and identity* (pp. 253–272). New York: Guilford.

Ryan, R. M., & Deci, E. L. (2004). Avoiding death or engaging life as accounts of meaning and culture: Commentary on Pyszczynski (2004). *Psychological Bulletin, 130*(3), 473–477.

Ryff, C. D., & Singer, B. (2002). From social structure to biology: Integrative science in pursuit of human health and well-being. In C. R. Snyder & S. J. Lopez (Eds.), *Handbook of positive psychology* (pp. 541–555). Oxford: Oxford University Press.

Salmivalli, C., Kaukiainen, A., & Lagerspetz, K. M. J. (1999). Self-evaluated self-esteem, peer evaluated self-esteem, and defensive egotism and predictors of adolescents' participation in bullying situations. *Personality and Social Psychology Bulletin, 25*(10), 1268–1278.

Sanford, L., & Donovan, E. (1984). *Women and self-esteem.* New York: Anchor Press/Doubleday.

Sappington, A. (1989). *Adjustment: Theory, research, and personal applications.* Pacific Grove, CA: Brooks/Cole.

Scheff, T. J., & Fearon, Jr., D. S. (2004). Cognition and emotion? The dead end in self-esteem research. *Journal for the Theory of Social Behavior, 34*(1), 73–90.

Scheff, T., Retzinger, S., & Ryan, M. (1989). Crime, violence, and self-esteem: Review and proposals. In A. M. Mecca, N. J. Smelser, & J. Vasconcellos (Eds.), *The social importance of self-esteem* (pp. 165–199). Berkeley: University of California Press.

Schneiderman, J. W., Furman, M., & Weber, J. (1989). Self-esteem and chronic welfare dependency. In A. M. Mecca, N. J. Smelser, & J. Vasconcellos (Eds.), *The social importance of self-esteem* (pp. 200–247). Berkeley: University of California Press.

Sedikides, C., Rudich, E. A., Gregg, A. P., Kumashiro, M., & Rusbult, C. (2004). Are normal narcissists psychologically healthy?: Self-esteem matters. *Journal of Personality and Social Psychology, 87*(3), 400–416.

Seligman, M. E. P. (1990). *Learned optimism: How to change your mind and your life.* New York: Simon & Schuster.

Seligman, M. E. P. (1995a). The effectiveness of psychotherapy: The consumer's report study. *American Psychologist, 40,* 965–974.

Seligman, M. E. P. (1995b). *The optimistic child: A proven program to safeguard children against depression and build lifelong resilience.* New York: HarperCollins.

Seligman, M. E. P. (1999). The president's address. *American Psychologist, 54*(8). Retrieved August 29, 2005, from Positive Psychology Center, http://www.positivepsychology.org/aparep98.htm.

Seligman, M. E. P. (2002). Positive psychology, positive prevention, and positive therapy. In C. R. Snyder & S. J. Lopez (Eds.), *Handbook of positive psychology* (pp. 3–9). Oxford: Oxford University Press.

Seligman, M. E. P., & Csikszentmihalyi, M. (2000). Positive psychology: An introduction. *American Psychologist, 55,* 5–14.

Sheldon, K. M., Elliot, A. J., Kim, Y., & Kasser, T. (2001). What is satisfying about satisfying events? Testing 10 candidate psychological needs. *Journal of Personality and Social Psychology, 80*(2), 325–339.

Sheldon, K. M., & Kasser, T. (2001). Goals, congruence, and positive well-being: New empirical support for humanistic theories. *Journal of Humanistic Psychology 41*(1), 30–50.

Sheldon, K. M., & King, L. (2001). Why is positive psychology necessary? *American Psychologist, 56,* 216–217.

Shrik, S., & Harter, S. (1996). Treatment of low self-esteem. In M. A. Reineke, F. M. Dattilio & M. Freeman (Eds.), *Cognitive therapy with children and adolescents: A casebook for clinical practice* (pp. 175–198). New York: Guilford.

Sigelman, C. S., & Shaffer, D. R. (1995). *Life-span human development* (2nd ed.). Belmont, CA: Brooks/Cole.

Silverstone, P. H., & Salsali, M. (2003). Low self-esteem and psychiatric patients: Part I—The relationship between low self-esteem and psychiatric diagnosis. *Annals of General Hospital Psychiatry, 2*(2), 1–9.

Smelser, N. J. (1989). Self-esteem and social problems: An introduction. In A. M. Mecca, N. J. Smelser & J. Vasconcellos (Eds.), *The social importance of self-esteem* (pp. 1–23). Berkeley: University of California Press.

Snyder, C. R., & Lopez, S. J. (2002). *Handbook of positive psychology.* Oxford: Oxford University Press.

Snyder, C. S. (1989). Reality negotiation: From excuses to hope and beyond. *Journal of Social and Clinical Psychology, 8,* 130–157.

Strauman, T. J., Lemieux, A. M., & Coe, C. (1993). Self-discrepancy natural killer cell activity: Immunological consequences of negative self-evaluation. *Journal of Personality and Social Psychology, 64,* 1042–1052.

Sue, D. W., & Sue, D. (1990). *Counseling the culturally different: Theory and practice*. New York: Wiley.

Sullivan, H. S. (1953). *The interpersonal theory of psychiatry*. Chicago: University of Chicago Press.

Swanston, H. Y., Tebbutt, J. S. , O'Toole, B. I., & Oates, R. K. (1997). Sexually abused children 5 years after presentation: A case-control study. *Pediatrics, 100*, 600–608.

Tafarodi, R. W., & Ho, C. (2003). In defense of insecurity. *Psychological Inquiry, 14*(1), 77–79.

Tafarodi, R. W., & Milne, A. B. (2002). Decomposing self-esteem, *Journal of Personality, 70*(4), 443–483.

Tafarodi, R. W., & Swann, W. B., Jr. (1995). Self-liking and self-competence as dimensions of global self-esteem: Initial validation of a measure. *Journal of Personality Assessment, 65*(2), 322–342.

Tafarodi, R. W., & Swann, W. B., Jr. (1996). Individualism-collectivism and global self-esteem: Evidence for a cultural trade-off. *Journal of Cross-Cultural Psychology, 27*(6), 651–672.

Tafarodi, R. W., & Swann, W. B., Jr. (2001). Two-dimensional self-esteem: theory and measurement. *Personality and Individual Differences, 31*, 653–673.

Tafarodi, R. W., Tam, J., & Milne, A. (2001). Selective memory and the persistence of paradoxical self-esteem. *Personality and Social Psychology Bulletin, 27*(9), 1179–1189.

Tafarodi, R. W., & Vu, C. (1997). Two-dimensional self-esteem and reactions to success and failure. *Personality and Social Psychology Bulletin, 23*(6), 626–635.

Tageson, C. W. (1982). *Humanistic psychology: A synthesis*. Homewood, IL: Dorsey Press.

Taylor, E. (2001). Positive psychology and humanistic psychology: A reply to Seligman. *Journal of Humanistic Psychology, 41*(1), 13–29.

Tennen, H., & Affleck, G. (1993). The puzzles of self-esteem: A clinical perspective. In R. Baumeister (Ed.), *Self-esteem: The puzzle of low self-regard* (pp. 241–263). New York: Plenum.

Tice, D. (1993). The social motivations of people with low self-esteem. In R. Baumeister (Ed.), *Self-esteem: The puzzle of low self-regard* (pp. 37–54). New York: Plenum.

Tryon, W. (1991). Uncertainty reduction as valid explanation. *Theoretical and Philosophical Psychology Bulletin, 11*, 2.

Trzesniewski, K. H., Robins, R. W., Roberts, B. W., & Caspi, A. (2004). Personality and self-esteem development across the life span. In P. T. Costa & I. C. Siegler (Eds.), *Psychology of Aging* (pp. 163–185). Amsterdam: Elsevier Science.

Twenge, J. M., & Campbell, W. K. (2002). Self-esteem and socioeconomic status: A meta-analytic review. *Personality and Social Psychology Review, 6*(1), 59–71.

Twenge, J. M., & Crocker, J. (2002). Race and self-esteem: Meta-analysis comparing Whites, Blacks, Hispanics, Asian, and American Indians. *Psychological Bulletin, 128*(3), 371–408.

Vaillant, G. (1995). *The wisdom of the ego: Sources of resilience in adult life.* Cambridge, MA: Belknap Press.

Vinogradov, S., & Yalom, I. D. (1989). *A concise guide to group psychotherapy.* Washington, DC: American Psychiatric Press.

Weissman, H., & Ritter K. (1970). Openness to experience, ego strength and self-description as a function of repression and sensitization. *Psychological Reports, 26,* 859–864.

Wells, E. L., & Marwell, G. (1976). *Self-esteem: Its conceptualization and measurement.* Beverly Hills, CA: Sage.

Wells, R. A. (1982). *Planned short-term treatment.* New York: Free Press.

Werner, E. E., & Smith, R. S. (1992). *Overcoming the odds: High-risk children from birth to adulthood.* Ithaca, NY: Cornell University Press.

Wertz, F. (1984). Procedures in phenomenological research and the question of validity. In C. Aanstoos (Ed.), *Exploring the lived world: Readings in phenomenological psychology* (Vol. 23, pp. 9–28). Atlanta: West Georgia College.

White, R. (1959). Motivation reconsidered: The concept of competence. *Psychological Review, 66,* 297–333.

White, R. (1963). Ego and reality in psychoanalytic theory: A proposal regarding independent ego energies. *Psychological Issues, 3,* 125–150.

Winnicott, D. (1953). Transitional objects and transitional phenomena. *International Journal of Psychoanalysis, 34,* 89–97.

Wood, J. V., Giordano-Beech, M., Taylor, K. L., Michela, J. L., & Gaus, V. (1994). Strategies of social comparison among people with low self-esteem: Self-protection and self-enhancement. *Journal of Personality and Social Psychology, 67*(4), 713–731.

Wylie, R. (1974). *The self-concept* (Vol. 1). Lincoln: University of Nebraska Press.

Index

285

From the Paperback Reprint Series

Being and Becoming

Arthur W. Combs, PhD

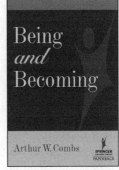

"**Being and Becoming**...*may well be on par with William James's and John Dewey's American infusion of psychological pragmatism into world thought...this book will provide a valuable guide to both the theoretician and practitioner in psychological science.*"

—**Franz B. Epting,** Professor of Psychology
University of Florida, Gainesville

In this outstanding volume, Dr. Combs updates his groundbreaking Field Theory of personality. This model grows out of Carl Rogers's ideas on client-centered therapy and has long been a major influence on theories of psychotherapy and personality within the humanistic and phenomenological traditions. He looks at who a person is, what he becomes, and how he behaves or misbehaves, and finally explores the nature and functions of our field of awareness and what it means for human growth and fulfillment.

In addition, Dr. Combs ties field psychology to the paradigm shifts in bio-physical sciences, and so provides a unifying frame of reference for all branches of psychology. His concise approach to the topic makes this book of practical interest to students, clinical psychologists, and counselors, as well as academics teaching upper-level or graduate courses in personality and on therapeutic techniques.

Partial Contents:

* Discovering the Self
* Challenge and Threat
* Human Capacity
* Learning and Change
* Self-Actualization and Health
* Troubled Selves
* Field Theory in Historical Perspective

2006 · 288pp · 0-8261-0262-X-0 · soft

From the Paperback Reprint Series

Zen and Psychotherapy
Integrating Traditional and Nontraditional Approaches

Christopher J. Mruk, PhD with Joan Hartzell, RN, MA

"The authors provide substance for the scholar and clinician alike. Mental health professionals, both seasoned and novice, will delight in the insightful blending of the lifetime of experience between the authors and the timeless practicality of Zen. A good reference for anyone dealing with the suffering of others."
— **Michael Jones,** PhD, Director
Psychological Associates, Houston, TX

With over 80 years of combined experience in the mental health field, Mruk and Hartzell explore the role of spirituality and religion in treatment and provide a sound clinical and academic rationale for integrating principles of Zen and traditional psychotherapy. They offer help to clinicians, supervisors, and educators in understanding specific Zen principles that can hold significant therapeutic value, and how they are compatible with traditional, empirically oriented, scientifically based education and training, regardless of one's particular academic or disciplinary orientation.

Partial Contents
Tradition, complementary, and Alternative Therapies • The Basic Principles of Zen and Their Psychotherapeutic Implications • From Realism to Idealism: Traditional Therapies and Zen • Practical Applications: Zen in the Clinical Setting • Integrating Zen and Psychotherapy: Connections and Limits

2006 ·264pp · 0-8261-2035-0 · soft

Differentiating Normal and Abnormal Personality

Second Edition

Stephen Strack, PhD

With graduate students and professionals new to the field, this book provides information about the central issues that are being addressed by researchers and clinicians in the realm of normal-abnormal personality today. In addition, it provides essential terminology, ideas, and methods that are unique to the field at large as well as basic tools needed to become a participant in normal-abnormal psychology.

Divided into three parts, the book presents an overview of major theories, statistical methods, and measurement instruments, including:

- Seven influential models of personality and psychopathology
- Four statistical methods for use in taxonomy, diagnosis, similarities and differences between normal and abnormal personality, and genetic and environmental influences
- Problems and pitfalls in designing empirical studies in the realm of normal-abnormal personality
- Empirically-based introductions and reviews of five widely-used instruments for assessing normal-abnormal personality

Partial Contents

Part I: Theoretical Perspectives • Interpersonal Theory and the Interpersonal Circumplex • Psychobiological Models and Issues • Differentiating Normal and Abnormal Personality from the Perspective of the DSM

Part II: Methodology • Principles of Exploratory Factor Analysis • Latent Variable Modeling • Taxometrics

Part III: Measurement and Assessment • Assessment of Maladaptive Personality Traits • The Personality Assessment Inventory and the Measurement of Normal and Abnormal Personality Constructs • Rorschach Assessment of Normal and Abnormal Personality

2006 · 656pp · 0-8261-3206-5 · hard

Anger-Related Disorders
A Practitioner's Guide to Comparative Treatments
Eva L. Feindler, PhD, Editor

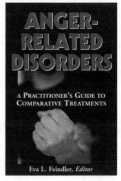

This volume addresses the treatment of adult anger disorders from the perspectives of clinical experts from different theoretical orientations.

The opening chapters describe diagnostic and assessment issues, empirical evidence for the treatment of anger disorders and cultural issues. Following a full description of the "Case of Anthony," case conceptualizations, treatment models and clinical issues are presented in chapters from a CBT, DBT, Psychoanalytic, family systems, Adlerian, assimilative integration and Buddhist perspectives. The final chapter succinctly summarizes the tenets and procedures of each approach and compares the proposed treatments.

This book is unusual in that it offers a number of proposed treatment approaches based upon very different theoretical foundations. Since all of the authors were asked to respond to the same clinical case material and address the same treatment concerns, the reader is able to compare and contrast the various approaches.

Partial Contents

Evidence for Effective Treatment of Anger Related Disorders • Dialectical Behavior Therapy for Anger Related Disorders • Couples and Family Treatment of Anger Difficulties • Psychopharmalogical Considerations in Anger Management • Emotion Focused Therapy (EFT) for Anger • Treating Anger with Wisdom and Compassion: A Buddhist Approach • An Adlerian Approach to the Treatment of Anger Disorders • Assimilative Psychodynamic Psychotherapy: An Integrative Approach to Anger Disorders • Multiple Perspectives on the Conceptualization and Treatment of Anger-Related Disorders

2006 · 400pp · 0-8261-4046-7 · hard